Applying an International Human Rights Framework to State Budget Allocations

AF695576

Human rights-based budget analysis projects have emerged at a time when the United Nations has asserted the indivisibility of all human rights and attention is increasingly focused on the role of non-judicial bodies in promoting and protecting human rights. This book seeks to develop the human rights framework for such budget analyses, by exploring the international law obligations of the International Covenant on Economic, Social and Cultural Rights (ICESCR) in relation to budgetary processes. The book outlines international experiences and comparative practice in relation to economic and social rights budget analysis and budgeting.

The book sets out an ICESCR-based methodology for analysing budget and resource allocations and focuses on the legal obligation imposed on state parties by article 2(1) of ICESCR to progressively realise economic and social rights to 'the maximum of available resources'. Taking Northern Ireland as a key case study, the book demonstrates and promotes the use of a 'rights-based' approach in budgetary decision-making.

The book will be relevant to a global audience currently considering how to engage in the budget process from a human rights perspective. It will be of interest to students and researchers of international human rights law and public law, as well as economic and social rights advocacy and lobbying groups.

Rory O'Connell is Professor of Human Rights and Constitutional Law at the Transitional Justice Institute/School of Law, University of Ulster. His research and teaching interests are in the areas of human rights, equality and constitutional law.

Aoife Nolan is Professor of International Human Rights Law at the School of Law, University of Nottingham. She has published extensively in the area of human rights, particularly in relation to economic and social rights and children's rights.

Colin Harvey is Professor of Human Rights Law, School of Law, Queen's University Belfast. He has written widely on human rights and constitutional law. He served as a Commissioner on the Northern Ireland Human Rights Commission (2005–2011) and is a former Head of the School of Law at Queen's (2007–2012).

Mira Dutschke has a postgraduate degree in Human Rights law and 10 years research experience in Southern Africa, Northern Ireland and the United States. She teaches at the University of Cape Town and works as an environmental news and film producer, and researcher.

Eoin Rooney is a social researcher. He is currently Coordinator of the Centre for Economic Empowerment, a think tank and skills development project within the Northern Ireland Council for Voluntary Action (NICVA).

Routledge Research in Human Rights Law

Available titles in this series include:

The Right to Development in International Law
The Case of Pakistan
Khurshid Iqbal

Global Health and Human Rights
Legal and Philosophical Perspectives
John Harrington and Maria Stuttaford

The Right to Religious Freedom in International Law
Between group rights and individual rights
Anat Scolnicov

Emerging Areas of Human Rights in the 21st Century
The role of the Universal Declaration of Human Rights
Marco Odello and Sofia Cavandoli

The Human Right to Water and its Application in the Occupied Palestinian Territories
Amanda Cahill

International Human Rights Law and Domestic Violence
The effectiveness of international human rights law
Ronagh McQuigg

Human Rights in the Asia-Pacific Region
Towards Institution Building
Hitoshi Nasu and Ben Saul

Human Rights Monitoring Mechanisms of the Council of Europe
Gauthier de Beco

The Positive Obligations of the State under the European Convention of Human Rights
Dimitris Xenos

Vindicating Socio-Economic Rights
International Standards and Comparative Experiences
Paul O'Connell

The EU as a 'Global Player' in Human Rights?
Jan Wetzel

Regulating Corporate Human Rights Violations
Humanizing Business
Surya Deva

The UN Committee on Economic, Social and Cultural Rights
The Law, Process and Practice
Marco Odello and Francesco Seatzu

State Security Regimes and the Right to Freedom of Religion and Belief
Changes in Europe Since 2001
Karen Murphy

The European Court of Human Rights in the Post-Cold War Era
Universality in Transition
James A. Sweeney

The United Nations Human Rights Council
A Critique and Early Assessment
Rosa Freedman

Children and International Human Rights Law
The Right of the Child to be Heard
Aisling Parkes

Litigating Transnational Human Rights Obligations
Alternative Judgements
Mark Gibney and Wouter Vandenhole

Reproductive Freedom, Torture and International Human Rights
Challenging the Masculinisation of Torture
Ronli Noa Sifris

Applying an International Human Rights Framework to State Budget Allocations
Rights and Resources
Rory O'Connell, Aoife Nolan, Colin Harvey, Mira Dutschke and Eoin Rooney

Forthcoming titles in this series include:

Jurisdiction, Immunity and Transnational Human Rights Litigation
Xiaodong Yang

Children's Lives in an Era of Children's Rights
The Progress of the Convention on the Rights of the Child in Africa
Afua Twum-Danso Imoh & Nicola Ansell

Applying an International Human Rights Framework to State Budget Allocations

Rights and Resources

Rory O'Connell, Aoife Nolan, Colin Harvey, Mira Dutschke and Eoin Rooney

Routledge
Taylor & Francis Group
LONDON AND NEW YORK

First published 2014 by Routledge

2 Park Square, Milton Park, Abingdon, Oxon OX14 4RN
711 Third Avenue, New York, NY 10017, USA

Routledge is an imprint of the Taylor & Francis Group, an informa business

First issued in paperback 2016

Copyright © 2014 Rory O'Connell, Aoife Nolan, Colin Harvey, Mira Dutschke, Eoin Rooney

The right of Rory O'Connell, Aoife Nolan, Colin Harvey, Mira Dutschke, Eoin Rooney to be identified as authors of this work has been asserted by them in accordance with sections 77 and 78 of the Copyright, Designs and Patents Act 1988.

All rights reserved. No part of this book may be reprinted or reproduced or utilised in any form or by any electronic, mechanical, or other means, now known or hereafter invented, including photocopying and recording, or in any information storage or retrieval system, without permission in writing from the publishers.

Notice:

Product or corporate names may be trademarks or registered trademarks, and are used only for identification and explanation without intent to infringe.

British Library Cataloguing in Publication Data
A catalogue record for this book is available from the British Library

Library of Congress Cataloging-in-Publication Data
O'Connell, Rory.
Applying an international human rights framework to state budget allocations: rights and resources/Rory O'Connell, Aoife Nolan, Colin Harvey, Mira Dutschke and Eoin Rooney.
pages cm – (Routledge research in human rights law)
Includes bibliographical references and index.
1. Human rights – Economic aspects. 2. Human rights – Economic aspects – Case studies. 3. Budget – Social aspects 4. Budget process – Moral and ethical aspects. 5. Northern Ireland – Appropriations and expenditures – Social aspects – Northern Ireland. 6. Human rights – Government policy. I. Nolan, Aoife. II. Harvey, Colin. III. Dutschke, Mira. IV. Rooney, Eoin. V. Title.
K3240.O346 2014
343'.034—dc23
2013028537

ISBN 978-1-138-66550-7 (pbk)
ISBN 978-0-415-52978-5 (hbk)
ISBN 978-0-203-79783-9 (ebk)

Typeset in Garamond 3 by
Florence Production Ltd, Stoodleigh, Devon, UK

Contents

Acknowledgements

This book is the product of a two-year research project on 'Budget Analysis and the Advancement of Economic and Social Rights in Northern Ireland'. Based at the School of Law at Queen's University Belfast, this project was undertaken by the authors. The project was made possible by funding from Atlantic Philanthropies and we are grateful for their support. We also acknowledge the invaluable assistance of our support staff on the project, Chris Wallace and Jennie Finlay.

The project team placed considerable emphasis on the peer review of its outputs in order to ensure that its outputs, including those discussed in this work, are complete, accurate and rigorous. In particular, extensive comments were provided by members of the project's International Advisory Board. Representatives of non-governmental organizations (including members of the project's Local Working Group) made many valuable suggestions, as did a number of other stakeholders. In addition, several experts in housing and economics offered comments on the findings presented in Chapters 5 and 6. The Northern Ireland Department for Social Development (DSD) and officials in the Department of Health Social Services and Public Safety (DHSSPS) also provided constructive suggestions. The project team acknowledges the time, effort and expertise of all these persons and is grateful for their assistance. The team would like to express particular gratitude to Ann Blyberg, Debbie Budlender, Fiona Crowley, Diane Elson, Oonagh Kane, Rosalind McKenna, Ignacio Saiz, Martín Sígal, Alex Tennant and Sally-Anne Way. We thank Marie Lynch for assistance with the proofreading. The authors would also like to thank our colleagues, families and friends for their support throughout the life of the project and beyond.

List of abbreviations

APRODEV	Association of World Council of Churches related Development Organizations in Europe
CAJ	Committee on the Administration of Justice
CAMH	Child and Adolescent Mental Health
CAMHS	Child and Adolescent Mental Health Services
CEDAW	Convention on the Elimination of All Forms of Discrimination Against Women
CERD	Convention on the Elimination of All Forms of Racial Discrimination
CESR	Center for Economic and Social Rights
CIH	Chartered Institute of Housing
Cmnd.	Command Paper
COHRE	Center on Housing Rights and Evictions
ComESCR	Committee on Economic, Social and Cultural Rights
CPI	Consumer Price Index
CRC	Convention on the Rights of the Child
CRPD	Convention on the Rights of Persons with Disabilities
DFP	Department of Finance and Personnel
DHSSPS	Department of Health, Social Services and Public Safety
DSD	Department for Social Development
ECHR	European Convention on Human Rights
ESC	European Social Charter
ESR	Economic and Social Rights
FAO	Food and Agriculture Organization of the United Nations
GB	Great Britain
GC	General Comment(s)
HAG	Housing Association Grant
HC	House of Commons
HL	House of Lords
HSC	Health and Social Care
IBP	International Budget Partnership
ICCPR	International Covenant on Civil and Political Rights

ICESCR	International Covenant on Economic, Social and Cultural Rights
IHRIP	International Human Rights Internship Program
IMF	International Monetary Fund
MAR	Maximum Available Resources
MI Principles	UN Principles for the Protection of Persons with Mental Illness and the Improvement of Mental Health Care
NGO	Non-governmental organization
NHRI	National Human Rights Institution
NI	Northern Ireland
NIA	Northern Ireland Assembly
NIFHA	Northern Ireland Federation of Housing Associations
NIHE	Northern Ireland Housing Executive
OFMdFM	Office of the First Minister and deputy First Minister
OHCHR	Office of the High Commissioner for Human Rights
ONS	Office of National Statistics
PESA	Public Expenditure Statistical Analysis
PFG	Programme for Government
PHC	Primary Health Care
PMH	Primary Mental Health
POC	Programme of Care
PPP	Public Private Partnership(s)
PPR	Participation and Practice of Rights
PR	Progressive Realization
PRS	Private Rented Sector
RBA	Rights Based Approach
UDHR	Universal Declaration of Human Rights
UUJ	University of Ulster at Jordanstown
UP	University Press
WHO	World Health Organization

List of tables and figures

Tables

Figures

Preface

The dry language of 'state budget allocations' may conjure up images of technical decisions made by anonymous bureaucrats (or – even worse – technocrats), presumably economists.[1] 'International human rights framework' similarly suggests the work of lawyers, diplomats and academics. The formal language and the images of elite professions obscure the fact that these matters concern the bread and butter – or even life and death – basics of human society. State budget allocations affect social security, health, education and security issues; they express in very practical and concrete terms the priorities of a political community. The grant or denial of funding may mean the difference between existence or not of maternity health clinics, literacy programs, social safety nets. Such decisions are not just matters of balancing the account books; they also express political choices.

Budget decisions are, however, not just matters of political choice; 'political' may, rightly or wrongly, suggest a purely interest-based approach to decision-making, and sometimes may even imply an essentially instrumental or Machiavellian approach to decision-making. As well as being economic and political issues, these matters are also fundamentally questions about human rights, i.e., the rights recognized as the universal entitlement of everyone by international human rights law. And this human rights dimension requires that we not merely address the economic and political dimension but also the legal dimension. As this book demonstrates, the international legal framework of human rights provides standards and guidelines for principled decision-making when rights are affected. We seek to spell out how that international legal framework requires us to approach budgetary decisions.

This book consists of two parts, broadly moving from a 'universal' or 'global' perspective to more 'local' case studies.[2] Part One consists of three

1 Steven G. Koven, *Ideological Budgeting: The Influence of Political Philosophy on Public Policy* (Praeger 1988) 3.

2 We borrow the language of 'global' and 'local' (as well as the specific understandings thereof) from Gráinne McKeever and Fionnuala Ní Aoláin, 'Thinking Globally, Acting Locally: Enforcing Socio-Economic Rights in Northern Ireland' [2004] *European Human Rights Law Review* 158.

chapters. The first chapter discusses the contexts relevant for understanding the approach to economic and social rights (ESR)-based budget analysis work in this book. The second chapter analyzes a selection of the existing budget analysis guidance documents and case studies that provide the background to our own approach. The third and fourth chapters build on this by developing in detail the human rights framework for budget analysis, using the International Covenant on Economic Social and Cultural Rights (ICESCR) as the guiding document.

While Chapters 1 to 4 focus on the global experience and universal standards, the chapters that make up the second part of the book switch to a more local perspective. Chapters 5 and 6 demonstrate how the universal principles discussed in Part One can be applied in specific contexts, using as our local focus, Northern Ireland. Chapter 5 examines how the ICESCR principles can be used generally in relation to mental health; Chapter 6 focuses in on the system for funding social housing and thus provides a more detailed case study. The research for these chapters covers the period of the distinct phases of the research project that forms the basis of this book; Chapter 5 covers the period from approximately 2004 to 2011; Chapter 6 covers the period from approximately 2003 to 2010. The raw data relates to those time periods, though where useful we have highlighted more recent developments, usually in footnotes. Finally, Chapter 7 draws out the lessons from the case studies.

We put forward the ICESCR framework and the specific cases studies as examples of how the general and abstract language of universal human rights treaties can be made relevant in local practical politics and economic decision-making.

Part One

1 Contexts

Introduction

This introductory chapter introduces the three elements that are fundamental to understanding the approach in this book to economic and social rights-based budget analysis work: international human rights law, budgets and human rights-based budget analysis, and our local jurisdictional focus (Northern Ireland).

This chapter first discusses the evolution of human rights law, highlighting in particular debates around economic and social rights (ESR), and the role of non-judicial institutions in protecting rights. The chapter then turns to the issues of budgets and human rights-based budget analysis. At this stage, we explain our reasons for choosing the International Covenant on Economic Social and Cultural Rights (ICESCR) as our key analytical framework and stress the importance of international human rights in the context of the global economic crisis. After the discussion of budgets and the choice of ICESCR, the chapter presents Northern Ireland as the jurisdictional focus chosen for this work. We explain the reasons for this choice. We proceed to discuss the history of Northern Ireland, as well as the experience of Northern Ireland as a devolved region within the United Kingdom. The chapter concludes with a consideration of the political institutions of this jurisdiction.

The evolution of human rights law and the emergence of ESR

The modern language of international human rights law can trace its antecedents among numerous traditions, localities and times.[1] For the purposes of understanding the role of economic and social rights and also the idea of budget analysis, the late-eighteenth-century revolutions in North America

1 Paul Gordon Lauren, *The Evolution of International Human Rights: Visions Seen* (3rd University of Pennsylvania Press 2011); Micheline Ishay, *The History of Human Rights: From Ancient Times to the Globalization Era* (University of California Press 2004); Thomas Buergenthal, 'International Human Rights in an Historical Perspective' in Janusz Symonides (ed) *Human Rights: Concepts and Standards* (Ashgate 2000).

and France are significant. These revolutions produced numerous innovations in politics and law; they were important in the evolution of constitutional law and formed one of the streams of thought that would produce international human law documents in the twentieth century. Among the revolutionary texts of this period were the diverse bills of rights of the different American states, the French Declaration of the Rights of Man and the Citizen 1789, the US federal Bill of Rights 1791 and the various French revolutionary declarations of the 1790s.

The American and French bills of rights were mainly, though not exclusively, liberal in character. Thus, they tended to focus on individual rights to non-interference by state agents: the right to be free from arbitrary execution, arrest, censorship, or expropriation. These were the 'rights of man' – or what we now call civil rights. Alongside these civil rights were a number of political rights; these were given especial prominence in the French Declaration. These political rights, although emerging in the same texts, were different from the individualistic civil rights. Political rights are necessarily collective in nature.[2]

Despite these differences, it has become commonplace to associate civil and political rights. Sometimes they are identified as the 'first generation' of rights; these first generation rights are then distinguished from the 'second generation' economic and social rights and the 'third generation' rights of peoples.[3] This language of generations has proven deeply problematic and even harmful to the principle of the indivisible nature of all human rights. The language of 'generations' suggests a neat chronological development which is at best an oversimplified account; furthermore the use of these distinctions may create a sense of hierarchy between the different generations.

The American and French revolutions also give us examples of different methods for the protection of rights. In both revolutions, the ideal was the political protection of rights; that is to say, rights would be best protected by a representative government, by citizens, and in extreme cases, by the right to rebel against tyranny. The French revolutionaries in particular were distrustful of judges, seeing them as frequently reactionary.[4] This predominantly political mode of protection remained commonplace in France but was quickly supplemented by a different innovation in the US. In 1803, the US Supreme Court asserted a power of judicial review over legislation, to assure its compatibility with the constitution.[5] This would lead to a much greater

2 Marx identified the distinction between political rights, which are necessarily communal, and the more individualistic rights of man: Karl Marx, 'On the Jewish Question' in Loyd Easton and Kurt Guddat (eds) *Writings of the Young Marx on Philosophy and Society* (Doubleday Books 1967, 1843), 225.

3 The language of generations seems to originate with Karel Vasak, 'A Thirty Year Struggle' (1977) 30 UNESCO Courier 29.

4 John P. Dawson, *The Oracles of the Law* (University of Michigan Press 1968) 375.

5 *Marbury v Madison* 5 US 137 Cranch 137 (1803).

emphasis on the judicial protection of constitutional provisions, including constitutional rights, in the US tradition. By contrast, the French continued to rely on political processes and to distrust judges.

These early constitutional developments are important for more than simply introducing the language of civil and political rights, or for highlighting different approaches to the protection of rights. A narrow focus on modern international human rights law obscures the historical reality that questions of budgets, finances and taxation have been critical to several of the important stages in the evolution of constitutional government.[6] The development of the English Parliament was closely linked to disputes about taxation powers, especially in the seventeenth century; the American revolutionaries' rallying cry was 'no taxation without representation', and it was a fiscal crisis that precipitated the French Revolution of 1789. The very innovation of a public budget originated in the fiscal crises of pre-Revolutionary France.[7] Later, the French Declaration of the Rights of Man and of the Citizen 1789 dealt with budgetary matters in several of its articles.

These developments in the revolutionary era are landmarks in terms of civil and political rights, the emergence of judicial and political means of protecting rights and even innovations in terms of budgets. However, an important element was largely missing. The late-eighteenth-century documents did not, for the most part,[8] address the economic and social rights that are the main concern of this book. Concern with economic and social justice pre-dates the late-eighteenth-century revolutions; Carozza discusses how the sixteenth-century missionary Las Casas was concerned with labour and health rights.[9] But it is the nineteenth century that sees the emergence of economic and social issues as claims of rights. They emerge as part of myriad nineteenth-century reform and protest movements; these movements included socialists, trade unionists and other reformers, who stressed working conditions, union activity, education, health, social security and welfare. The struggles of these reformers were complemented, ironically, by policies of more conservative mainstream political parties and politicians such as Bismarck in Germany and the Liberal Party in the United Kingdom.[10] Even the Catholic Church, which had

6 Philip T. Hoffman and Kathryn Norberg, *Fiscal Crises, Liberty, and Representative Government, 1450–1789* (Stanford UP 1994); Rory O'Connell, 'Recovering the History of Human Rights: Public Finances and Human Rights' in Aoife Nolan, Rory O'Connell and Colin Harvey (eds) *Human Rights and Public Finance* (Hart 2013).

7 Jacques Godechot, *France and the Atlantic Revolution of the Eighteenth Century, 1770–1799* (Free Press 1965) 69.

8 As a notable exception, the French 1793 Declaration contained provisions on occupation, slavery and education.

9 Paolo Carozza, 'From Conquest to Constitutions: Retrieving a Latin American Tradition of the Idea of Human Rights' (2003) 25 *Human Rights Quarterly* 281, 295.

10 See Micheline Ishay, *The History of Human Rights: From Ancient Times to the Globalization Era* (University of California Press 2004).

condemned liberalism,[11] urged the need to protect the rights of workers.[12] While these policy proposals may well have been intended to undermine revolutionary agitation, they also served to consolidate the notion that economic and social claims could be conceived of as entitlements and therefore, perhaps, rights. Such developments were not unique to Europe, but also took place in the US (in the guise of progressivism) and in Latin America.[13]

In the early twentieth century these economic and social interests were increasingly recognized as rights. The turmoil produced by the First World War – the collapse of empires and the rise of a communist regime – was the catalyst for important international and national developments.

At the international level, the end of the First World War witnessed two significant innovations. The International Labour Organization (ILO) was created alongside the League of Nations. The ILO owed its origins to the efforts made by workers and unions during the First World War, and responded to demands by labour leaders for an international charter of labour rights.[14] The ILO was seen as both a reward for workers' sacrifices during the War, but also a bulwark against communism.[15] Subsequently the ILO would come to use the language of labour rights: the 1944 Declaration of Philadelphia speaks of freedom of expression and association and the right to pursue material well-being and spiritual development.[16] The use of rights language has become even more prominent in the work of the ILO since then.[17] Also at the international level, the system of minority rights treaties adopted in the new countries formed from the debris of defeated imperial powers recognized minority rights including important minority cultural rights (religion, language, and education).[18]

Returning to national level developments: the Mexican Constitution of 1917 was the first to recognize economic and social interests as constitutional

11 *Syllabus Errorum*, 1864.

12 *Rerum Novarum*, 1891, cited in Paolo Carozza, 'From Conquest to Constitutions: Retrieving a Latin American Tradition of the Idea of Human Rights' (2003) 25 Human Rights Quarterly 281, 308.

13 Carozza, ibid 307.

14 Roger Normand and Sarah Zaidi, *Human Rights at the UN: The Political History of Universal Justice* (Indiana UP 2008) 57.

15 Susan L. Kang, 'The Unsettled Relationship of Economic and Social Rights and the West: a Response to Whelan and Donnelly' (2009) 31 Human Rights Quarterly 1006, 1018; Roger Normand and Sarah Zaidi, *Human Rights at the UN: The Political History of Universal Justice* (Indiana UP 2008) 56–7.

16 ILO Declaration of Philadelphia 1944: www.ilo.org/dyn/normlex/en/f?p=1000:62:0::NO:62:P62_LIST_ENTRIE_ID:2453907:NO (accessed 1 May 2013).

17 See for example Declaration on Fundamental Principles and Rights at Work 1998 www.ilo.org/declaration/thedeclaration/textdeclaration/lang–en/index.htm (accessed 1 May 2013).

18 Hurst Hannum, 'The Rights of Persons belonging to Minorities' in Janusz Symonides (ed) *Human Rights: Concepts and Standards* (Ashgate 2000) 278–80.

rights.[19] Other texts followed suit, such as the Soviet Union's Declaration of the Rights of Working People and the Exploited. Later interwar constitutions such as the Weimar 1919 Constitution and the Irish 1937 Constitution included economic and social interests and, in some cases, treated these as rights. The Weimar Constitution included detailed provisions on education and the economy. The Irish Constitution also included provisions on education and the economy, carefully distinguishing between enforceable rights (education) and non-enforceable guiding principles ('Directive Principles').[20] During the Second World War, President Roosevelt highlighted the importance of economic and social rights in two important State of the Union addresses. In the first, he proclaimed the need to recognize the 'four freedoms', which included freedom from want and freedom from fear;[21] while in a subsequent State of the Union address he announced the need for a Second Bill of Rights, one that would complete the 1791 Bill of Rights with its focus on civil and political rights. With an eye to the emergence of authoritarian and totalitarian regimes after the First Word War, Roosevelt warned that 'People who are hungry and out of a job are the stuff of which dictatorships are made.'[22] To complete the link with the late-eighteenth-century revolutions, in France the 1946 Constitution recognized the fundamental importance of economic and social rights in its Preamble.

Most of these developments took place within national contexts; the various rights were contemplated in relation to national constitutional texts and traditions, and not international law. While the period 1917–45 witnessed significant international law developments,[23] it was only after the Second World War and the atrocities associated with it, that modern international human rights law was born. The most significant step was the proclamation by the United Nations General Assembly of the Universal Declaration of Human Rights (UDHR) on 10 December 1948, a date now marked as Human Rights Day.

The drafting and adoption of the UDHR was a remarkable achievement: the states of the UN adopted the Declaration by a vote of forty-eight in favour

19 See Paolo Carozza, 'From Conquest to Constitutions: Retrieving a Latin American Tradition of the Idea of Human Rights' (2003) 25 *Human Rights Quarterly* 281, 303 on social liberalism in the Mexican example.

20 Jill Cottrell, 'Ensuring Equal Rights in Constitutions: Public Participation in Drafting Economic Social and Cultural rights' in Jody Heymann and Adele Cassola (eds) *Making Equal Rights Real* (Cambridge UP 2012) 52–3.

21 Franklin Delano Roosevelt 'State of the Union Address' (1941) www.presidency.ucsb.edu/ws/index.php?pid=16518 (accessed 8 May 2013).

22 Franklin Delano Roosevelt 'State of the Union Address' (1944) Available at www.presidency.ucsb.edu/ws/index.php?pid=16518 (accessed 8 May 2013).

23 Paul Gordon Lauren, *The Evolution of International Human Rights: Visions Seen* (University of Pennsylvania Press 2011) Chapter 4.

and none against, with eight abstentions.[24] The Declaration was conceived of as a non-binding proclamation, i.e., it did not give rise to legally enforceable rights; accordingly it does not include any enforcement mechanisms. And undoubtedly the non-binding nature encouraged agreement by states which may have had qualms about binding legal engagements. Nevertheless, it remains an impressive achievement, not least because it integrates the different types of human rights that had emerged – civil and political, economic and social and, indeed, cultural rights.[25] The text does not establish any hierarchy among the categories of rights.[26] Rather, an impressive unity of rights – civil, cultural, economic, social and political – is envisaged. We might say that they were regarded as indivisible.

The story of human rights law after the Universal Declaration is an oft-told one.[27] During the Cold War period the unity of the various rights announced in the UDHR was sundered, with separate texts emerging in the UN, Europe and the Americas to deal with civil and political rights on the one hand and economic and social (and cultural) rights on the other. The separation was never perfect, but the trend towards separation is evident at both UN and regional levels. The UN adopted two Covenants in 1966: the International Covenant on Economic Social and Cultural Rights (ICESCR) and the International Covenant on Civil and Political Rights (ICCPR); the Council of Europe also adopted separate mechanisms: the European Convention on Human Rights 1950 and the European Social Charter 1961; finally, the Organization of American States adopted the American Convention on Human Rights 1969 and the later Protocol of San Salvador 1988.

This separation was based on a perception that the implementation mechanisms for economic and social rights needed to be different from those

24 A detailed study is available in Johannes Morsink, *The Universal Declaration of Human Rights: Origins, Drafting and Intent* (University of Pennsylvania Press 2000). Saudi Arabia, South Africa, the Soviet Union and five other socialist states abstained. Morsink discusses the abstentions at 21–7, highlighting that even the abstainers did not condemn the project.

25 Latin American countries were instrumental in making sure that economic and social rights were included: Morsink, ibid 130–1.

26 While no hierarchy is established, the economic, social and cultural rights are grouped in Articles 22–28, and there is some language in Article 22 which acts as a mini-preamble for this part of the Declaration. There is however no formal division of headings.

27 Roger Normand and Sarah Zaidi, *Human Rights at the UN: the Political History of Universal Justice* (Indiana UP 2008); Whelan challenges the conventional interpretation that the split into two Covenants was primarily about ideological divisions between East and West: Daniel J. Whelan, *Indivisible Human Rights: A History* (University of Pennsylvania Press 2010) 134. See also Daniel Whelan and Jack Donnelly, 'The West, Economic and Social Rights, and the Global Human Rights Regime: Setting the Record Straight' (2007) 29 *Human Rights Quarterly* 908; Alex Kirkup and Tony Evans, 'The Myth of Western Opposition to Economic, Social, and Cultural Rights?: A Reply to Whelan and Donnelly' (2009) 31 *Human Rights Quarterly* 221; Daniel J. Whelan and Jack Donnelly, 'Yes, a Myth: A Reply to Kirkup and Evans' (2009) 31 *Human Rights Quarterly* 239.

for civil and political rights; thus, it was argued that only civil and political rights were amenable to *immediate, judicial* protection, i.e., only they were justiciable rights. Economic and social rights, it was said, were primarily political aspirations and could only be protected as part of long-term programmes.[28] These arguments were also tied into debates about the supposed differences between negative and positive rights.[29]

This controversy[30] manifested itself in the texts themselves, especially in the UN and the Council of Europe. The ICCPR included an immediate obligation to respect the rights therein and was accompanied by an optional communications or complaints mechanism. By way of contrast, ICESCR had no complaints mechanism. Indeed, uniquely among the core UN human rights treaties, ICESCR did not even establish a dedicated treaty-monitoring body;[31] instead monitoring was entrusted to the Economic and Social Committee. Subsequently a specialized ICESCR Committee was established by ECOSOC Resolution 1985/17 of 28 May 1985. Moreover, the umbrella obligation in ICESCR was couched in very specific language, which we will have reason to return to throughout this book:

> Article 2
>
> 1. Each State Party to the present Covenant undertakes to take steps, individually and through international assistance and co-operation, especially economic and technical, to the maximum of its available resources, with a view to achieving progressively the full realization of the rights recognized in the present Covenant by all appropriate means, including particularly the adoption of legislative measures.

28 Whelan and Donnelly make the point that no state argued against the idea that economic and social rights required a different implementation approach: Daniel Whelan and Jack Donnelly, 'The West, Economic and Social Rights, and the Global Human Rights Regime: Setting the Record Straight' (2007) 29 *Human Rights Quarterly* 908, 935.

29 Roger Normand and Sarah Zaidi, *Human Rights at the UN: the Political History of Universal Justice* (Indiana UP 2008) 209. The arguments against social and economic rights or positive rights were rehearsed again after the end of the Cold War: see Cass Sunstein, 'Against Positive Rights: Why Social and Economic Rights Don't Belong in the Constitutions of Eastern Europe' (1993) (Winter) *East European Constitutional Review* 35; Sunstein would later change his position on protecting social and economic rights: Cass Sunstein, *The Second Bill of Rights: FDR's Unfinished Revolution and Why We Need It More Than Ever* (Basic Books 2004).

30 The literature on this point is voluminous; Chapter 4 of Henry Steiner, Philip Alston and Ryan Goodman, *International Human Rights in Context* (Oxford UP 2008) includes excerpts reflecting different perspectives on the debate over the differences between these groups of rights.

31 Whelan and Donnelly describe this as 'unjustifiable': Daniel Whelan and Jack Donnelly, 'The West, Economic and Social Rights, and the Global Human Rights Regime: Setting the Record Straight' (2007) 29 *Human Rights Quarterly* 908, 936.

> 2. The States Parties to the present Covenant undertake to guarantee that the rights enunciated in the present Covenant will be exercised without discrimination of any kind as to race, colour, sex, language, religion, political or other opinion, national or social origin, property, birth or other status.
>
> 3. Developing countries, with due regard to human rights and their national economy, may determine to what extent they would guarantee the economic rights recognized in the present Covenant to non-nationals.

Article 2(1) ICESCR contains much more qualified language than is found in the equivalent Article 2 ICCPR. In particular the language of maximum available resources, progressive realization, taking steps, all suggest a less onerous obligation than Article 2 ICCPR, which speaks of an obligation 'to respect and to ensure' and to provide a remedy for violations.

The end of the Cold War saw important changes in approaches to human rights. Two developments are key to understanding the emergence of ESR-based budget analysis. First, the Vienna Declaration and Programme of Action 1993 reaffirmed the principle that all human rights are indivisible; it proclaimed that 'All human rights are universal, indivisible and interdependent and interrelated.'[32] This position is now the default position of international human rights law (as is evidenced in the post-1993 UN human rights instruments), though not necessarily national practice. While there are many good grounds for reasserting this unity, one important reason is the realization that economic and social rights can be treated as justiciable rights. Numerous authors have demolished the claim that economic and social rights are non-justiciable,[33] while in practice courts and quasi-judicial bodies have growing experience in dealing with economic and social rights claims.[34] Furthermore, courts and commentators recognize that civil and political rights have positive dimensions and that economic and social rights have negative ones; this also entails that all rights have resource implications. As a matter of international human rights law, it is no longer possible to sustain any argument of a hierarchy between civil and political rights on the one hand and economic and social ones on the other.

The second important development, perhaps ironically, is a shift in focus away from judicial protection of human rights. The latter part of the twentieth

32 Paragraph 5.

33 See for example Aoife Nolan, Malcolm Langford and Bruce Porter, 'The Justiciability of Social and Economic Rights: an Updated Appraisal' (2007) NYU Centre for Human Rights and Global Justice Working Paper Series.

34 See Malcolm Langford (ed), *Social Rights Jurisprudence: Emerging Trends in International and Comparative Law* (Cambridge UP 2009). Chapters 3 and 4 will consider some examples of courts from around the world that have addressed social and economic rights.

century saw much emphasis on the role of judges. Partly this was down to the prestige of the US 'Warren Court' era of constitutional jurisprudence, when liberal decisions on equal protection, free speech and religious liberty produced headline reactions and even virulent counter-reactions. But it was not just the US; courts or constitutional tribunals assumed greater importance in many jurisdictions, frequently in the aftermath of major constitutional transitions. This was true at the end of the Second World War (Germany, Italy), but also with the demise of fascist states in Europe (Spain, Portugal), authoritarian regimes in Latin America, communist dictatorships in Eastern Europe and the Apartheid regime in South Africa. Many countries embraced a greater role for judges in protecting constitutional rights. Several of these courts or tribunals have been willing to intervene dramatically in budgetary[35] or social security and welfare policy.[36]

The judicial protection of human and constitutional rights remains vital, but the last few decades have seen increased awareness of the need to develop *non-judicial* means to protect rights. This is in response to perceived weaknesses in the judicial model for protecting rights. The traditional judicial process suffers from important limitations.[37] An applicant needs to satisfy procedural requirements such as standing to even get into court. An applicant seeking redress in the courts may face problems in terms of lack of knowledge or confidence, cost, delay or gathering evidence. The litigation model tends to deal with problems retrospectively. The traditional litigation model focuses on matters affecting the individual litigants, and may not be suited to dealing with more complex problems. The frequently individual-focused nature of litigation means that an important law suit may be settled and, hence, an important precedent avoided. Even if a court hears a case, the judges may feel they need to tread with caution and show deference, institutional respect or a margin of appreciation to public authorities. Even where an applicant is successful a court may be constrained in relation to the types of remedies that it can offer; it may be limited to offering redress only for the individual litigant rather than changing relevant structures; it may offer a remedy but then not continue with any sustained supervision of problems that may be on-going.

35 A number of courts have struck down budgetary provisions on procedural or substantive grounds: the Hungarian Constitutional Court in Decision 4/2006; the Portuguese Constitutional Court in Decision 187/2013. For more on such cases, see Aoife Nolan (ed), *Economic and Social Rights After the Global Financial Crisis* (Cambridge UP 2014).

36 Hirschl argues that this activism gives rise to a 'juristocracy': Ran Hirschl, *Towards Juristocracy: The Origins and Consequences of the New Constitutionalism* (Harvard UP 2004).

37 The problems with traditional litigation models, and the responses of public law or public interest models are discussed in Abram Chayes, 'The Role of the Judge in Public Law Litigation' (1976) 89 *Harvard Law Review* 1281; PN Bhagwati, 'Judicial Activism and Public Interest Litigation' (1985) 23 *Columbia Journal of Transnational Law* 561.

These problems are arguably even more striking at an international level when international courts or court-like bodies are involved. An international dimension may involve a new layer of procedural obstacles, a greater degree of judicial deference and even more delay.[38]

To some extent, the development of 'public law'[39] models of adjudication involving class actions, public interest litigation or social action litigation, seeks to address these problems. An alternative is to look for change beyond the courts. This does not mean, however, simply a return to the notion that the ordinary democratic political process suffices to protect rights; rather, it takes the form of new institutions or procedures.

This may take the form of new institutions for the protection and promotion of human rights, such as specialist human rights committees in Parliament[40] or the development of National Human Rights Institutions (NHRIs).[41]

Apart from changing the judicial process or introducing new institutions, there is a third possible response to the deficits of a court-centred model.[42] This is to change the way existing political and administrative institutions approach their responsibilities so as to incorporate human rights protection and promotion into their daily work and thinking. This is manifested in the idea of mainstreaming.[43]

38 The Open Society Justice Initiative has produced reports on the challenges of implementing international human rights decisions: Open Society Justice Initiative, *From Rights to Remedies: Structures and Strategies for Implementing International Human Rights Decisions* (Open Society 2013); Open Society Justice Initiative, *From Judgment to Justice: Implementing International and Regional Human Rights Decisions* (Open Society 2010).

39 See the landmark discussion of different models of adjudication in Abram Chayes, 'The Role of the Judge in Public Law Litigation' (1976) 89 *Harvard Law Review* 1281.

40 The UK's Joint Committee on Human Rights is a notable example: Murray Hunt, 'Enhancing Parliament's Role in Relation to Economic and Social Rights' (2010) *European Human Rights Law Review* 242.

41 NHRIs developed from earlier institutions such as independent ombudsman or mediator offices, or consultative committee on human rights. By the 1990s they became recognised as a distinctive type of state institution, created and funded by the state, but with guarantees of independence and special legal powers. The requirements to be an independent and effective NHRI were set out by the UN in the Paris Principles, 1993: Principles relating to the Status of National Institutions for the Promotion and Protection of Human Rights ['Paris Principles'] 1993 GA Res. 48, UN GAOR, A/Res/48/134 A/RES/48/134. On NHRIs see Anne Smith, 'The Unique Position of National Human Rights Institutions: A Mixed Blessing' (2006) 28 *Human Rights Quarterly* 904; Thomas Pegram, 'Diffusion Across Political Systems: The Global Spread of National Human Rights Institutions' (2010) 32 *Human Rights Quarterly* 729; Stephen Livingstone and Rachel Murray, 'The Effectiveness of National Human Rights Institutions' in Simon Halliday and Patrick Schmidt (eds) *Human Rights Brought Home* (Hart 2004).

42 For the avoidance of doubt: these approaches are not exclusive and can all be pursued in tandem.

43 Mainstreaming ideas have been popular in relation to specific sectors. Thus, gender mainstreaming has become especially prominent, and indeed there have been gender budgeting initiatives; the same is true also of child-centred approaches. More recently, this has been

The need for approaches that are not court-centric can be found in the Universal Declaration of Human Rights itself. The UDHR was conceived as a hortatory proclamation, and its preamble speaks of the need for,

> every individual and every organ of society, keeping this Declaration constantly in mind, shall strive by teaching and education to promote respect for these rights and freedoms and by progressive measures, national and international, to secure their universal and effective recognition and observance . . .

This preambular exhortation does not speak about courts, but about every organ of society (and indeed individuals); it highlights the need to keep the universal rights in mind, and envisages teaching and education but also progressive measures to ensure that rights are universally and effectively protected. The Preamble thus signals the importance of one of the final rights listed in the Declaration: the entitlement to a 'social and international order in which the rights and freedoms set forth in this Declaration can be fully realized' (Article 28). This is not a goal that can be fully achieved by even the most interventionist or activist of courts; rather, it requires concerted effort on the part of politicians, public servants, civil society and citizens.

It is within this context that rights-based budget analysis projects have developed: a realization that human rights are not just the business of courts, but that other institutions have a role – indeed, probably the key role – in protecting and promoting human rights. Bearing this in mind, we now need to say more on budgets and budget analysis.

Budgets and human rights budget analysis

Before looking at the notion of budget analysis, we have to make a few important observations about budgets and public finances in general. This is necessarily a fairly abstract discussion, as practices, procedures and institutions will differ from country to country, depending on matters such as the

expanded into the broader idea of equality mainstreaming. The mainstreaming ideal seeks to combat the notion that policymaking and service delivery are distinct somehow from the promotion of gender equality, child-centred policies or equality. The disadvantages of treating these factors as different is that they tend to be marginalized and forgotten about during the core work of the relevant public body; this may lead to a gender, child or equality dimension being 'tacked on' to a policy that has largely been designed and delivered with entirely different or even potentially incompatible goals in mind. The mainstreaming model requires that all public authorities treat gender equality, child-centred approaches or equality as central to their core mission. On mainstreaming and ESR budget analysis see Eoin Rooney and Colin Harvey, 'Better on the Margins? A Critique of Mainstreaming Economic and Social Rights' in Aoife Nolan, Rory O'Connell and Colin Harvey (eds) *Human Rights and Public Finance* (Hart 2013).

constitutional structure, presence of natural resources, importance of developmental aid.[44]

The field of budgets and public finances covers the processes by which a country generates income, secures financial resources (taxation, borrowing, development aid), manages the taxation system, allocates those resources to distinct agents or purposes, expends those resources and monitors the use of the resources. The budgetary process also includes executive explanations of the broader economic context, with predictions for how the economy will develop.[45]

Thus, the budget is really a process over a period of time, typically a year.[46] It involves distinct stages of formulation by the executive, approval by the legislature, execution by government, and a final stage of auditing and evaluation.[47] Within each stage there may be different budgetary documents to consider.[48] Thus, at the level of formulation, even before the government produces a formal budget proposal, it may publish pre-budget documentation.[49]

When the executive produces a formal budget proposal, this includes a formal legislative proposal (an appropriations or budget bill) as the budget typically needs legislative sanction.[50] The formal budget proposal will include, among much other information, details about how resources will be expended.[51] The next stage is the formal, approved budget, which is typically a legislative act. The formal approval of the budget is by no means the final stage in the process, however. Rather, it is followed by periodic reviews of the budget, some minor but others more in the nature of a 'comprehensive assessment of the government's fiscal performance'.[52] This latter, more strategic document, may

44 Vivek Ramkumar and Isaac Shapiro, *Guide to Transparency in Government Budget Reports: Why are Budget Reports Important, and What Should They Include?* (International Budget Partnership 2010) 14.

45 Ibid 12.

46 Andrew Norton and Diane Elson, *What's Behind the Budget?: Politics, Rights and Accountability in the Budget Process* (Overseas Development Institute 2002) 7.

47 Vivek Ramkumar and Isaac Shapiro, *Guide to Transparency in Government Budget Reports: Why are Budget Reports Important, and What Should They Include?* (International Budget Partnership 2010) 4–5. Even within this four-stage process there are many different elements; Norton and Elson identify eleven different stages within this broad four-stage cycle: Norton, Andrew and Diane Elson, *What's Behind the Budget?: Politics, Rights and Accountability in the Budget Process* (Overseas Development Institute 2002) 8.

48 Ramkumar and Shapiro ibid 5.

49 Ramkumar and Shapiro ibid 6.

50 Ramkumar and Shapiro ibid 12. According to these authors the budget should also include a budget speech, a summary, the formal bill, a description of economic developments, discussion of fiscal strategy, explanation as to how the budget will be financed, details on the debt, details on publicly owned assets, details of other fiscal matters, and an overview of the state-owned corporations; ibid.

51 Ramkumar and Shapiro ibid 12.

52 Ramkumar and Shapiro ibid 27.

make adjustments to the budget in the light of economic conditions, performance, or other changes in circumstance.[53]

Centralization, technocracy, complexity

Unsurprisingly, budgetary processes differ from country to country.[54] As we will discuss below, in many states, the process is highly centralized; it may also be regarded as highly technocratic and complex, calling for technical expertise rather than politics.

The centralized and technocratic nature of budget processes is expressed in numerous ways. Historically, control over finances has been linked to representative political institutions;[55] while this may well imply a major role for parliaments in the budgetary process, in practice the extent of parliamentary involvement differs considerably.[56] In many countries the process is often centralized in that the executive branch of central government will take the lead.[57] For the representative institution to exercise effective control it requires appropriate powers, organization (e.g., a strong committee system) and access to information. It is rare for a representative institution to benefit from all of these; a 2003 survey of forty-three countries found that only the US Congress, and to a lesser degree the Swedish and Norwegian parliaments, possessed all three requirements to a significant extent.[58] In the absence of these features, the role of the representative institution is likely to be secondary to the central executive. And even if the representative institution possesses formal powers these may be of limited effectiveness due to practical or political considerations.[59]

53 Ramkumar and Shapiro ibid 31.

54 Comparative surveys are found in Rick Stapenhurst, Riccardo Pelizzo, David M. Olson and Lisa von Tapp, *Legislative Oversight and Budgeting: a World Perspective* (World Bank 2008); Ian Lienert, *Who Controls the Budget: the Legislature or the Executive?* (International Monetary Fund Working Paper 05/115 2005).

55 Rick Stapenhurst, 'The Legislature and the Budget' in Riccardo Pelizzo, Rick Stapenhurst and David Olson (eds) *The Role of Parliaments in the Budget Process* (World Bank Institute, Washington, DC 2008) 51.

56 Joachim Wehner, 'Legislative Arrangements for Financial Scrutiny: Explaining Cross-National Variation' in Riccardo Pelizzo, Rick Stapenhurst and David Olson (eds) *The Role of Parliaments in the Budget Process* (World Bank Institute, Washington, DC 2005) 2.

57 Andrew Norton and Diane Elson, *What's Behind the Budget?: Politics, Rights and Accountability in the Budget Process* (Overseas Development Institute 2002) 9.

58 Joachim Wehner, 'Legislative Arrangements for Financial Scrutiny: Explaining Cross-National Variation' in Riccardo Pelizzo, Rick Stapenhurst and David Olson (eds) *The Role of Parliaments in the Budget Process* (World Bank Institute, Washington, DC 2005) 3–4.

59 Carolyn Forestiere and Riccardo Pelizzo, 'Does the Parliament Make a Difference? The Role of the Italian Parliament in Financial Policy' in Riccardo Pelizzo, Rick Stapenhurst and David Olson (eds) *The Role of Parliaments in the Budget Process* (World Bank Institute, Washington, DC 2005) 29–30.

Even within the executive branch of government, budgetary processes may be concentrated within one department, typically the finance ministry,[60] and other executive ministers may have limited influence over the budget. Schick explains that:

> Putting together the budget and overseeing its implementation engages a vast enterprise of specialists centred in the Finance Ministry or a similar organization at the top of government. This ministry's reach extends to all governmental departments and agencies, and entails sifting through vast amounts of financial and operational data. To do its job well, the Finance Ministry must also assess political demands and interests, as well as the efficiency of expenditure. When the budget is submitted, the Finance Ministry knows a great deal about the public finances and the legislature knows very little other than what the government wants of it.[61]

This leads to a phenomenon whereby the finance minister is necessarily one of the most powerful members of the executive, while the finance ministry will necessarily have a pre-eminent position among all the ministries.

Further, the process is a highly complex and technical one and the focus may be on the specifically economic skills required. The complex technical character of the process will frequently impact on the ability of ordinary citizens and even parliamentarians[62] to comment intelligently on the budgetary process. This effectively means that much of the decision-making process regarding the budget takes place among civil servants and politicians in a small number of ministries, with the finance ministry predominating. The process may well be accompanied by other factors, such as secrecy or severe time constraints.[63]

The centralized and technocratic character of the process may play out in other ways. Important economic decisions may be delegated to non-governmental bodies, e.g., Central Banks charged with the role of combating

60 Andrew Norton and Diane Elson, *What's Behind the Budget?: Politics, Rights and Accountability in the Budget Process* (Overseas Development Institute 2002) 10.

61 Allen Schick, 'Can National Legislatures Regain an Effective Voice in Budget Policy?' (2002) 1 (3) *OECD Journal on Budgeting* 15, 22.

62 Some countries may have specialist bodies which provide the representative institution with independent budgetary analysis such as the US Congressional Budget Office: Barry Anderson, 'The Value of a Nonpartisan, Independent, Objective Analytic Unit to the Legislative Role in Budget Preparation' in Riccardo Pelizzo, Rick Stapenhurst and David Olson (eds) *The Role of Parliaments in the Budget Process* (World Bank Institute, Washington, DC 2008).

63 Representative institutions need information provided to them in a timely and appropriate manner: Katherine Barraclough and Bill Dorotinsky, 'The Role of the Legislature in the Budget Drafting Process: A Comparative Review' in Riccardo Pelizzo, Rick Stapenhurst and David Olson (eds) *The Role of Parliaments in the Budget Process* (World Bank Institute, Washington, DC 2008) 105.

inflation. This process may reflect a view that politicians – especially elected representatives – will make decisions on political grounds that have the effect of creating fiscal problems.[64] Such a process reinforces the perceived technical and therefore supposedly politically neutral nature of budgetary and economic policymaking; at the same time, the creation of independent institutions necessarily reduces the level of political control, as well as attenuating the lines of democratic political accountability. This process of delegating responsibility for important political and economic decisions to independent national and even international organizations[65] has been aptly summed up at the 'rise of the unelected.'[66]

These features of centralization and technocratic expertise lead to a high degree of complexity that makes participation by, and accountability to, the citizenry difficult. While these features of budgetary processes may seem hostile to a human rights approach (which, as we will discuss later in this book, emphasises the principles of transparency, participation and accountability), there have been some important efforts to remedy this, as well as to introduce social justice dimensions. Norton and Elson emphasize that there is a growing awareness that questions of public expenditure are not merely technical exercises but involve political decisions.[67] A move towards greater openness and accountability is one example of this. Ramkumar and Shapiro suggest that governments need to take responsibility to produce 'Citizens Budgets',

64 Allen Schick, 'Can National Legislatures Regain an Effective Voice in Budget Policy?' (2002) 1 (3) *OECD Journal on Budgeting* 15, 16; Rick Stapenhurst, 'The Legislature and the Budget' in Riccardo Pelizzo, Rick Stapenhurst and David Olson (eds) *The Role of Parliaments in the Budget Process* (World Bank Institute, Washington, DC 2008) 54.

65 In some cases budgetary and economic decisions are directed by international or regional economic actors. Countries in the developing world have long been used to the idea of 'conditionality' whereby International Monetary Fund (IMF) or World Bank loans are accompanied by conditions as to 'structural adjustment'. On arguments that these policies violate human rights see Adam McBeth, 'A Right by Any Other Name: The Evasive Engagement of International Financial Institutions with Human Rights' [2009] *George Washington International Law Review* 40 and Adam McBeth, *International Economic Actors and Human Rights* (Routledge 2010) 184–96; Mac Darrow, *Between Light and Shadow: the World Bank, the International Monetary Fund and International Human Rights Law* (Hart 2003) 68–72. More recently, a number of European Union countries have agreed to limitations on their economic sovereignty and thus limited their freedom of action in relation to budgets. See the Treaty on Stability, Coordination and Governance (Fiscal Compact) available at http://european-council.europa.eu/media/639235/st00tscg26_en 12.pdf (accessed 10 June 2013); discussed in Leonard F.M. Besselink and Jan Herman Reestman, 'The Fiscal Compact and the European Constitutions: "Europe Speaking German"' (2012) 8 *European Constitutional Law Review* 1.

66 Frank Vibert, *The Rise of the Unelected: Democracy and the New Separation of Powers* (Cambridge UP 2007).

67 Andrew Norton and Diane Elson, *What's Behind the Budget?: Politics, Rights and Accountability in the Budget Process* (Overseas Development Institute 2002) vi.

'a simplified summary of the budget designed to facilitate discussion.'[68] They highlight the important work of the Open Budget Survey in fostering more openness and the adoption by the International Monetary Fund of this principle in its own guidance documents.[69] Alongside this work to enhance the openness of budgetary processes, some countries are attempting to redress the balance between the executive and legislative branches of government in order to enhance the influence of the representative institution[70] or even to introduce more participatory practices.[71] Sanjeev, de Renzio and Fung suggest that these positive moves towards greater transparency and accountability may be traced to different stimuli, including political transitions, economic crises, cases of corruption and certain external factors.[72] Norton and Elson identify a range of measures to include a social justice dimension in budgetary processes including pro-poor budgeting and gender budgeting.[73]

It is within this challenging but evolving terrain that we seek to develop a notion of human rights (specifically ESR)-based budget analysis.

Human rights-based budget analysis

Human rights-based budget analysis[74] concerns analyzing the process and outcomes of public finances in terms of substantive human rights obligations.

68 Vivek Ramkumar and Isaac Shapiro, *Guide to Transparency in Government Budget Reports: Why are Budget Reports Important, and What Should They Include?* (International Budget Partnership 2010) 18.

69 Ibid. See also Murray Petrie and Jon Shields, 'Producing a Citizens' Guide to the Budget: Why, What and How?' (2010) *OECD Journal on Budgeting* 2. The OECD has also produced a document on *Best Practices for Budget Transparency* (OECD, 2001).

70 Allen Schick, 'Can National Legislatures Regain an Effective Voice in Budget Policy?' (2002) 1 (3) *OECD Journal on Budgeting* 15–42; Barry Anderson, 'The Changing Role of Parliament in the Budget Process' (2009) 2009 *OECD Journal on Budgeting* 1; Rick Stapenhurst, 'The Legislature and the Budget' in Riccardo Pelizzo, Rick Stapenhurst and David Olson (eds) *The Role of Parliaments in the Budget Process* (World Bank Institute, Washington, DC 2008) 53.

71 Anwar Shah, *Participatory Budgeting* (World Bank 2007). For a UK example of participatory budgeting, see the work of the Participatory Budgeting Unit, www.participatorybudgeting.org.uk (accessed 5 November 2013).

72 Sanjeev Khagram, Paolo de Renzio and Archon Fung, 'Overview and Synthesis: The Political Economy of Fiscal Transparency, Participation, and Accountability around the World' in Sanjeev Khagram, Archon Fung and Paolo de Renzio (eds) *Open Budgets: The Political Economy of Transparency, Participation, and Accountability* (Brookings Institution Press 2013) 3.

73 Andrew Norton and Diane Elson, *What's Behind the Budget?: Politics, Rights and Accountability in the Budget Process* (Overseas Development Institute 2002) 35–45.

74 Blyberg uses 'budget analysis' more narrowly to cover 'number crunching' on revenue, allocation and expenditure figures; she uses the term 'budget work' to cover budget analysis, costing, tracking, audits, impact assessments and budget advocacy: Ann Blyberg, 'Government Budgets and Rights Implementation: Experience from Around the World' in Jody Heymann and Adele Cassola (eds) *Making Equal Rights Real* (Cambridge UP 2012) 198.

As we will explore further later on in this book, such activity may entail looking at:

- How governments manage the economy and development (macro-economic questions).
- How governments generate resources (direct taxation, indirect taxation, borrowing, grants from elsewhere including development aid).
- How governments allocate financial and other resources.
- How governments actually spend the resources (expenditure).
- The outcomes achieved by government expenditure.
- The processes of government in making these decisions.

Non-governmental organizations (NGOs), especially in developing countries, have been the trailblazers in developing budget-analysis projects. There has also been work carried out in developed countries (albeit to a more limited extent). Development, human rights and economics academics have also contributed to budget analysis work. We examine in more detail some of these contributions in Chapter 2.

Budget analysis work depends heavily on the choice of a framework to analyze the budget. In the next section, we explain our reasons for choosing a specific framework – ICESCR – and also highlight the importance of the ICESCR rights during a global economic crisis.

Choice of ICESCR as the relevant human rights framework

The framework applied in the project that formed the basis of this book is rooted in the International Covenant on Economic Social and Cultural Rights (ICESCR). The employment of ICESCR for the development of a framework for ESR-based budget analysis is appropriate for a number of reasons.

First, our focus is on one of the jurisdictions within the United Kingdom. The UK has signed and ratified ICESCR and is therefore obliged under international law to realize the rights in the Covenant. Second, although the UK has ratified the European Social Charter (1961), it has not ratified the Revised European Social Charter (1996), which accords protection to a more extensive range of social rights than the primarily labour rights-focused 1961 instrument. The UK has also ratified a number of other international treaties that might be used to supplement the provisions of ICESCR. These include the United Nations Convention on the Rights of the Child (CRC), the Convention on the Elimination of All Forms of Discrimination against Women (CEDAW) and the Convention on the Rights of Persons with Disabilities (CRPD). The primary focus of this book is on ICESCR.

A human rights framework need not necessarily be based on international law. However, as in many other jurisdictions, the national human rights framework in the UK fails to provide comprehensive protection to international

ESR obligations set out in ICESCR. The UK has not incorporated the provisions of ICESCR or any other treaties dealing extensively with ESR into domestic law.[75] This is despite the fact that the ComESCR has repeatedly called on the UK to do so.[76] Indeed, the UK's failure to do so is inconsistent with the view expressed by the ComESCR in General Comment No. 9 on the Domestic Application of the Covenant that direct incorporation of ICESCR is desirable.[77] This is not likely to change under any forthcoming Bill of Rights for the UK.[78] The Human Rights Act 1998 incorporates the European Convention on Human Rights. However, the ESR afforded protection by this instrument are narrow in scope and do not correspond, or afford coverage, to the wide range of ESR set out in ICESCR.[79] Therefore, it makes sense to focus on the state's international law obligations under ICESCR.

In defending its refusal to incorporate the provisions of ICESCR into its domestic legal system, the UK has historically argued that ESR are nothing more than programmatic objectives and are only matters of policy.[80] The UK has claimed that the national legal system is incompatible with the notion of judicially enforceable ESR.[81] It has also argued that statutes protecting ESR already ensured their domestic realization.[82] In fact, however, by signing and ratifying ICESCR, the UK (like any signatory) is obliged to make the provisions contained therein practical and effective – even if this implies burdens for the state.[83]

75 UN Committee on Economic, Social and Cultural Rights (ComESCR), *UN Committee on Economic, Social and Cultural Rights: Concluding Observations, United Kingdom of Great Britain and Northern Ireland* E/C.12/1/Add 79, 5 June 2002 paragraph 10.

76 Ibid, paragraphs 12–13.

77 ComESCR, *The Domestic Application of the Covenant, General Comment No 9* E/C.12/1998/24, 3 December 1998 paragraphs 8 and 10.

78 A commission produced a split report on a UK Bill of Rights in 2012: Commission on a Bill of Rights, *Final Report: A UK Bill of Rights? The Choice Before Us* (Commission on a Bill of Rights, UK 2012). As of May 2013 there does not appear to be any move towards adopting a UK Bill of Rights, although there are occasional threats to amend the Human Rights Act 1998 or even to leave the European Convention on Human Rights.

79 For an account of the limited protection accorded to ESR by UK public law prior to the introduction of the HRA 1998, see Ellie Palmer, *Judicial Review, Socio-Economic Rights and the Human Rights Act* (Hart 2009).

80 ComESCR, *UN Committee on Economic, Social and Cultural Rights: Concluding Observations, United Kingdom of Great Britain and Northern Ireland* E/C.12/1/Add 79, 5 June 2002 paragraph 11.

81 Joint Committee on Human Rights, *The International Covenant on Economic, Social and Cultural Rights: Twenty-First Report* (HL 183, HC 1188 2003–04) 52. See Ed Bates, 'The United Kingdom and the International Covenant on Economic, Social and Cultural Rights' in Mashood Baderin and Robert McCorquodale (eds), *Economic, Social and Cultural Rights in Action* (Oxford UP 2007) 280.

82 Ibid 260.

83 María Magdalena Sepúlveda Carmona, *The Nature of the Obligations under the International Covenant on Economic, Social and Cultural Rights* (Intersentia 2003) 80.

The refusal to incorporate ESR into the domestic legal system effectively excludes the courts and the legislature from the realm of ESR to a large extent.[84] Much has been written about the role of the judiciary and its role in remedying ESR violations. However, the legislature and the executive should not be ignored; in discharging their functions they have a crucial impact on the effective enjoyment of human rights. Admittedly, socio-economic rights are generally formulated as being imposed on 'the state' generally. However, the reality that the elected branches have primary responsibility for giving effect to socio-economic rights is recognized in the language of, for example, Article 2(1) of ICESCR. As highlighted above, this provision refers to the obligation of states' parties to 'take steps . . . with a view to achieving progressively the full realization of the rights recognized in the present Covenant by all appropriate means, *including particularly the adoption of legislative measures*' (emphasis added). Legislatures are representative bodies that provide a mechanism by which citizens participate in public affairs and government; they are also forums in which governments can be held accountable for their conduct; and they are (more or less) deliberative law-making bodies. In discharging each of these functions, they can affect the enjoyment of human rights.[85] Despite the UK's position, existing UK law fails to protect fully the rights found in ICESCR.

The *Limbuela* case[86] is but one example of such a failure. The case deals with Section 55 of the Nationality, Immigration and Asylum Act 2002, enabling the Secretary of State to withhold assistance from certain groups of asylum seekers. Not surprisingly, given its lack of enforceability at the domestic level, ICESCR is not mentioned in the judgment. The House of Lords found that individuals should not be reduced to living in conditions that would amount to 'inhuman and degrading treatment' – a right found in Article 3 of the European Convention on Human Rights (ECHR) and incorporated into the UK's domestic law by the Human Rights Act 1998. One Law Lord mentioned that mere 'rough-sleeping' alone would not suffice for Article 3 ECHR to apply.[87] According to another member of the House of Lords, that minimum threshold may be crossed when a person is left destitute by the deliberate

84 Jeff King, 'United Kingdom: Asserting Social Rights in a Multi-layered System' in Malcolm Langford (ed), *Social Rights Jurisprudence: Emerging Trends in Comparative and International Law* (Cambridge UP 2009) 276–91 deals with the justiciability of welfare rights in the UK in detail.

85 Carolyn Evans and Simon Evans, 'Evaluating the Human Rights Performance of Legislatures' (2006) 6 *Human Rights Law Review* 545, 548.

86 *R (on the application of Limbuela) v Secretary of State for the Home Department* [2005] UKHL 66.

87 See also Lord Bingham at paragraph 7, 'A general public duty to house the homeless or provide for the destitute cannot be spelled out of Article 3. But I have no doubt that the threshold may be crossed if a late applicant with no means and no alternative sources of support, unable to support himself, is, by the deliberate action of the State, denied shelter, food or the most basic necessities of life'.

action of the state and may therefore be driven to prostitution or begging.[88] This would seem to fall significantly short of the right to an adequate standard of living as set out in Article 11 ICESCR.[89]

The adoption of ICESCR seems a suitable framework, and the need to develop this framework is made all the more urgent by the global economic crisis and recession of the last few years.

Rights in a time of recession

The development of a framework based on international human rights law to assess government's employment of resources towards the realization of economic and social rights (ESR) through the budget is particularly topical in the current economic climate. Key intergovernmental forums around the crisis have barely mentioned human rights, let alone ESR specifically. This is despite the central role that such rights ought to play in both addressing the crisis and in relation to the process by which the crisis is addressed.[90] For human rights advocates this is a critical moment to highlight basic human rights principles, when decisions about how to resolve the economic crisis are being debated.[91]

Budget analysis based on ICESCR and other international law treaties are particularly relevant in the current context since they include human rights which, in order to be fully realized, are likely to have relatively high resource demands. ICESCR is especially pertinent because of its requirement that rights generally should be realized progressively using the maximum of resources available.[92] This is discussed in more detail in Chapter 3, but by way of an introduction, this provision legally requires states to do whatever they can to avoid taking retrogressive measures in the realization of the rights in that treaty.[93] In addition, a key provision of ICESCR requires that states ensure the enjoyment of rights without discrimination.[94]

88 Lord Hope's judgment paragraphs 59–60.

89 Bates argues that the court could have invoked aspects of ICESCR: Ed Bates, 'The United Kingdom and the International Covenant on Economic, Social and Cultural Rights' in Mashood Baderin and Robert McCorquodale (eds), *Economic, Social and Cultural Rights in Action* (Oxford UP 2007) 290. See also Joint Committee on Human Rights, *The International Covenant on Economic, Social and Cultural Rights Twenty-First Report*, (2003–2004 HL 183 / HC 1188) 120.

90 Ignacio Saiz 'Rights in Recession? Challenges for Economic and Social Rights Enforcement in Times of Crisis' (2009) 1 *Journal of Human Rights in Practice* 277, 281. The author refers specifically to the Stiglitz Commission. The report on the UN Conference on the World Financial and Economic Crisis and its Impact on Development can be found at www.un-ngls.org/IMG/pdf_dod.pdf (accessed 7 September 2010).

91 Saiz ibid 282.

92 Article 2(1) ICESCR.

93 ComESCR, *General Comment No. 3, The Nature of States Parties Obligations* UN Doc E/1991/23 annex III at 86 (1990) paragraph 9.

94 Article 2(2).

The potential benefit of drawing on ICESCR in the UK in general and in Northern Ireland in particular can be illustrated by a brief review of the key responses to the 2010 budget introduced by the then new Conservative Liberal Democrat coalition.[95] Initial analysis by the Institute for Fiscal Studies indicated that the overall effects of the reforms announced in the 2010 Budget were regressive.[96] Significant expenditure cuts set out in the budget entail both reductions in welfare payments and departmental spending.[97] The anticipated cuts in welfare spending were likely to affect low-income households of working age the most.[98] Further, benefits make up a higher percentage of the income of women than of men and so cuts to benefits will have a gender impact.[99] These disparate impacts fly in the face of the non-discrimination principles in ICESCR and in particular the requirement spelled out by the ComESCR that:

> even in times of severe resources constraints whether caused by a process of adjustment, of economic recession, [. . .] the vulnerable members of society can and indeed must be protected by the adoption of relatively low-cost targeted programmes.[100]

The cuts in public sector spending are likely to have a devastating effect on public service jobs across the UK,[101] possibly causing 730,000 job losses in

95 Please note that this is intended to serve as an illustration only and is by no means a complete analysis of the 2010 budget. This would be beyond the scope and the purpose of this book.

96 Institute for Fiscal Studies *The Distributional Effect of Tax and Benefit Reforms to be Introduced between June 2010 and April 2014: A Revised Assessment*; J. Browne and P. Levell (eds) IFS Briefing Note BN108 (2010) 1 available at www.ifs.org.uk/bns/bn108.pdf (accessed 16 September 2010).

97 Economic Research Institute Northern Ireland/ Oxford Economics *Cutting Carefully – How Repairing UK Finances Will Impact NI: A report for NICVA*, July 2010 page 5 available at www.donegallpass.org/Oxford_Economics_Report_-_impact_on_NI_July_2010.pdf (accessed 14 September 2010).

98 Institute for Fiscal Studies, *The Distributional Effect of Tax and Benefit Reforms to be Introduced between June 2010 and April 2014: A Revised Assessment*; J. Browne and P. Levell (eds) IFS Briefing Note BN108 (2010) page 1 available at www.ifs.org.uk/bns/bn108.pdf (accessed 16 September 2010).

99 Women's Budget Group, *The Impact on Women of the Budget 2012* (Women's Budget Group 2012) available at http://wbg.org.uk/pdfs/The-Impact-on-Women-of-the-Budget-2012-FINAL.pdf (accessed 14 June 2013).

100 ComESCR, *General Comment No. 3, The Nature of States Parties Obligations* UN Doc E/1991/23 annex III at 86 (1990) paragraph 12.

101 Economic Research Institute Northern Ireland/ Oxford Economics *Cutting Carefully – How Repairing UK Finances Will Impact NI: A Report for NICVA* July 2010 page 5 available at www.donegallpass.org/Oxford_Economics_Report_-_impact_on_NI_July_2010.pdf (accessed 14 September 2010).

the public sector between 2011 and 2017.[102] They are, however, also likely to have a particularly significant impact on Northern Ireland – a region that depends more heavily on the public sector than elsewhere in the UK.[103] This also seems likely to have serious effects on equality between men and women; approximately two-thirds of the public sector workforce are female, resulting in women being disproportionately affected by the public sector cuts as well as reductions in benefits.[104] In contrast to this, Article 3 of ICESCR states specifically that 'States Parties to the present Covenant undertake to ensure the equal rights of men and women to the enjoyment of all economic, social and cultural rights set forth in the present Covenant.'

The need for a human rights analysis of budgetary decisions is therefore timely – indeed, urgent. Having introduced some of the wider contexts, the next section provides an introduction to the jurisdiction in which our chosen case studies are based – Northern Ireland, which is an example of devolution within the United Kingdom.

Northern Ireland

In this section we discuss our reasons for selecting Northern Ireland as the local context for the purposes of this book. We outline the historical background to Northern Ireland, highlight Northern Ireland as an example of a devolved sub-national jurisdiction within the UK, and then introduce some of the important features of the constitutional structures and budgetary arrangements of this jurisdiction.

Choice of local focus: Why Northern Ireland?

While much that we write in Chapters 2 and 3 will not relate specifically to Northern Ireland, our empirical budget analysis case studies in Part Two will focus more particularly on that jurisdiction – although the points made in them are certainly not limited to that region. There are some very specific aspects of the local arrangements that need to be discussed, but first we should

102 Women's Budget Group, *The Impact on Women of the Budget 2012* (Women's Budget Group 2012) available at http://wbg.org.uk/pdfs/The-Impact-on-Women-of-the-Budget-2012-FINAL.pdf (accessed 14 June 2013).

103 NI has 31 per cent of employment in public services compared to 25.9 per cent in the UK. NI's dependence on public spending is even clearer with public expenditure close to 70 per cent relative to GVA compared to a UK figure of 43 per cent. ERINI ibid page 6, 7.

104 Women's Budget Group, *The Impact on Women of the Budget 2012* (Women's Budget Group 2012) available at http://wbg.org.uk/pdfs/The-Impact-on-Women-of-the-Budget-2012-FINAL.pdf (accessed 14 June 2013).

explain the rationale for the focus on Northern Ireland and outline how that jurisdiction's experiences are nevertheless generalizable.

Northern Ireland offered a valuable jurisdictional focus for our work as an example of a devolved sub-national region. While there are peculiar limitations involved in focusing on this particular type of polity, it is not unique in having this status. Its experiences may therefore be directly relevant to other sub-national authorities.

Furthermore, some of the experiences that have shaped the Northern Irish political system will be familiar to persons in other jurisdictions. As we will see in Chapter 6, one key phenomenon in the housing context in Northern Ireland has been the shift from a model of public provision of housing to one that emphasizes more the role of the market and private financing. Far from being distinctive to Northern Ireland, this shift from public provision to market values has been experienced in many countries over the last four decades and across many social spheres. Similarly, to the extent that the case studies reveal problems about the processes and data used in budgetary decision-making, we believe these experiences will resonate with observers elsewhere.

Apart from these experiences that may be generalizable, there were reasons peculiar to Northern Ireland for its selection. The region was an attractive choice as well because it had relatively new political arrangements. The Northern Irish devolution system had been suspended during the period 2002–07. It has effectively only been running since 2007; our project hoped to influence the development of new systems. Furthermore, the history of the conflict was an important consideration. Human rights violations were key to that conflict, both in precipitating it and prolonging it. The end of the conflict was associated with the need to develop new human rights institutions and protections.[105] The peace process and early period of devolution saw the introduction of a NHRI in Northern Ireland (the Northern Ireland Human Rights Commission), as well as innovations in terms of an Equality Commission, a Children's Commissioner and an as-yet-unfinished debate about a bill of rights for Northern Ireland. Northern Ireland was one of the pioneers in equality mainstreaming.[106] This seemed fertile ground for introducing human rights-based budget analysis as a novel human rights initiative in a novel political context.

105 Brice Dickson, 'The Protection of Human Rights – Lessons from Northern Ireland' (2000) *European Human Rights Law Review* 213.

106 Christopher McCrudden, 'Mainstreaming Equality in the Governance of Northern Ireland' (1999) 22 *Fordham International Law Journal* 1696.

Northern Ireland: Brief history[107]

The 1800 Acts of Union, passed by the British and Irish Parliaments, created the United Kingdom of Great Britain and Ireland. Throughout the nineteenth and early twentieth centuries there were repeated efforts by Irish nationalists to undo this union.[108] Moderate movements sought 'Home Rule' (what we now call devolution), i.e., a separate Parliament in Dublin for domestic Irish affairs but with Ireland remaining within the United Kingdom. There were also stronger demands made by militant nationalist groups for Irish independence. During this time, but especially towards the end of the nineteenth century,[109] unionist politicians argued in favour of keeping the union with Britain.[110] Unionists were concentrated in the north-east of the island, though also spread throughout the island. These political divisions mirrored sectarian divisions: while there were exceptions, unionists tended to adhere to different Protestant faiths, while nationalists tended to be Catholic.

Matters climaxed in the early twentieth century, with increased militarization in both unionist and nationalist camps. During 1919–21, a guerrilla war was fought between militant Irish nationalists (now grouped under the labels of the Irish Republican Army (IRA) and Sinn Féin (SF)) and the UK forces. This resulted in a more-or-less independent Irish state in 1921, but a partitioned island. Northern Ireland, with its unionist and Protestant majority, remained within the UK, with its own separate Parliament for domestic affairs.[111]

The southern twenty-six counties of Ireland formed the Irish Free State, which had dominion status within the British Empire (later Common-

107 There are many publications on the history of Northern Ireland and especially the conflict. Any account needs to acknowledge that there are very different interpretations of this history; overviews of differing interpretations are provided in John Whyte, *Interpreting Northern Ireland* (Clarendon 1991) and John McGarry and Brendan O'Leary, *Explaining Northern Ireland: Broken Images* (Blackwell 1995). Histories of Northern Ireland include Patrick Buckland, *A History of Northern Ireland* (Gill & Macmillan 1981); Paul Bew, Peter Gibbon and Henry Patterson, *Northern Ireland 1921–2001: Political Forces and Social Classes* (Rev. and updated Serif 2002); Thomas Hennessey, *A History of Northern Ireland, 1920–1996* (Macmillan 1997). See Claire Palley, 'The Evolution, Disintegration and Possible Reconstruction of the Northern Ireland Constitution' (1972) 1 *Anglo-American Law Review* 368 for the constitutional background and an analysis of developments in the important period prior to 1972.

108 Alvin Jackson, *Ireland, 1798–1998: Politics and War (A History of the Modern British Isles)* (Blackwell 1999).

109 The unsuccessful introduction of a Home Rule Bill in 1886 galvanized unionist opposition: John Darby, 'The Historical Background' in John Darby (ed) *Northern Ireland: The Background to the Conflict* (Syracuse UP 1983) 18.

110 Claire Palley, 'The Evolution, Disintegration and Possible Reconstruction of the Northern Ireland Constitution' (1972) 1 *Anglo-American Law Review* 368, 368–375.

111 Government of Ireland Act 1920.

wealth).[112] In 1937, the Free State adopted a new Constitution, which removed most of the remaining links with the UK and adopted the name 'Ireland'.[113] Many of the provisions of the 1937 Constitution included distinctively nationalist language,[114] and Christian, even Catholic, overtones;[115] in addition, the Constitution included a territorial claim to Northern Ireland.[116] In 1948, Ireland formally left the Commonwealth and described itself as a Republic.[117] The response of the UK was to pass the Ireland Act 1949 to guarantee that the constitutional position of Northern Ireland would not be changed without the consent of the Northern Ireland Parliament.[118]

The Northern Ireland devolved regime 1921–72 was thus the UK's first experiment with devolution. Its beginnings were inauspicious in many ways. It was born 'amid bloodshed and communal disorder';[119] its southern neighbour was hostile to its existence; and its own population was deeply divided. Northern Ireland was constructed with an effectively permanent unionist and Protestant majority, but with a very substantial nationalist and Catholic minority.

Throughout the period 1921–72, the Unionist Party dominated politics; no other party held power in this time. For most of it, the opposition Nationalist Party did not take its seats in the Parliament and so the Unionist Party governed effectively without opposition.[120] Northern Ireland experienced periodic outbursts of civil unrest and political violence. Discrimination manifested itself in politics, security matters, public and private employment and housing.[121] The education system was effectively segregated.[122]

112 Anglo-Irish Treaty 1921 available at www.nationalarchives.ie/topics/anglo_irish/dfaexhib2.html (accessed 31 May 2013).

113 'Ireland' is the name of the twenty-six-county state; it is also the name of the island.

114 See the Preamble, Articles 1–3, Article 8 (national language is Irish) of the original 1937 Constitution.

115 The original 1937 Constitution included a provision in Article 44 recognizing the 'special position' of the Catholic Church. This was deleted following a referendum in 1972.

116 Articles 2 and 3 of the original Constitution.

117 Republic of Ireland Act 1948 (Ireland).

118 The Ireland Act 1949 also specified that Irish citizens were not to be treated as foreigners in UK law.

119 John Darby, 'The Historical Background' in John Darby (ed) *Northern Ireland: the Background to the Conflict* (Syracuse UP 1983) 21.

120 The Nationalist Party withdrew from the Parliament in 1932: From 1958–65 the official opposition consisted of four Northern Ireland Labour Party MPs. The Nationalist Party took their seats from 1965–8. Patrick Buckland, *A History of Northern Ireland* (Gill & Macmillan 1981) 70, 108.

121 On discrimination during this period see John Whyte, 'How much Discrimination was there under the Unionist Regime, 1921–68?' in Tom Gallagher and James O'Connell (eds) *Contemporary Irish Studies* (Manchester UP 1983); Cameron Report, *Disturbances in Northern Ireland: Report of the Commission appointed by the Governor of Northern Ireland* (HMSO, Belfast 1969) Cmnd 532.

122 Patrick Buckland, *A History of Northern Ireland* (Gill & Macmillan 1981) 77, 90.

Following the Second World War, the UK, including Northern Ireland, adopted numerous welfare state initiatives. This lead to a growing emphasis on secondary and tertiary education and a greater involvement of the state in housing provision.[123] Housing was important not only in economic and social terms; it was also significant politically. The distribution of the population was tied into systems of political gerrymandering.[124] Thus, political involvement in the allocation of housing inevitably lead to discrimination and segregation. This provoked an important reaction in the 1960s: civil rights protesters conducted marches to highlight discrimination in Northern Ireland. They were met with opposition from unionist and Protestant organizations. Civil unrest escalated in 1968–9 leading to the momentous decision to introduce UK armed forces on to the streets of Northern Ireland in August 1969. While initially welcomed by the nationalist minority, relations quickly deteriorated. The Irish Republican Army (IRA) split and the newly formed 'Provisional' IRA re-launched a campaign to end what it termed the British occupation of Ireland.[125] The Provisional IRA was the most significant paramilitary organization during the conflict but it was not the only one. There were also other nationalist or 'republican' paramilitary groups. As well as nationalist groups, a number of paramilitary organizations emerged to defend the union with Britain; these are frequently called 'loyalist' organizations.

Thus the conflict, euphemistically termed the 'Troubles', was born.[126] The Northern Ireland and UK governments responded with a series of important reforms and security measures. The reforms included political reform, security reform and reforms affecting housing. For instance, an independent Housing Executive was created to end political control over housing allocation decisions.[127] Later, the UK Government established a Standing Advisory Committee on Human Rights (SACHR) and introduced laws banning religious and political discrimination in employment.[128]

Security responses included internment without trial,[129] the use of inhuman and degrading treatment in interrogations[130] and the use of force by the security

123 Patrick Buckland, *A History of Northern Ireland* (Gill & Macmillan 1981) 89–91, 116.

124 Buckland, ibid 101.

125 There are numerous histories of the IRA including Ed Moloney, *A Secret History of the IRA* (Penguin 2003); Tim Pat Coogan, *The IRA* (Palgrave for St Martin's Press 2002); Richard English, *Armed Struggle: the History of the IRA* (Oxford UP 2003).

126 Accounts of the conflict include David McKittrick and David McVea, *Making Sense of the Troubles: A History of the Northern Ireland Conflict* (Rev. ed. Viking 2012); Paul Dixon, *Northern Ireland: The Politics of War and Peace* (Palgrave 2001); J. Bowyer Bell, *The Irish Troubles: A Generation of Political Violence, 1967–1992* (St Martin's Press 1993); Tim Pat Coogan, *The Troubles: Ireland's Ordeal, 1966–1996 and the Search for Peace* (Arrow 1996).

127 Housing Executive Act (NI) 1971.

128 Fair Employment (Northern Ireland) Act 1976.

129 Kevin Boyle, Tom Hadden and Paddy Hillyard, *Law and State: The Case of Northern Ireland* (Robertson 1975).

130 The European Court of Human Rights found that some internees had been subjected to inhuman and degrading treatment in *Ireland v United Kingdom* (1978) 2 EHRR 25.

forces.[131] In 1972, the UK Government concluded that the Northern Ireland Parliament and Government could no longer respond adequately to the crisis. The Northern Ireland Parliament was prorogued[132] and a lengthy period of 'direct rule' instituted. Direct rule did not treat Northern Ireland as an integral part of the UK. Rather, Northern Ireland was treated as a devolved jurisdiction but administered by a UK minister, aided by the civil service.[133] This suspended a situation where the Unionist party in Northern Ireland dominated political arrangements, but also considerably weakened the normal processes of democratic control and accountability.

Following the introduction of direct rule in 1972, there were repeated initiatives to find a political solution to the conflict; these frequently recognized the need for a power-sharing or consociational dimension (i.e., unionist and nationalist politicians would share power in an executive coalition) and some sort of link with Ireland.[134] All these efforts failed until the important decision in 1994 of the IRA and other paramilitary organizations to declare a ceasefire. While the IRA later broke this ceasefire, the arrival of a New Labour Government in the UK in 1997 created the opportunity for a renewed ceasefire and renewed efforts at a negotiated end to the conflict. Coincidentally, the New Labour Government was elected on a platform to introduce greater measures of devolution within the UK. The Northern Irish settlement thus has to be seen both in the context of the history of conflict and within the context of the 1998 devolution reforms introduced by New Labour. This set the stage for the 1998 or Belfast/Good Friday Agreement.

We turn next to examine UK devolution and the institutions established after 1998, but we first highlight here the costs of the conflict. During the conflict, actors on all sides violated human rights. More than 3500 people were killed in Northern Ireland (and elsewhere) during this time.[135] The majority of the victims were civilians, i.e., did not belong to security forces or paramilitary groups.[136] A conservative estimate of the numbers physically

131 Fionnuala Ní Aoláin, *The Politics of Force* (Blackstaff Press 2000).

132 Northern Ireland (Temporary Provisions) Act 1972.

133 Claire Palley, 'The Evolution, Disintegration and Possible Reconstruction of the Northern Ireland Constitution' (1972) 1 *Anglo-American Law Review* 368, 445–450.

134 John Morison and Stephen Livingstone, *Reshaping Public Power* (Sweet & Maxwell 1995) discusses the key features of constitutional proposals during this period.

135 The exact figure for deaths is uncertain but lies somewhere between 3500 and 4000: Marie-Therese Fay, Mike Morrissey and Marie Smyth, *Northern Ireland's Troubles: The Human Costs* (Pluto Press in association with The Cost of the Troubles Study 1999) 127. CAIN publishes Malcolm Sutton's *An Index of Death from the Conflict in Ireland* 1969–2001, indicating a death toll of 3530 available at http://cain.ulst.ac.uk/sutton/ (accessed 3 June 2013). David McKittrick, *Lost Lives: The Stories of the Men, Women and Children who Died as a Result of the Northern Ireland Troubles* (Mainstream 2001) records the details of everyone who was killed during the conflict.

136 Marie-Therese Fay, Mike Morrissey and Marie Smyth, *Northern Ireland's Troubles: The Human Costs* (Pluto Press in association with The Cost of the Troubles Study 1999) 168.

injured by the conflict during the period 1971–96 is 37,541.[137] These figures need to be considered in the context of a small population of less than 2 million. Despite enormous improvements since the ceasefires and the 1998 Agreement, the Northern Ireland of the twenty-first century is still affected by this legacy of discrimination, segregation and violence.[138] Thus, for instance, in 2010 it was reported that sixteen of the twenty most deprived wards were Catholic;[139] in 2011 more than a third of wards were 'single community' areas (this is a decrease from fifty per cent in 2001);[140] sectarian attacks averaged 3.4 a day in 2011–12.[141] The cost of policing Northern Ireland is proportionately more than double the cost in England and Wales.[142]

Northern Ireland and UK devolution

Northern Ireland is a devolved jurisdiction within the United Kingdom. This is part of the phenomenon of 'multi-level governance'. Even if the central national level dominates budgetary discussions, relevant budgetary decisions are often made within a state at provincial or local level. Indeed the process of multi-level governance, which highlights the role of international and regional arrangements, also shows the importance of provincial or local levels of government. Some countries have decentralized political powers to provincial or local authorities. This may take the form of strongly developed local government arrangements, as in Italy. At the most developed stage, this decentralization includes states with federal arrangements such as India, Mexico, South Africa and the United States. Between decentralisation and federalism lies the category of devolution, which is our concern in this book.

The introduction of devolution across the UK is a relatively recent phenomenon, apart from the Northern Ireland experiment. As part of a series of constitutional reforms,[143] the Labour Government elected in 1997 embarked

137 Fay, Morrissey and Smyth ibid 160.

138 See Deloitte, *Research into the Financial Cost of the Northern Ireland Divide* (2008); Paul Nolan, *Northern Ireland Peace Monitoring Report: Number One* (Community Relations Council 2012); Paul Nolan, *Northern Ireland Peace Monitoring Report: Number Two* (Community Relations Council 2013).

139 Paul Nolan, *Northern Ireland Peace Monitoring Report: Number Two* (Community Relations Council 2013) 92.

140 Paul Nolan, *Northern Ireland Peace Monitoring Report: Number Two* (Community Relations Council 2013) 120.

141 Paul Nolan, *Northern Ireland Peace Monitoring Report: Number Two* (Community Relations Council 2013) 49.

142 While not easy to quantify, this could represent an additional annual cost for Northern Ireland of as much as £504 million: Deloitte, *Research into the Financial Cost of the Northern Ireland Divide* (2008) 41, 49.

143 For accounts of the devolution system, see Vernon Bogdanor, *The New British Constitution* (Hart Publishing 2009); Anthony Stephen King, *The British Constitution* (Oxford UP 2007); Brigid Hadfield, 'Devolution: A National Conversation?' in Jeffrey Jowell and Dawn Oliver (eds) *The Changing Constitution* (7th Oxford UP 2011).

on an important process of devolution, creating a Parliament in Scotland,[144] an Assembly in Northern Ireland[145] and a National Assembly in Wales.[146]

There are a number of features of devolution in the UK that require highlighting. First, there is no single codified document that functions as an entrenched written constitution (or, as is commonly said, the UK has no written constitution). This means that there is no formal document *binding the central political authorities* as well as devolved authorities so as to entrench any particular division of competences as between the centre and the devolved regions. This is a key difference with traditional federal systems where the central authorities cannot unilaterally change the balance of powers with the states or provinces of the federal state. Connected with this is the distinctive UK concept of parliamentary sovereignty; the central UK Parliament, based at Westminster, is legally competent to enact any law, and in theory can interfere with, amend, suspend or abolish provincial governance arrangements unilaterally.

It is important, though, to remember that political conventions and soft law arrangements play a significant role in the actual practice of devolution. Therefore the theoretical legislative omnicompetence of the central Parliament is, in practice if not in theory, limited.[147] The devolved assembles were created by Acts of Parliament, but subsequent to referenda in the devolved regions approving the principles of devolution. The legitimacy of these institutions is rooted therefore in popular consent and not purely an exercise of parliamentary sovereignty.[148] In the case of Northern Ireland, this was even more complex: the devolution arrangements followed a peace agreement which involved negotiations between Northern Irish political parties as well as an international treaty between the UK and Ireland; this peace agreement was approved by referenda both in Northern Ireland and Ireland; Ireland changed its own Constitution on the basis of this agreement. This background of popular approval in referenda would make difficult in practice any arbitrary exercise of the central Parliament's will. Furthermore, political conventions preclude the central political institutions from interfering in the areas of devolved competence without the consent of the devolved authorities.[149] Finally there are numerous soft law arrangements between the central and devolved authorities to facilitate governing.

A third feature of devolution in the UK is that the system is in in a state of flux; it is an ongoing project with major legislative changes to the framework

144 Scotland Act 1998.

145 Northern Ireland Act 1998.

146 Government of Wales Act 1998.

147 Vernon Bogdanor, *The New British Constitution* (Allen Lane 2008) 112.

148 Brigid Hadfield, 'Devolution: A National Conversation?' in Jeffrey Jowell and Dawn Oliver (ed) *The Changing Constitution* (7th Oxford UP 2011) 218.

149 For example, the Sewel convention in respect of Scotland: Hadfield, ibid 217; Vernon Bogdanor, *The New British Constitution* (Allen Lane 2008) 112.

being introduced in a piecemeal and ad hoc fashion. Thus the Welsh system was the subject of a major reform with the Government of Wales Act 2006. The Scottish system has recently been reformed with the Scotland Act 2012 and that jurisdiction is preparing for a referendum on independence in 2014. The Northern Ireland system has been the subject of repeated reform,[150] suspension,[151] renegotiation[152] and yet more reform.[153]

A fourth feature is that devolution in the UK is *asymmetrical*;[154] this indeed is signalled in the different names chosen for the different assemblies. The devolution regimes in Scotland, Northern Ireland and Wales are different in terms of their structure, their legislative competences and, to varying extents, their budgetary and economic powers. Despite the variability, there is a commonality in that all the devolved regimes depend heavily on allocation of funds from the central UK Treasury for their financing. Funding is allocated to the devolved regions according to a predetermined formula, the Barnett formula.[155] As regards Northern Ireland, more than ninety per cent of the Northern Irish budget comes from this central block grant. The remainder comes from limited local taxation powers and borrowing powers.

The 1998 Agreement and the institutional context

We have discussed Northern Ireland above in relation to the devolution regime introduced into the UK by the 1997 Labour Government. This should not detract from the unique political conjuncture that produced the Northern Irish political system. The history of a deeply divided society, the relationship with the neighbouring sovereign state of Ireland, the existence of a decades-long violent conflict; all of these mean that Northern Ireland is not a typical instance of devolution within the UK.[156]

The system of governance in Northern Ireland (NI) was agreed by a number of Northern Ireland political parties and the governments of the UK and Ireland in 1998.[157] The Northern Irish parties included what was then the largest

150 E.g. Northern Ireland Act 2000.

151 Pursuant to the Northern Ireland Act 2000, the Assembly was suspended for several months in 2000, for a day (twice) in 2001, and for a period of more than four years from 2002–07.

152 Most notably in the St Andrews Agreement negotiations of 2006.

153 Northern Ireland (St Andrews Agreement) Act 2006.

154 Vernon Bogdanor, *The New British Constitution* (Allen Lane 2008) 93.

155 Select Committee on the Barnett Formula, *The Barnett Formula* (HL 2008–2009 139).

156 Colm Campbell, Fionnuala Ní Aoláin and Colin Harvey, 'The Frontiers of Legal Analysis: Reframing the Transition in Northern Ireland' (2003) 66 *Modern Law Review* 317, 318. Also highlighting the differences between the British constitutional tradition and the Northern Ireland settlement, see Christopher McCrudden, 'Northern Ireland, The Belfast Agreement, and the British Constitution' in Jeffrey Jowell and Dawn Oliver (eds) *The Changing Constitution* (Oxford UP 2007).

157 On the 1998 Agreement see Special Issue, 'Northern Ireland, the Belfast/Good Friday Agreement' (1999) 22 *Fordham International Law Journal*; Michael Cox, Adrian Guelke and Fiona Stephen, *A Farewell to Arms? Beyond the Good Friday Agreement* (Manchester UP 2006).

unionist party (the Ulster Unionists), smaller loyalist political parties, the two main nationalist parties (Social Democratic and Labour Party, Sinn Féin), and the bipartisan Alliance Party and Women's coalition; the Democratic Unionist Party (then the second-largest unionist party) was not a participant, though it would later negotiate the St Andrews Agreement (2006).

The 1998 Belfast/Good Friday Agreement[158] was approved by referendums in both jurisdictions of Ireland and legislated for in the Northern Ireland Act 1998, adopted by the UK Parliament. The 1998 Act has been amended by the Northern Ireland (St Andrews Agreement) Act 2006 in the wake of the political agreement at St Andrews.

The Agreement consists of commitments under different headings: Declaration of Support; Constitutional Issues; Strand One: Democratic Institutions in Northern Ireland; Strand Two: North/South Ministerial Council; Strand Three: British–Irish Council and British–Irish Intergovernmental Conference; Rights, Safeguards and Equality of Opportunity; Decommissioning; Security; Policing and Justice. While Strand One institutions will be our key focus, some of these other features deserve highlighting. The Agreement recognizes Northern Ireland as part of the United Kingdom, but also adopts the self-determination principle: the people of Northern Ireland can choose to unite with Ireland.[159] Also, as part of the constitutional dimension, Ireland agreed to hold a referendum to remove the territorial claim to Northern Ireland from its Constitution. Strand Two recognizes the relationship between Northern Ireland and the island of Ireland, while Strand Three deals with the relationship between the governments and parliaments in the two islands.

The Agreement contains numerous commitments regarding human rights, equality, and policing and justice reforms. These include a statutory equality duty, enacted in Section 75 of the Northern Ireland Act, which requires designated public authorities to have due regard to the need to promote equality of opportunity on a number of different grounds. As part of this statutory duty, public authorities must conduct equality impact assessments and provide opportunities for consultation by affected groups and individuals.

The research in this book is primarily concerned with the Strand One institutions established by the Agreement and the subsequent Northern Ireland Act 1998, as amended. The Act establishes a devolved system of governance for Northern Ireland within the UK. The Westminster Parliament remains the supreme law-making authority in the UK, but under these Acts it has devolved certain competences to institutions in Northern Ireland. These

158 The Agreement is available at www.gov.uk/government/uploads/system/uploads/attachment_data/file/136652/agreement.pdf (accessed 30 May 2013). There are two agreements. One is the agreement between the different parties to the talks; the other is a formal international treaty between the UK and Ireland.

159 Northern Ireland Act 1998, s 1.

institutions include a legislative body, the Northern Ireland Assembly, and an executive body, the NI Executive. Those areas of policy for which the devolved system is responsible are known as 'transferred' or 'devolved' matters. Those areas that remain under the remit of UK Parliament are categorized as either 'excepted' or 'reserved'.[160] Excepted matters include foreign affairs, military affairs and taxation. Reserved matters are those that may be transferred to the NI Assembly at some point in the future, while excepted matters are expected to remain with the UK Parliament. The Secretary of State for Northern Ireland (conventionally a member of the UK Cabinet) is responsible for reserved matters, which until 2010 included policing and criminal justice. The Department of Justice Act (Northern Ireland) 2010 transferred these functions to the NI Department of Justice, which came into existence on 12 April 2010.

Spending on excepted matters is categorized as UK 'national' expenditure. The most important of these is social security, which is paid according to the status of the individual claimants irrespective of their geographical location.[161] Some spending on national expenditure – such as social security – is channelled through the Northern Ireland Assembly (NIA) through various agencies such as the Northern Ireland Social Security Agency or the Northern Ireland Housing Executive.

The devolved institutions follow a 'consociational' model in which power is shared between Unionists and Nationalist political representatives. One of the key decision-making institutions established by the 1998 Act is a devolved Northern Ireland Assembly (NIA) with 108 elected members, called Members of the Legislative Assembly (MLAs).[162] Each MLA must self-designate as Nationalist, Unionist, or Other.[163] For certain decisions of the Assembly, 'cross community' support is required: the measure must receive support from a majority of MLAs, a majority of Nationalist MLAs and a majority of Unionist MLAs or an overall majority of at least sixty per cent of MLAs with over forty per cent support from both Nationalists and Unionists.[164]

The Executive is headed by the First Minister (currently Peter Robinson of the Democratic Unionist Party) and the deputy First Minister (currently Martin McGuinness of Sinn Féin) who carry out their work through the Office of the First and deputy First Minister (OFMdFM).[165] The largest party in the largest designation in the Assembly designates the First Minister, while

160 These are listed in Schedules 2 and 3 of the Northern Ireland Act 1998.

161 House of Lords Select Committee on the Barnett Formula, *The Barnett Formula: 1st Report of Session 2008–09* (HL 2008–2009 139) 13.

162 Northern Ireland Act, s 33.

163 Northern Ireland Act 1998, s 4.

164 Northern Ireland Act, 1998, s 4(5).

165 Northern Ireland Act, s 16A. Responsibilities include equality.

the largest party in the second-largest designation selects the deputy First Minister.[166] Despite the adjective 'deputy', OFMdFM is a joint office and the two members must act jointly.

The Executive body is comprised of five political parties, with Ministers proportionately shared among political parties in the Assembly on the basis of the d'Hondt system.[167] Ministers are nominated by the political parties (not OFMdFM) and can only be removed by their political parties[168] or in exceptional cases by a cross-community vote in the Assembly.[169] Eleven government departments are in operation, with the Minister of each represented on the Executive. Each Executive Department is shadowed by an Assembly Committee.[170] The Departments are: Department of Agriculture and Rural Development (DARD); Department of Culture, Arts and Leisure (DCAL); Department of Education (DENI); Department for Employment and Learning; Department of Enterprise, Trade and Investment; Department of the Environment; Department of Finance and Personnel (DFP); Department of Health, Social Services and Public Safety (DHSSPS); Department for Regional Development; Department for Social Development (DSD)[171] and the Department of Justice.

The Executive tries to take decisions by consensus but, failing this, a vote may be taken. This vote may use the cross-community voting rules if three Executive members so request.[172] Executive Ministers take a pledge of office 'to serve all the people of Northern Ireland equally, and to act in accordance with the general obligations on government to promote equality and prevent discrimination'.[173] The Executive is under a statutory duty to 'adopt a strategy setting out how it proposes to tackle poverty, social exclusion and patterns of deprivation based on objective need.'[174]

Turning to the general funding context, we note that there is widespread agreement that in the UK the executive dominates budgetary decision-making: 'Nowhere is the budgetary decline of Parliament more noticeable than in Britain.'[175] Thus, the Northern Ireland institutions inherited a tradition

166 Northern Ireland Act, 1998, s 16A as amended by the Northern Ireland (St. Andrews Agreement) Act ss 8 and 27.

167 A formula which apportions posts on the basis of a party's electoral strength; Northern Ireland Act, 1998, s 18. The Minister for Justice is not selected using D'Hondt but by a cross-community vote.

168 Northern Ireland Act, s 18(9).

169 Northern Ireland Act, s 30.

170 Northern Ireland Act, s 29.

171 Responsibilities include housing, the subject matter of Chapter 6.

172 Northern Ireland Act 1998, s 28A(8).

173 Northern Ireland Act 1998, sch 4.

174 Northern Ireland Act 1998, s 28E.

175 Allen Schick, 'Can National Legislatures Regain an Effective Voice in Budget Policy?' (2002) 1 (3) *OECD Journal on Budgeting* 15, 27.

that is unfavourable to processes of participation and accountability in budgeting.

In terms of the resources available to it, the Assembly receives its funding from four main sources. The most significant is the 'block grant' from the United Kingdom Treasury (approximately ninety-two per cent). The size of the block grant is largely determined through the 'Barnett Formula'. The second source is Regional Rates (approximately six per cent); this is a form of local taxation determined by property values. Borrowing is the third source; this is worth approximately two per cent. Under the Reinvestment and Reform Initiative[176] NIA borrowing must be used for capital investment and financed by an increase in regional rates. Finally, EU Special Programmes provide less than one per cent of the funding available to the Northern Ireland authorities.

In 2010–11, the difference between total public expenditure in Northern Ireland (£23.2 billion) and receipts collected (£12.7 billion) was approximately £10.5 billion.[177] This means that in that year, the UK invested £10.5 billion more in Northern Ireland than it received from the region in taxes. This difference is termed the UK 'subvention'.

The size of the Northern Ireland budget is thus largely determined by decisions made at central government level in London. This was brought home in the reaction to the global economic crisis. In response to the global economic crisis of 2008–9, the then Labour UK government, faced with threats to the banking system, borrowed money on a large scale to fund measures to save the banking system. This resulted in a dramatic increase in public debt. The Conservative–Liberal Democrat coalition, which replaced the Labour government in May 2010, committed itself to eliminating this debt by decreasing total public expenditure. The new administration's 'emergency budget' of June 2010 reduced planned UK public expenditure for 2010/11 by £6 billion, £128 million of which came from the Northern Ireland budget.[178]

Conclusion

Human rights (and specifically ESR)-based budget analysis projects have emerged at a time when the indivisibility of all human rights has been reasserted by the United Nations, and also when attention is increasingly

176 This Initiative was negotiated with the Westminster Treasury by the Executive in 2002. It includes an investment strategy for Northern Ireland, a Strategic Investment Board to oversee the strategy, a programme of public sector reform, the establishment of borrowing criteria for the Executive and the transfer of a number of military sites from the Ministry of Defence and the Northern Ireland Office to the Executive for regeneration.

177 Paul Nolan, *Northern Ireland Peace Monitoring Report: Number Two* (Community Relations Council 2013) 27.

178 Oxford Economics and ERINI, *Cutting Carefully – How Repairing UK Finances Will Impact NI* (2010) 4.

focused on the role of non-judicial bodies in promoting and protecting human rights. Budget analysis has been taken up by practitioners and scholars across the world. This book seeks to develop the human rights framework for such budget analysis, and to demonstrate how this might be applied in a particular local context, Northern Ireland.

We will now turn to practitioners and commentators elsewhere; in Chapter 2 we review and analyze a selection of the ESR-based budget analysis case studies and guidance documents that have been developed across the globe.

2 Economic and social rights-based budget analysis

An overview

Introduction

This chapter reviews selected existing guidance and case studies on economic and social rights (ESR) budget analysis. The main purpose of this review is to inform the development of a human rights framework for ESR budget analysis outlined in Chapters 3 and 4. It also serves as an overview of previous work in the field for all those interested in ESR budget analysis. By identifying the key elements – as well as some of the gaps – in ESR-based budget analysis practice, the review provides guidance to local and global efforts to employ such a methodology.[1]

We begin by introducing the fourteen different reports that are the central focus of this chapter. We then proceed to analyze these reports. In doing so, we investigate which instruments are used, which aspects of budgets are analyzed, the relationship established in the documents between budgets and ESR principles (or not), the degree to which the reports refer to other human rights principles, and the challenges faced by those seeking to carry out ESR budget analysis. The fourth section of the chapter focuses on the budget analysis tools developed and employed in the reports. The chapter concludes with a discussion of the principal lessons that can be derived from the analysis of these reports.

ESR-based budget analysis practice: An overview

The fourteen ESR budget analysis papers considered here were selected on the basis that they constituted the best-known, most comprehensive and most influential English-language examples of ESR-based budget analysis at the

1 Please note that a more detailed analysis of the specific reports addressed in this chapter can be found in QUB Budget Analysis Project, '*Budget Analysis and Economic and Social Rights: A Review of Selected Case Studies and Guidance*' (Belfast, Queen's University Belfast, 2010), 17–81: available at www.qub.ac.uk/schools/SchoolofLaw/Research/HumanRightsCentre/ResearchProjects/BudgetAnalysis/Documents/filestore/Filetoupload,210765,en.pdf (accessed 14 June 2013).

time of the review.[2] Table 2.1, below, identifies the papers considered in the review. It shows that of these fourteen documents, five provided case studies and nine offered guidance. This emphasis on guidance highlights the relatively

Table 2.1 ESR-based budget analysis reports.

Report Number	*Author*	*Title*	*Type*	*Year*
1	Diokno	A Rights-Based Approach towards Budget Analysis	Guidance	1999
2	NYCWR and HRDP	Hunger is No Accident: New York and Federal Welfare Policies Violate the Human Right to Food	Case Study	2000
3	Fundar	Health Care: A Question of Human Rights, Not Charity	Case Study	2002
4	Shultz	Promises to Keep: Using Public Budgets as a Tool to Advance Economic, Social and Cultural Rights	Guidance	2002
5	IDASA	Budgeting for Child Socio-Economic Rights: Government Obligations and the Child's Right to Social Security and Education	Guidance	2002
6	IDASA	Monitoring Government Budget to Advance Child Rights: A Guide for NGO's	Guidance	2003
7	Fundar, IBP and IHRIP	Dignity Counts: A Guide to Using Budget Analysis to Advance Human Rights	Guidance	2004
8	IDASA	Comparative Provincial Housing Brief	Case Study	2004
9	IDASA	Child Specific Spending on the Right to Health in MTEF 2004/05 – An Identification Problem	Case Study	2004
10	IDASA	Provincial Budgets for Developmental Social Welfare Services	Case Study	2005
11	Elson	Budgeting for Women's Rights: Monitoring Government Budgets for Compliance with CEDAW	Guidance	2006
12	APRODEV	Budgeting Human Rights: Join the Efforts to Budget Human Rights	Guidance	2007
13	FAO	Budget Work to Advance the Right to Food: Many a Slip	Guidance	2009
14	IBP & IHRIP	Reading the Books: Governments' budgets and the right to education	Guidance	2010

2 This chapter is based on a review of ESR-based budget analysis work that was completed in October 2010. For details on subsequent work in this area, see the resources at http://internationalbudget.org/ and www.humanrightsbudgetwork.org/ (accessed 26 August 2013).

recent nature of the development of rights-based budget analysis methodologies. It also reflects a perceived need to educate advocates, public servants and others on the nature of human rights obligations, the relationship of such to budgets, and measures of compliance.

The papers that we examined come from a range of organizations across the globe. The majority were produced by non-governmental organizations, particularly ones based in the US, Mexico and South Africa. However, some were authored by international organizations such as the Food and Agriculture Organization (FAO) or academic practitioners.

One of the earliest contributions was Maria Diokno's *A Rights Based Approach towards Budget Analysis*.[3] This is a wide-ranging paper that examines a number of aspects of rights-based budget analysis including its value with regard to litigation and activism. The author acknowledges that the paper offers a 'beginning framework' that is 'neither definitive nor exhaustive' and that its 'limitations and gaps will likely become more evident as the rights-based approach is tested'.[4]

The New York City Welfare Reform and the Human Rights Documentation Project produced *Hunger is No Accident: New York and Federal Welfare Policies Violate the Human Right to Food* in 2000.[5] This report focuses on the implementation of the right to food in New York, with particular reference to the Personal Responsibility Act 1996, which weakened the New York Federal Food Stamp Program. It alleges a range of violations of the right to food on behalf of the New York City, New York State and Federal governments. Budgetary data is used to support a number of these alleged violations.

Fundar is a civil society organization, established in Mexico in 1999. Budget analysis forms a key component of the organization's work, which has included the monitoring of federal health and anti-poverty programmes. *Health Care: A Question of Human Rights, Not Charity* is one of Fundar's few papers published in English.[6] The paper begins by setting out a rights framework and then discusses the policy context. The report examines past health expenditure and budget allocations for 2002. It also includes data on health outputs and outcomes.

Promises to Keep: Using Public Budgets as a Tool to Advance Economic Social and Cultural Rights was produced following a three-day conference that was held in Mexico City, convened by the Ford Foundation and Fundar, and attended by human rights and budget activists.[7] It describes government budgets as

3 Maria Diokno, *A Rights-Based Approach towards Budget Analysis* (International Human Rights Internship Program 1999).

4 Ibid 5.

5 New York City Welfare Reform and Human Rights Documentation Project, *Hunger is no Accident* (2000).

6 Fundar, *Health Care: A Question of Human Rights, Not Charity* (2002).

7 Jim Schultz, *Promises to Keep: Using Public Budgets as a Tool to Advance Economic, Social and Cultural Rights* (Fundar 2002) 7.

'mechanisms for allocating public resources and, therefore, often the chief instruments through which governments either comply or fail to comply with these rights'.[8] The paper is primarily geared towards civil society organizations that seek to carry out budget analysis.

Regarded as 'one of the most experienced budget groups around the world'[9] the South African organization IDASA described itself as 'an independent public interest organization committed to promoting sustainable democracy based on active citizenship, democratic institutions and social justice'.[10] *Budgeting for Child Socio-Economic Rights* sets out a model for assessing the extent to which government budgets comply with children's socio-economic rights, particularly the rights to social security and to basic education.[11] This study is described as 'a first attempt at budget analysis from a child socio-economic rights perspective and as such, suffers from limitations and will benefit from on-going improvement'.[12] IDASA followed up with *Monitoring Government Budgets to Advance Child Rights: A Guide for NGOs* in 2003.[13] This paper outlines a framework for analysis of government budgets in relation to the Convention on the Rights of the Child (CRC).[14] It also outlines three examples of research studies by IDASA in relation to child rights.

In 2004, IDASA produced a *Comparative Provincial Housing Brief*. This paper provides a briefing on expenditure in relation to the right of access to adequate housing. The analysis focuses on spending in each of South Africa's nine provinces. Subsequently IDASA published *Child Specific Spending on the Right to Health in MTEF 2004/05* (2004). This paper sought to examine planned spending for the financial period 2004/05–06/07 in relation to the right of children, to basic health care services. A 2005 paper from IDASA, *Provincial Budgets for Developmental Social Welfare Services* concentrates on the right of children in South Africa to 'social welfare' services. These three papers from IDASA do not rely on ICESCR principles as their central framework. Rather, they employ instead the South African constitutional framework, which contains ESR, as well as domestic judicial interpretations of that framework.

Fundar and the International Human Rights Internship Program jointly produced *Dignity Counts: A Guide to Using Budget Analysis to Advance Human*

8 Ibid 7.

9 Helena Hofbauer, *Sustained Work and Dedicated Capacity* (2006) 31.

10 Source: www.idasa.org.za. IDASA announced in 2013 that it would have to close.

11 IDASA and Judith Streak, *Budgeting for Child Socio-Economic Rights: Government Obligations and the Child's Right to Social Security and Education* (IDASA 2002).

12 IDASA, *Budgeting for Child Socio-Economic Rights: Government Obligations and the Child's Right to Social Security and Education* (IDASA 2002) 57.

13 IDASA and Judith Streak, *Monitoring Government Budgets to Advance Child Rights: A Guide for NGOs* (IDASA 2003).

14 A subsequent section of the report on analyzing budget allocations is primarily focused on technical issues such as adjusting expenditure in different years for inflation.

Rights in 2004.[15] *Dignity Counts* was developed following a workshop attended by budget analysis practitioners and human rights activists in Mexico. It sets out how civil society organizations, in particular, can use budget analysis in order to assess a government's compliance with economic, social and cultural rights obligations. The report uses the Fundar case study *Health Care: A Question of Rights Not Charity* in order to demonstrate the meaning of the ESR concepts referred to.

Within the broad arena of human rights and equality work, there has been considerable interest in the ideas of gender mainstreaming including gender budgeting, and so we examine a report on gender budgeting. Diane Elson wrote *Budgeting for Women's Rights: Monitoring Government Budgets for Compliance with CEDAW* (2006) to provide 'a framework for applying a rights-based approach to budgets from a gender perspective'.[16] CEDAW does not itself establish specific ESR guarantees but it contains a range of ESR-related equality/non-discrimination requirements. The report engages with these extensively.

In 2007, APRODEV[17] Rights and Development Group published *Budgeting Human Rights: Join the Efforts to Budget Human Rights*. This is a short paper produced following an international workshop on 'Budgeting the Rights' in Geneva and is mainly concerned with establishing the cost (i.e., the resources required) to realize economic, social and cultural rights, and 'frontloading' these costs into budgets.

The Food and Agriculture Organization (FAO) produced *Budget Work to Advance the Right to Food: Many a Slip* in 2009. The objective of this paper was to build on *Dignity Counts*[18] with particular reference to using budget analysis in order to assess a government's compliance with its right to food obligations. The title 'many a slip' refers to the gap between a government's rhetoric and what it actually delivers[19] with budget analysis understood as a tool for examining the dissonance between the two. The report provides guidance on identifying and building a budget-related right to food case, the performance of budget analysis, as well as on how to present a right to food claim in order to ensure that those carrying out the analysis are understood – and their concerns heard. The report includes a number of examples of right to food-based budget analysis exercises.

The International Human Rights Internship Program and Institute of International Education published the final report that we examine – *Reading*

15 Helena Hofbauer, Ann Blyberg and Warren Krafchik, *Dignity Counts* (Fundar; International Budget Project and the International Human Rights Internship Program, 2004).

16 Diane Elson, *Budgeting for Women's Rights: Monitoring Government Budgets for Compliance with CEDAW* (2006) 1.

17 Association of World Council of Churches related Development Organizations in Europe.

18 Fundar, International Budget Project, International Human Rights Internship Program, *Dignity Counts: A Guide to Using Budget Analysis to Advance Human Rights* (2004).

19 FAO, *Budget Work to Advance the Right to Food: Many a Slip* (2009) 5.

the Books: Governments' Budgets and the Right to Education (2010).[20] This report seeks to address 'a gap in the literature'[21] by providing 'an in-depth look at how to relate international human rights standards on the right to education to government budgets and budget processes, and how to use these standards in research and advocacy.'[22]

In doing so, it draws heavily on *Budget Work to Advance the Right to Food: Many a Slip*, adapting the approach to ESR budget work set out in that earlier publication and applying it to the example of the right to education. The publication also includes an introduction to the costing of right to education-related programmes.

Analysis of ESR-based budget analysis reports

We will now provide an in-depth analysis of the fourteen ESR budget analysis documents. In doing so, we focus on five key issues. First, we address the human rights instruments cited. We then consider the aspects of the budget analyzed. Third, we discuss how the different reports have addressed (or not) the relationship between budgets and ESR principles, before going on to demonstrate how other human rights have constituted important principles for the purposes of ESR-based budget work. The section concludes with a discussion of the challenges faced by those seeking to carry out ESR budget analysis that the various reports have identified.

Human rights instruments cited

Table 2.2 below shows that eleven documents used the International Covenant on Economic, Social and Cultural Rights (ICESCR) and General Comments of the Committee on Economic, Social and Cultural Rights (GC) as points of reference. A smaller number of documents invoked other UN human rights instruments; nine texts cited the Convention on the Rights of the Child (CRC) and seven documents cited the International Covenant on Civil and Political Rights (ICCPR). Seven separate documents referred to national constitutional texts (six references to South Africa and two to Mexico).

It is thus clear that, while ESR-based budget analysis has not been exclusively based on the international ESR framework, ICESCR and other international standards have constituted a central element of many ESR-based budget analysis efforts. It is striking that, even where domestic standards are available (and/or, in fact, constitute the primary analytical schema in a particular instance of budget analysis work) international standards will also

20 IBP and IHRIP, *Reading the Books: Governments' Budgets and the Right to Education* (2010).
21 Ibid 1.
22 Ibid.

Table 2.2 Human rights instruments identified.

Paper	*ESR Instrument*							
	International						*National/Regional*	
	ICESCR/ GC	*UDHR*	*CRC*	*CEDAW*	*CERD*	*ICCPR*	*Mexico Constitution*	*SA Constitution*
1	X							
2	X	X	X			X		
3	X						X	
4	X	X	X	X				
5	X		X					X
6	X		X			X		X
7	X		X	X	X	X		
8								X
9								X
10								X
11	X	X	X	X	X	X	X	X
12	X	X	X	X	X	X		
13	X	X	X	X		X		
14	X	X	X	X		X		
Total	11	6	9	6	3	7	2	6

often be referred to.[23] There is thus a clear awareness of the implications of 'global' human rights standards on the part of those carrying out ESR-based budget analysis work at the local level.

Aspects of budget analyzed

A budget is a plan of revenue and expenditure over a period of time.[24] As Table 2.3 shows, ESR budget analysis documents have examined a range of different dimensions of budgets. All of the papers reviewed refer to the allocation of resources, while past expenditure is discussed by thirteen of the fourteen documents. Budget outcomes (the impact that the budget has on the enjoyment of ESR) are considered in twelve. Budget outputs (the goods and services produced by the budget) are identified in nine reports, while budget revenue streams are cited in eight papers. Only four papers discuss the macroeconomics of the budget.

These findings suggest a historical reluctance on the part of those carrying out budget analysis work to move beyond the allocation and expenditure

23 See, for example, Judith Streak, *Budgeting for Child Socio-Economic Rights: Government Obligations and the Child's Right to Social Security and Education* (IDASA, 2002).

24 See Chapter 1.

Table 2.3 Aspects of budget analyzed.

Paper	*Macro-economics*	*Revenue*	*Expenditure*	*Allocation*	*Outputs*	*Outcomes*
1	X	X	X	X		X
2			X	X	X	X
3			X	X	X	X
4		X	X	X		X
5		X	X	X	X	X
6	X	X	X	X	X	X
7		X	X	X		X
8			X	X	X	X
9				X	X	
10			X	X	X	
11	X	X	X	X		X
12			X	X		X
13	X	X	X	X	X	X
14		X	X	X	X	X
Total	4	8	13	14	9	12

elements to engage with issues around revenue and macroeconomics. This is perhaps unsurprising given the general complexity (and opaqueness) of macroeconomic fiscal decision-making processes, as well as the role played in the areas of revenue and macroeconomics by supranational bodies such as international financial institutions whose human rights obligations remain uncertain.

Although more recent work on these issues is to be welcomed,[25] they remain key lacunae in budget analysis work.

Relationship between budgets and ESR principles

An assessment of how practitioners made the link between budgetary decision-making and ESR principles constituted a key element of our review. The relationship between budgets and ESR obligations is explored in greater detail

25 For an example of a recently developed methodology designed to evaluate macroeconomic policies from an ESR perspective, see Radhika Balakrishnan, Diane Elson and Raj Patel, *Rethinking Macroeconomic Strategies from a Human Rights Perspective (Why MES with Human Rights II)* (New York, Marymount Manhattan College/ US Human Rights Network 2009) and Diane Elson, Radhika Balakrishnan and James Heintz, 'Public Finance, Maximum Available Resources and Human Rights' in Aoife Nolan, Rory O'Connell and Colin Harvey (eds) *Human Rights and Public Finance* (Hart 2013). For a discussion of budget analysis from a revenue perspective, see Ignacio Saiz, 'Resourcing Rights: Combating Tax Injustice from a Human Rights Perspective' in Aoife Nolan, Rory O'Connell and Colin Harvey (eds), *Human Rights and Public Finance: Budgets and the Promotion of Economic and Social Rights* (Hart 2013).

in Chapters 3 and 4. Here, however, we will demonstrate the links made by practitioners between budgets and specific ESR obligations in the context of assessing the compliance of the former with the latter.

As such, Tables 2.4–2.9 identify the measures that the fourteen papers used to assess compliance with specific ICESCR obligations. Where possible, it also includes the budget tool that the reports recommend to establish these measures of compliance. We will return to the issue of budget tools in the next section.

Table 2.4 shows that a relatively small number of measures have been developed in relation to compliance with the tripartite obligation on states

Table 2.4 Reports that cite the 'tripartite typology' of 'respect, protect, fulfil'.

ESR Obligation	*Measures of Compliance*	*Budget Tool*
Respect	State does not fund measures which interfere with ESR (2, 14).	Examine budget lines for expenditure programmes which interfere with existing ESR enjoyment (1).
	State mainly uses direct rather than indirect taxes to raise revenue (1).	
	Taxes do not impinge on current enjoyment of ESR (14).	
Protect	Adequate funding for regulatory bodies (13, 14).	Adequacy could be ascertained by carrying out a costing exercise to determine if the funds available allow for adequate staffing and operations (13).
Fulfil	Adequate funding for provision of basics (13, 14).	Examine budget lines for expenditure programmes which fulfil ESR (6, 13).
		Compare expenditure likely to be required to fulfil ESR against actual allocation (13).
	Government raises sufficient revenue to adequately fund ESR (14).	
	Allocated funds are fully expended (14).	
	Expenditure results in greater enjoyment of ESR (14).	
	Programmes which raise awareness of ESR are funded and increased over time (14).	

to respect, protect and fulfil ESR.[26] In relation to the obligation to respect, measures of compliance expressed as 'State does not fund measures which interfere with ESR' suggest that compliance requires non-interference with existing access. This has also been called a 'negative obligation'. However, such an approach fails to recognize that, as will be discussed further in Chapter 4, in some cases the obligation to respect ESR can also require positive action. In addition, the obligation to fulfil can be subdivided into the duties to facilitate, promote and provide. These duties are likely to have distinct budgetary implications but the reports do not explore this.

The obligation of progressive realization is not simply reducible to resources but resources do play a key role in limiting states' ability to advance ESR achievement.[27] Given the budgetary focus of the reports reviewed, it is unsurprising that measures for compliance with the duty of progressive realization are primarily conceptualized in terms of resources. Indeed, the key theme that emerges from Table 2.5 is increasing allocation of resources to ESR over time, whether in terms of the quality of those resources, the amount

Table 2.5 Progressive realization.

Measures of Compliance	*Budget Tool*
Increase in expenditure on ESR over time (1, 7, 14).	Calculate change in ESR expenditure over time (1, 5, 7).
Increase in number of beneficiaries of a policy/ programme (5).	Identify number of people who benefit from a government-funded programme (5).
Increase in level or quality of services over time (5).	Calculate change in number of programme beneficiaries over time (5).
Increase in level of enjoyment of ESR over time (5, 14).	Examine indicators of enjoyment of ESR (5).
Funded programmes actually contribute to the realization of ESR (1).	
A clear plan for how resources will be mobilized to progressively realize the ESR (4, 5).	Check that strategies for resource use are in place to realize right (4, 5).
Loan repayments or conditions (such as expenditure constraints) do not undermine the capacity of the state to progressively realize ESR (1).	
Revenue increased to the extent necessary to progressively increase ESR allocation (14).	Compare revenue increases with inflation and population growth (14).

26 For more on these obligations, see Chapter 4.

27 For more on this point, see Chapter 3.

Table 2.6 Retrogressive measures.

Measures of Compliance	*Budget Tool*
Reduction in enjoyment of ESR over time (1, 4, 5)	
Fall in quality of services over time (6)	
Reduction/termination of expenditure for an ESR programme or overall (1, 4) despite stable/growing need (2)	Compare level of spend in ESR over time (1, 4) relative to need (2)
Government funds a programme which directly or indirectly obstructs realization of ESR or existing enjoyment of ESR (1)	Examine each expenditure line in order to identify any programmes which obstruct ESR (1)

of resources, or the extent to which they are effectively used in actually realizing ESR. It seems important, however, that an assessment of compliance with 'progressive realization' should recognize that increasing resources need to be considered in the context of other factors, such as the resources available, the extent to which people already enjoy ESR and a changing population.

Just as the reports tend to understand the obligation of progressive realization as requiring increasing resources over time, they appear to regard the obligation not to take retrogressive measures to imply the prohibition of a diminution of resources directed towards ESR enjoyment. Importantly, Table 2.6 refers to the need to factor in the level of need, as determined by the extent to which the ESR in question is enjoyed, when assessing state budgetary compliance with the prohibition on impermissible retrogressive measures.[28] Thus, a reduction in resources may be justified if the enjoyment of ESR continues to increase.

The measures utilized by the fourteen reports to examine budgetary compliance with the minimum core obligation seem less well developed relative to the other obligations. As will be discussed in Chapter 3, the content of the minimum core obligation is not clear-cut and this may well impact upon the willingness of practitioners to engage with it when assessing state compliance with ESR.[29] The existence of 'large numbers of people in high levels of need' would indeed suggest a failure to provide the minimum core, but the budgetary implications of the obligation need further clarification. If the content of the minimum core was more explicitly defined in the reports,

28 For more on this point, see Chapter 3.

29 For a discussion of human rights advocates' reluctance to employ a minimum core obligations approach to human rights monitoring and advocacy more generally, see Audrey Chapman, 'The Status of Efforts to Monitor Economic, Social and Cultural Rights' in Shareen Hertel and Lanse Minkler (eds), *Economic Rights: Conceptual, Measurement and Policy Issues* (Cambridge UP 2007) 154–5.

Table 2.7 Minimum core.

Measures of Compliance	*Budget Tool*
Basic services prioritized in budget (5)	
Absence of large number of people in high level of need (2, 4, 3, 8)	
Per capita spend on ESR compares with national minimum thresholds (5)	
Allocation is adequate to ensure that minimum core is provided (2, 6)	Compare social security benefit levels with poverty threshold (2)

Table 2.8 Non-discrimination.

Measures of Compliance	*Budget Tool*
State mainly uses direct rather than indirect taxes to raise revenue (1)	
Differences in per capita expenditure between social groups is perpetuating inequality in outcomes (2, 11)	Identify which groups are likely to be the main beneficiaries of a programme or the primary victims of budget cuts (2)
Per capita expenditure congruent with need/level of ESR realization (1, 7, 11)	Establish the region/group's share of expenditure using disaggregated expenditure incidence analysis. Compare this with the group's need/level of ESR realization (1, 5, 7, 11, 13)
Increase over time in expenditure on disadvantaged groups or on programmes likely to reduce inequality (5, 7, 11)	Calculate allocation to programmes likely to reduce inequality over time (5, 7, 11)
Programmes which promote equality, including translation services, adequately funded (2,11)	Determine the cost of activities necessary to promote equality and compare with actual allocation (11)
Funding for equality programmes spent on intended purpose (11)	Expenditure tracking (11)
Intended beneficiaries of funded equality programme are satisfied (11)	Beneficiary assessments (11)
Funded programmes don't have a discriminatory impact/deliver better equality outcomes (2,11)	Establish make up of programme beneficiaries in order to ascertain which social groups are likely to gain most from increases in expenditure or suffer most from budget cuts (2)
	Compare outcome indicators with budget analysis data (11)
Access to government funded services is restricted to some social groups (2)	Examine eligibility criteria (2)
Revenue raised, allocated and spend in a non-discriminatory fashion (14)	
No discrimination in distribution of benefits from government expenditure (14)	Realization of enjoyment of ESR (such as test scores in relation to right to education) improve (14)

it might then be possible to ascertain the extent to which the funding of basic services related to ESR ensure that no one falls below such thresholds.

Table 2.8 provides a fairly large number of compliance measures and budget tools associated with the principles of equality and non-discrimination. In terms of compliance measures, it is important to note that (consistent with international human rights law understandings of equality and non-discrimination)[30] they encompass both formal and substantive conceptions of equality. This is evidenced by, for instance, the focus on programmes which seek to promote equality of historically marginalized groups. Measures of compliance also reflect a concern with preventing direct and indirect discrimination; for example, by highlighting how state use of indirect taxes may have a disproportionate impact on those who have less disposable income.[31]

Given the papers' focus on budgets – and hence resource-related issues – it is unsurprising that the obligation that receives the greatest attention from practitioners in their work is that of maximum available resources.[32] Compliance measures included in Table 2.9 relate to both the amount of resources allocated to ESR and to how those resources are used. The amount of spending on ESR could be compared with spending on non-ESR areas and with the size of the economy. The usage of resources can refer to their efficient and effective use.

Thus far, we have largely discussed the various ESR obligations and the measures of compliance corresponding to them in isolation. It is important, however, to get a sense of how budget analysis practitioners address different aspects of ESR frameworks within their work as whole. Table 2.10 below provides a summary of the ICESCR obligations cited in each report, and assesses the extent to which the report authors attempt to relate the obligation to budgetary data. The case study papers are shaded. A further attempt has been made to distinguish between 'weak' and 'strong' efforts. 'Weak' attempts are those that suggest relatively general guidance. For example, in order to assess

30 For more on international human rights law standards on equality and non-discrimination in the context of ESR, see Chapter 4 and ComESCR, *General Comment No. 20, Non-Discrimination in Economic, Social and Cultural Rights*.

31 As Diokno highlights: 'Direct taxes are computed on the basis of the taxpayer's income or personal assets such that those with greater income pay a larger tax. . . . Indirect taxes, on the other hand, are those paid by persons other than the one on whom the tax is legally imposed. Persons liable for indirect taxation may shift or transfer their tax burden to others as part of the purchasing price of a commodity or part of compensation for services rendered. In countries where income is inequitably distributed, indirect taxation increases inequality in society. This is because when the poor pay the same amount of taxes as the rich, the poor are actually paying proportionately more taxes than the rich are. The indirect tax is a bigger share of the income of the poor, and the poor have less to spend for their needs than the rich do.' Maria Diokno, *A Rights-Based Approach towards Budget Analysis* (1999) 35.

32 See Tables 2.10 and 2.11 below.

Table 2.9 Maximum available resources.

Measures of Compliance	*Budget Tool*
Spending on ESR as a proportion of budget increases over time (7, 10, 13)	Calculate ESR expenditure as a proportion of budget over time (7, 10, 13)
Surplus finance re-invested in ESR (2, 4, 7)	Examine whether surplus finance is allocated to ESR or non-ESR programmes (2, 4)
	See which departments underspent and overspent. Those which overspent are those which were assigned additional resources (7)
Allocation for ESR fully spent (1, 5, 13, 14)	Compare expenditure plans with end-of-year audit reports (1, 5, 6, 13)
Spending on ESR congruent with size/rate of growth of the economy (1, 7, 11, 13, 14)	Calculate budget as a share of GDP over time (13)
	Compare realization of ESR with State's level of development (1, 13)
	Comparative analysis of expenditure on ESR between governments with similar levels of development (1, 13)
ESR spending significantly higher than non-ESR spending (13)	Comparative analysis of government expenditure on ESR and non-ESR items over time (13)
Taxation system raises maximum funding for allocation to ESR (1)	
Spending on ESR as proportion of GDP/total government spending increases over time (7)	Calculate ESR expenditure as a percentage of GDP/total government expenditure over time (7)
Resources spend efficiently and effectively (5)	
Costs of service delivery stable or decrease over time (5)	Calculate costs of administering services over time (5)
Expenditures have the maximum beneficial impact on the enjoyment of ESR (14)	

progressive realization, Diokno advocates a consideration of whether the 'status'[33] of rights improves over time. We categorize this as 'weak'. We categorize *Dignity Counts* as 'strong' because it goes beyond this generality, providing a specific example to illustrate its point. It states that between 1998

33 Maria Diokno, *A Rights-Based Approach towards Budget Analysis* (1999) 33.

Table 2.10 Elements of ICESCR obligations by report.

Paper	*ICESCR Obligations*							
	Respect	*Protect*	*Fulfil*	*PR*	*RM*	*MAR*	*MC*	*ND*
1	XX	XX	XX	XX	XXX	XX		XX
2	X	X	X	XX	XXX	XXX	XXX	XX
3				XX		X	X	XXX
4	X	X	X	XX	XX	XX	X	XX
5	X	X	X	XX	XX	XX	X	X
6	X	XX	XX	X	XX	XX	X	X
7	X	X	X	XXX	X	XXX		XX
8				X		X		
9								
10				X		X		
11	X	X	XX	X	X	XX	X	XXX
12	X	X	X	X	X	X	X	X
13	XXX	XX	XXX	XXX	XX	XXX	X	XX
14	XXX	XXX	XXX	XXX	X	XXX		XXX

X – Obligation cited but no attempt to relate to budget
XX – Weak attempt to relate obligation to budget
XXX – Strong attempt to relate obligation to budget

and 2002 'inflation-adjusted health care spending rose in two years, fell slightly in one, and fell sharply in the last year'[34] suggesting that although 'there is some indication of progressive achievement, that progress essentially evaporates by the end of 2002'.[35]

A summary of the above findings is provided in Table 2.11 below.

Tables 2.10 and 2.11 suggest that the three ESR-related obligations that have most often been related to budgets in the reviewed literature are maximum available resources (nine links), progressive realization (eight) and non-discrimination (eight). It further indicates that the two obligations that have been least often related to government budgets are minimum core (related in one), respect (related in three) and protect (related in four). This is of concern, given that, as we will see in Chapters 3 and 4, the minimum core and the obligations to respect and protect are very important aspects of a state's ESR obligations.

We have already highlighted the uncertainty that exists with regard to what the minimum core entails and how this may impact on practitioner willingness to utilize that standard: without a clear benchmark it is hard to measure compliance. Arguably, part of the explanation for the weak connection between

34 Fundar International Budget Project, International Human Rights Internship Program, *Dignity Counts: A Guide to Using Budget Analysis to Advance Human Rights* (2004) 34–5.
35 Ibid 35.

Table 2.11 Summary of elements of ESR obligations.

Paper	*ICESCR Obligations*							
	Respect	*Protect*	*Fulfil*	*PR*	*RM*	*MAR*	*MC*	*ND*
Absent	4	4	4	1	4	1	6	3
Cited	7	6	5	5	4	4	7	3
Weak Attempt	1	3	3	5	4	5	0	5
Strong Attempt	2	1	2	3	2	4	1	3

the obligation to protect and government budgets, is that this obligation requires the state to prevent third parties from interfering with ESR. It might be thought that government regulation of third parties can be carried out in the form of legal frameworks and policy interventions, which might be regarded as 'cost free'. This is due to the fact that such measures often form part of the existing infrastructural framework of a state. Thus, in practice, it may not be the fact that measures required to give effect to the obligation to protect ESR are cost free, but that they may not be '*ESR-specific*', that has led to relatively limited consideration of the 'obligation to protect ESR' in a budgetary context.

So where does this leave us? Looking at the five case studies, three (8–10) made very weak attempts to directly link budget analysis with ESR obligations. If the principles underpinning rights-based budget analysis are to be improved, and economic analysis is truly to be rights-based, it is important that they be applied to and tested in specific cases. We will return to this point in the chapter conclusions.

Other human rights principles

The reports reviewed in this chapter highlighted transparency, accountability and participation as important rights-based budget principles in terms of ESR-based budget work (see Table 2.12). As will be discussed further in Chapter 4, failure to satisfy such procedural requirements may also amount to a violation of international obligations. The inclusion of these principles in the papers under review is unsurprising given that one of the key foci of budget work is budgetary processes. While the reports reviewed did not focus on issues such as participatory budgeting, all budget work – indeed, all human rights work – is fundamentally underpinned by a concern with accountability, transparency and participation.

Difficulties in ESR budget analysis

A number of the documents highlighted challenges faced by those seeking to carry out ESR budget analysis. As Table 2.13 shows, five papers cited a lack

Table 2.12 Other human rights principles.

Report	*Transparency*	*Accountability*	*Participation*
1	X	X	X
2	-	-	-
3	-	-	-
4	X	-	-
5	-	-	-
6	X	X	X
7	X	X	-
8	-	-	-
9	-	-	-
10	-	-	-
11	X	X	X
12	X	X	X
13	X	X	X
14	-	-	X
Total	7	6	6

Table 2.13 Difficulties cited.

Report	*Availability of Data*	*Vagueness of ESR Principles*	*Technical Expertise*
1	-	-	-
2	-	-	-
3	-	-	-
4	-	-	X
5	X	X	-
6	-	-	X
7	X	X	X
8	-	-	-
9	X	-	-
10	X	-	-
11	-	X	-
12	X	X	-
13	-	-	-
14	-	X	-
Total	5	5	3

of data with which to carry out budget analysis. Five documents referred to a general lack of clarity surrounding ESR principles. Three reports mentioned issues around the technical skills required for budget analysis.

We will return to relevant lessons from this analysis in the final section of this chapter. It is enough at this point to highlight the challenges that have been identified by practitioners. We will now turn to consider the tools used by those carrying out budget analysis to assess the compliance of budgets with ESR standards.

Budget analysis tools

The guidance and case studies reviewed in this paper suggest that a formal set of analytical tools are not clearly associated with ESR budget analysis. This contrasts with, for instance, the more established field of gender budgeting (or gender-based budget analysis), in which tools of analysis are well established.[36] That said, our review indicated a number of tools that have been regularly used in budget analysis work.

Several examples emphasized analyzing specific budget lines to see which projects were supported and which were not. First, some case studies tried to identify budget lines that were inimical to the enjoyment of ESR,[37] or which were not involved in the realization of ESR (i.e., their effect was neutral).[38] It could then be argued that these were resources that would be better used to realize ESR (in the case of budget lines inimical to ESR) or more subtle uses might be feasible. For instance, Hofbauer and others identified that an overspend in the Ministries of Tourism, Finance and Foreign Affairs was enough to fund a particular project aimed at realizing ESR.[39] Both these examples relate to the ICESCR obligation to devote the maximum of available resources to realizing ESR but such an approach to budget lines could also be employed when considering whether measures or programmes violate the obligation to respect or the prohibition on impermissible retrogressive measures.

Of course, ESR-based budget analysis work is not solely concerned with budget lines that do not advance ESR enjoyment. The reports also addressed the need to identify budget lines that were involved in the realization of ESR. Such budget lines may serve as key indicators of whether the state is giving effect to its obligation to fulfil ESR. This exercise may well mean identifying budget lines that are concerned with the provision of ESR-related goods and

36 See Diane Elson, *Budgeting for Women's Rights: Monitoring Government Budgets for Compliance with CEDAW* (2006) 171. For more evidence of this, see Table 8 for evidence of the large number of budget tools associated with the principles of equality and non-discrimination in an ESR context. This range of tools seems likely to reflect the fact that the tools which have been developed within the specific field of gender budgeting, such as beneficiary assessments, are transferable to equality and non-discrimination issues in an ESR context. For more on this, see James Harrison and Mary-Ann Stephenson, 'Assessing the Impact of the Public Spending Cuts: Taking Human Rights and Equality Seriously' in Aoife Nolan, Rory O'Connell and Colin Harvey (eds), *Human Rights and Public Finance: Budgets and the Promotion of Economic and Social Rights* (Hart 2013).

37 Diokno gave the example of subsidies for the tobacco industry: Maria Diokno, *A Rights-Based Approach towards Budget Analysis* (International Human Rights Internship Program 1999) 8.

38 For instance, these might be expenditures on the tourism, finance, or foreign affairs departments: Helena Hofbauer, Ann Blyberg and Warren Krafchik, *Dignity Counts* (Fundar; International Budget Project and the International Human Rights Internship Program, 2004) 37.

39 Ibid.

services. However, it is also important to examine other budget lines that are important ancillaries to the realization of ESR. For instance, is there a budget to facilitate processes that are transparent, accountable and participatory? Is there a budget for promotional activities? Is there a budget for the necessary planning that is required for the realization of ESR (i.e., the obligation to take steps)? Is there a budget to support those agencies necessary to realize, and monitor the realization of, ESR?[40]

However, identifying relevant budget lines was only a preliminary step. Frequently, this task needed to be combined with other tools.

A number of reports focussed on determining whether there had been underspends or overspends, or diversions of allocations to non-ESR-related projects. If money has been allocated to an ESR-related project or programme and not spent or fully spent for that purpose then this is a failure to use the maximum of available resources.[41] From the perspective of this obligation, if an ESR-related programme has underspent then the resources should be reallocated to realizing ESR. Alternatively, if a non-ESR-related programme has overspent then those are resources that could have been used to realize ESR, and accordingly suggest a failure to use the maximum of available resources. Furthermore, where funds have been diverted due to corruption, incompetence or inefficiency then ICESCR obligations have been violated.[42] These points also indicate the importance of linking human rights budget work to the work of audit offices and ombudspersons. Thus, analyzing overspend, underspend and diversion in relation to ESR-related budgetary processes is a crucial tool for evaluation of state compliance with its ESR obligations.

Other tools go beyond focussing on whether money is spent on ESR projects; rather, they are concerned with establishing whether expenditure is efficient and effective. Thus, for instance, the South African group IDASA stresses the need to implement cost-effective measures, to reduce costs and to avoid waste.[43] If monies are being spent inefficiently or wastefully then there is likely to have been a failure to use maximum available resources and to ensure that ESR are being progressively realized at an adequate rate.

40 This last point has been especially relevant to the UK and Ireland in recent years, where there have been serious budget cuts to the GB Equality and Human Rights Commission, the NI Human Rights Commission and the Irish Human Rights Commission and Equality Authority.

41 Maria Diokno, *A Rights-Based Approach towards Budget Analysis* (International Human Rights Internship Program 1999) 33; New York City Welfare Reform and Human Rights Documentation Project, *Hunger is no Accident* (2000) 42.

42 For more on this point, see Chapter 3.

43 IDASA and Judith Streak, *Budgeting for Child Socio-Economic Rights: Government Obligations and the Child's Right to Social Security and Education* (IDASA 2002) 14, 35; IDASA and Judith Streak, *Monitoring Government Budgets to Advance Child Rights: A Guide for NGOs* (IDASA 2003) 11.

One tool employed widely in the reports is the examination of how funding for an ESR-related budget line changes over time. This is an important (albeit not perfect) proxy for determining whether the state is progressively realizing ESR. It may also serve to indicate that there is retrogression in the implementation of ESR. In either case, there are caveats. First, it is important to allow for inflation so that any change can be assessed in real terms. This requires a decision to be made about which measure of inflation to use,[44] and also requires competence in the necessary mathematical skills. Second, expenditure can only be a proxy for what is important, i.e., changes in outcome in terms of ESR realization. An increase in allocations does not necessarily mean there is any improvement in terms of the realization of rights. Third, even if a decrease in allocation suggests a possible retrogressive measure, then it has to be remembered that retrogressive measures may be justifiable or permissible in terms of human rights law.[45] Fourth, it may be necessary to match any changes to changes in demography or indeed need. Fifth, a decrease may reflect a change in the available resources; or a modest increase might obscure a missed opportunity. For example, if a country experiences a significant increase in its resources or budget but only makes modest increases in respect of ESR, this may indicate a failure to prioritize ESR.

For these reasons, examining individual budget lines and how they alter over time may not give a full picture. To obtain a better contextual understanding, it may be helpful to analyze an ESR-oriented budget allocation as a percentage of the overall budget[46] or governmental expenditure, or as a percentage of the Gross Domestic Product. These measures can be useful in demonstrating how the state prioritizes expenditure on ESR compared to other expenditure or alternatively whether it is making maximum use of available resources. In the first instance, if a state is increasing its proportionate expenditure on defence, foreign affairs or tourism, while decreasing its proportionate expenditure on ESR-related areas (for instance, health, education and social security), then this may signal a worrying failure to prioritize human rights, especially ESR. In the second case, an increasing GDP may indicate that more 'real resources' are available to the state and that it is failing to make full use of them; alternatively, if GDP, is contracting it may indicate a genuine problem of lack of resources.

44 IDASA identified three different measures: the Consumer Price Index, a Producer Price Index and a measure of Gross Domestic Product inflation: IDASA and Judith Streak, *Monitoring Government Budgets to Advance Child Rights: A Guide for NGOs* (IDASA 2003) 80.

45 For more on this point, see Chapter 3.

46 IDASA and Judith Streak, *Monitoring Government Budgets to Advance Child Rights: A Guide for NGOs* (IDASA, 2003); Helena Hofbauer, Ann Blyberg and Warren Krafchik, *Dignity Counts* (Fundar; International Budget Project and the International Human Rights Internship Program 2004) 36–8.

The reports reviewed made it clear that measuring a state's expenditure on ESR as a percentage of GDP may also be worthwhile in other ways. For instance, it may be useful to compare such percentages to the equivalent percentages in neighbouring countries or those with a similar level of development. If comparator countries can afford to devote more resources to ESR then it raises the question as to why the state under scrutiny cannot. Alternatively, it may be possible to compare the percentage allocation to that recommended by international organizations or UN expert bodies.

Benchmarks may also be important in another very different way; namely, in determining whether a state is observing its minimum core obligations. Benchmarks can, of course, be international in nature, but often it may be more appropriate to rely on country-specific standards. Diokno, for example, suggests that ESR rights expenditure should be analyzed to see if it provides expenditures equal to or greater than specific measures of access to food, poverty, daily minimum wage, or daily cost of living.[47]

Another tool that is used in a range of reports is the assessment of allocations against need. This has been employed in the context of ensuring that states are complying with their obligations in relation to non-discrimination and progressive realization. With regard to the latter, this determination is key to discovering whether the state is taking steps with a view to progressively realizing the relevant rights. Human rights law requires that there be a concrete plan to realize human rights.[48] In order to do this it is necessary to assess the nature and degree of the relevant need, and to assess whether programmes are expected to deal with the problem.[49]

Some groups have looked to see how governments raise revenue (taxation), and, in particular, whether revenue is raised in ways likely to harm the less well-off. Others have considered budgetary processes in terms of tax avoidance and tax evasion. Another way in which budget analysis practitioners have examined the ESR-related implications of revenue is by comparing the approach to taxation with suitable comparators. If a state generates significantly less taxation than comparator states then this may indicate there is a failure to use the maximum of available resources. It is also possible to evaluate how a state provides exemptions and subsidies.[50]

47 Maria Diokno, *A Rights-Based Approach towards Budget Analysis* (International Human Rights Internship Program 1999) 18–19.

48 Jim Schultz, *Promises to Keep: Using Public Budgets as a Tool to Advance Economic, Social and Cultural Rights* (Fundar 2002) 30.

49 IDASA and Judith Streak, *Budgeting for Child Socio-Economic Rights: Government Obligations and the Child's Right to Social Security and Education* (IDASA 2002) 15–19.

50 In a report which post-dates the research for this chapter, CESR has determined for instance that the exemptions and subsidies offered by Guatemala actually outweigh the amount of money received in taxation: Center for Economic and Social Rights, *Assessing Fiscal Policies from a Human Rights Perspective: Methodological case study on the use of available resources to realize economic, social and cultural rights in Guatemala* (CESR 2012) 20.

A final budget tool that has been employed in reports under review is the examination of who the beneficiaries of programmes or changes in public expenditure are: do certain programmes benefit people depending on their wealth or income, their sex, their race/ethnicity, whether they are children, whether they have a disability or where they live?[51] Such work is essential to evaluating budgets from the perspective of the immediate and cross-cutting obligation of non-discrimination, and the related concepts of equality and equity. This kind of analysis may be somewhat technical, but it can also be approached in a more participative manner, by surveying the intended beneficiaries of government programmes.[52]

This section has demonstrated that there are a wide range of tools that have been, and may be, applied in ESR-based budget analysis work. In Chapters 5 and 6 we will demonstrate how these tools were applied to assess the compliance of budget decisions in Northern Ireland with the right to the highest attainable standard of mental health and the right to adequate housing.

Conclusions

A number of key conclusions can be drawn from our analysis that should be taken into account in future ESR-based budget analysis efforts. Notably, the analysis of ESR case studies and guidance materials suggest that this area of study would benefit from more comprehensive definitions of ESR principles such as those delineated in the context of the ICESCR. In particular, given the inconsistent way in which these principles are applied to budgets, there is a need for their budgetary implications to be clarified. This task, of developing a consistent understanding of the relationship between budgets and ESR obligations, is complicated by the need for such an understanding to accommodate variations across countries, periods and socio-economic contexts.

Indeed, it is worth noting that the documents reviewed give little indication of the changing context of public expenditure over the period that they span (1999–2009). For example, the international dominance of 'neoliberal' economic models is associated with particular patterns of revenue (such as less progressive taxation[53]) and expenditure (such as reductions in social security) and particular forms of ownership and delivery (such as public–private partnerships). These phenomena have profound implications for ESR.

51 M. Diokno, *A Rights-Based Approach Towards Budget Analysis* (International Human Rights Internship Program 1999) 11.

52 IDASA for instance stresses the need to find out children's experience of poverty and their experience of relevant service delivery: IDASA and Judith Streak, *Monitoring Government Budgets to Advance Child Rights: A Guide for NGOs* (IDASA 2003) 103–23.

53 A progressive taxation system is one in which the tax rate increases with increasing wealth or income.

However, they receive little attention in the documents reviewed. Three of the papers,[54] all guidance documents, make reference to the power of non-state actors such as corporations and international organizations such as the International Monetary Fund. *Budgeting for Women's Rights* mentions privatization[55] and *Budget Work to Advance the Right to Food* alludes to trade liberalization.[56] If rights-based budget analysis is to prove relevant in the long term, it is important that it recognizes and responds to the constantly changing global and national contexts in which government budgets operate.[57]

Having clarified the relationship between ESR and budgets, indicators of compliance are required. As Table 2.4 demonstrates, a range of measures have been suggested or applied. However, they seem somewhat ad hoc and incomplete. For example, is growing expenditure on an ESR area in and of itself sufficient evidence of compliance with progressive realization? Or does progressive realization have to be considered in terms of outcomes; that is, the extent to which the expenditure contributes to the enjoyment of the right? Further, it can be argued that the measures set out in Tables 2.4–2.9 require development if they are to provide applicable human rights indicators that allow for comprehensive measurement of ESR obligations. For example, one of the measures of compliance refers to 'adequate funding for regulatory bodies' in relation to the obligation to protect (Table 2.4). However, it is not clear what level of funding would qualify as 'adequate' in terms of international human rights law. For the measures set out in Tables 2.4–2.9 to progress into a rigorous model of budgetary compliance with ESR obligations, concepts such as 'adequacy' will have to be developed. Those carrying out this task would benefit from a consideration of various indicators that have been developed at the international level.[58]

Bearing these issues in mind, in the next two chapters we turn to the task of clarifying the relevant obligations in international human rights law, focusing particularly on the International Covenant on Economic Social and Cultural Rights.

54 Maria Diokno, *A Rights-Based Approach towards Budget Analysis* (1999); Jim Schultz, *Promises to Keep: Using Public Budgets as a Tool to Advance Economic, Social and Cultural Rights* (2002); and Fundar, *International Budget Project, International Human Rights Internship Program Dignity Counts: A Guide to Using Budget Analysis to Advance Human Rights* (2004).

55 Diane Elson, *Budgeting for Women's Rights: Monitoring Government Budgets for Compliance with CEDAW* (2006) 35.

56 FAO, *Budget Work to Advance the Right to Food: Many a Slip* (2009) 21.

57 As noted in footnote 25, examples of contributions on these issues can be found in contributions to Aoife Nolan, Rory O'Connell and Colin Harvey (eds), *Human Rights and Public Finance: Budgets and the Promotion of Economic and Social Rights* (Hart 2013).

58 See, for example, indicators developed in relation to the right to adequate housing by the UN Habitat and OHCHR, *Monitoring Housing Rights* Discussion Paper Prepared for Expert Group Meeting on Housing Rights Monitoring Geneva 26–28 November 2003.

3 A human rights framework

Part 1: Exploring Article 2(1) ICESCR obligations

Introduction

Having identified some of the key elements – and lacunae – in ESR-based budget analysis practice in Chapter 2, this chapter and the following one address the broader human rights issues that are relevant to the development of ESR budget analysis methodology. In using the International Covenant on Economic, Social and Cultural Rights (ICESCR) and the various analytical frameworks that have been employed by the Committee on Economic, Social and Cultural Rights (ComESCR) to categorize ESR obligations, this chapter and Chapter 4 link these to budgetary decisions and processes.

The chapter opens with a discussion of how the ESR obligations imposed on the state can be defined. We then proceed to set out the various analytical frameworks that have been employed by the ComESCR and others to categorize ESR obligations. The remainder of the chapter is devoted to the key umbrella obligation under ICESCR, Article 2(1). We delineate the obligations imposed by that provision and relate them, where possible, to budgetary decisions and processes.

Measuring what? A question of rights and obligations

Before measuring whether a state party to ICESCR has complied with its ESR obligations (including those related to budgets), there has to be conceptual clarity about what is to be measured.[1] This determination involves two keys steps. First, the substantive content of the particular ESR under analysis must be established. Second, the legal obligations that are imposed by the right must be defined. In outlining ESR and the duties imposed by them with increasing precision and clarity, their precise implications with regard to resources and budget decisions become increasingly evident. Ultimately, this contributes to greater understanding and acceptance of the obligations they impose on the part of both rights and duty-bearers.

1 Judith V. Welling, 'International Indicators and Economic, Social and Cultural Rights' (2008) 30 *Human Rights Quarterly* 933, 948.

When seeking to determine the full content of the rights set out in ICESCR, the primary reference point will be the work of the ComESCR, including the General Comments and Concluding Observations issued by that body. The General Comments are not binding but have taken on an important 'law-making' type function by providing extensive interpretations of the provisions in ICESCR.[2] For example, the ComESCR has expanded the meaning of the right to an adequate standard of living in Article 11 of ICESCR considerably by issuing two General Comments elaborating on different aspects of the right to adequate housing as a component of the right to an adequate standard of living.[3] That body has also issued two General Comments on the right to adequate food and water as components of the right to an adequate standard of living.[4]

The Reporting Guidelines set out by ComESCR are another, less direct, source of information on the substantive content of Covenant rights.[5] They indicate the type of information that states should include in their country reports.[6] The information contained in these reports provides the basis upon which the ComESCR ascertains the extent to which a country has given effect to its obligations under ICESCR and are therefore indicative of what is expected of states in the realization of the rights in that treaty. The Concluding Observations made by the ComESCR on individual state reports are also reflective of the extent to which states are fulfilling their obligations and provide valuable insights into how states should implement international ESR obligations at the domestic level.[7] Other relevant sources include the work of the

2 Conway Blake, 'Normative Instruments in International Human Rights Law: Locating the General Comment' Centre for Human Rights and Global Justice Working Papers No. 17 (2008) New York University, School of Law 9.

3 ComESCR, *General Comment No 4: Right to Adequate Housing* (1991) UN Doc E/1992 /23 annex III at 114; ComESCR, *General Comment No 7: Right to Adequate Housing – Forced Evictions* (1997) UN Doc E/1998/22, annex IV at 113.

4 ComESCR, *General Comment No 12: The Right to Adequate Food* (Art.11) United Nations 1999) UN Doc E/C.12/1999/5; *General Comment No 15: The Right to Water* (arts. 11 and 12 of the Covenant) 2002.

5 ComESCR, *The Guidelines on Treaty-Specific Documents to be Submitted by State Parties under Articles 16 and 17 of the International Covenant on Economic, Social and Cultural Rights* UN Doc E/C.12/2008/2 (2008).

6 See Ibid section 2: 'The purpose of reporting guidelines is to advise States parties on the form and content of their reports, so as to facilitate the preparation of reports and ensure that reports are comprehensive and presented in a uniform manner by States parties.'

7 For example, the ComESCR has recommended that the UK should take immediate measures to improve the situation of the large number of people living in poor housing conditions and to relieve the situation of those that are 'fuel poor'. This indicates that adequate fuel for heating is an element of the right to adequate housing and an adequate standard of living generally. See ComESCR, *Concluding Observations of the Committee on Economic, Social and Cultural Rights: United Kingdom of Great Britain and Northern Ireland* UN Doc E/C.12/1/Add.79 (2002) paragraph 39.

UN Special Procedures with specific ESR-related mandates (for instance, the Special Rapporteur on the Right to the Highest Attainable Standard of Health[8] and the Special Rapporteur on the Right to Adequate Housing as a Component of the Right to an Adequate Standard of Living[9]), the jurisprudence of other international and regional human rights bodies with an ESR-related mandate,[10] and the work of academic commentators.[11]

Furthermore, in addition to looking at the international framework, the scope and content of ESR can be clarified by looking at the ways in which they have been interpreted and applied in various jurisdictions by implementation bodies, courts and academics.

Notably, many of the legally binding and non-binding international standards discussed above have been applied by national, regional and international courts in their decision-making. Such instances can serve to highlight how these principles may be applied in specific domestic or regional contexts. While the approach of these judicial and quasi-judicial bodies in construing these principles cannot be assumed to conform with the approach that the ComESCR would adopt when doing so, such decisions can provide a useful sense of how ESR-related obligations should operate in practice. We now turn to the obligations under ICESCR.

Different frameworks for defining the legal obligations imposed by ESR

Various frameworks have been used to describe the state's obligations under ICESCR. These frameworks overlap and interact to varying extents.

8 See for example the work done of linking health systems with the right to the highest attainable standard of health in General Assembly, *Report of the Special Rapporteur on the Right of Everyone to the Enjoyment of the Highest Attainable Standard of Physical and Mental Health, Paul Hunt* A/HRC/7/11 (2008).

9 See for example the work done on indicators in General Assembly, *Report of the Special Rapporteur on Adequate Housing as a Component of the Right to an Adequate Standard of Living, Miloon Kothari* A/HRC/4/18 (2007).

10 The importance of the ComESCR has already been established. Other relevant international human rights bodies include the Committee on the Rights of the Child, the Committee on the Elimination of Discrimination against Women, the Committee on the Rights of Persons with Disabilities and the Committee on the Elimination of All Forms of Racial Discrimination. The jurisprudence of regional bodies, in particular the European Court on Human Rights and the European Committee on Social Rights, may also be relevant.

11 See in particular the 'Maastricht Guidelines on Violations of Economic, Social and Cultural Rights' (1998) 20 *Human Rights Quarterly* 691 and the 'Limburg Principles on the Implementation of the International Covenant on Economic, Social and Cultural Rights' (1987) 9 *Human Rights Quarterly* 122 and UN Doc E/CN.4/1987/17, Annex.

The first framework relates to the language of the Covenant in Article 2(1), which states that:

> [e]ach State Party to the present Covenant undertakes to take steps, [. . .], especially economic and technical, to the maximum of its available resources, with a view to achieving progressively the full realization of the rights recognized in the present Covenant by all appropriate means, including particularly the adoption of legislative measures.

This duty of progressive realization necessarily imposes a corresponding prohibition on retrogressive measures in nearly all circumstances.[12] Where government cuts existing benefits, increases prices of government goods and services, or removes legislative protection, this may amount to a retrogressive measure.[13] The same principle should be applied to deliberate steps backwards with regard to the allocation of resources. Indeed, governments are likely to be held to a stricter test in relation to available resources with regard to retrogressive measures than they will with regard to the failure to take positive steps to create or enhance programmes.[14]

Logically, because the prohibition on taking retrogressive steps applies to existing measures of implementation of ESR, it has to be of effect immediately, in order to provide effective protection. Other duties also apply immediately regardless of available resources, for example, the so-called 'minimum core' obligations imposed by economic and social rights. These immediate obligations will be dealt with further below. Suffice to say for now that ICESCR obligations can be distinguished between those that are immediate and those that are progressive in nature.

12 See ComESCR, *General Comment No. 3, The Nature of States Parties Obligations* UN Doc E/1991/23 annex III at 86 (1990) paragraph 9.

13 Aoife Nolan, Bruce Porter and Malcolm Langford. 'The Justiciability of Social and Economic Rights: An Updates Appraisal' (2007) 15 Centre for Human Rights and Global Justice Working Paper 31.

14 Ibid 35. See also ComESCR, *General Comment No. 3, The Nature of States Parties Obligations* UN Doc E/1991/23 annex III at 86 (1990) at paragraph 9 which states that: 'any deliberately retrogressive measures in that regard would require the most careful consideration and would need to be fully justified by reference to the totality of the rights provided for in the Covenant and in the context of the full use of the maximum available resources.' ComESCR, *General Comment No. 13, The Right to Education* UN Doc E/C.12/1999/10 (1999) paragraph 55 states that there is a strong presumption of impermissibility of any retrogressive measures taken in relation to the right to education, as well as other rights enunciated in the Covenant. States bear the burden of proof if any deliberately retrogressive measures are taken, the state party has the burden of proving that they have been introduced after the most careful consideration of all alternatives. See also ComESCR *General Comment No. 14, on the Right to the Highest Attainable Standard of Health* E/C.12/2000/4 (2000) paragraph 32 and ComESCR *General Comment No. 15, The Right to Water (Article 11 and 12)* UN Doc E/C.12/2002/11 (2002) paragraph 19.

As well as the Article 2(1) obligation, the rights found in ICESCR are often analyzed in terms of a second framework: the tripartite typology. This is so called because, under this approach, the state's obligations are categorized in terms of three layers, namely, the obligations to *respect*, *protect* and *fulfil* ESR. As will be discussed in Chapter 4, this distinction allows for an analysis of the more precise obligations on the state. It also points to the actions the state has to take or has to refrain from taking in order to comply with ICESCR, depending on the situation at hand. For the present purpose, the typology is useful because each action required has to be resourced. This framework is also relevant because it can be applied to civil, political and cultural rights as well as ESR, thereby supporting the indivisibility of rights.[15]

Finally, a third schema for analyzing the ICESCR obligations is to classify them in terms of 'obligations of conduct' and 'obligations of result'. According to Eide, an obligation of *conduct* (active or passive) points to behaviour that the duty-holder should follow or abstain from. An obligation of *result* is less concerned with the choice of the line of action taken, but more concerned with the results, which the duty-holder should achieve or avoid.[16] The Maastricht Guidelines assert that '[t]he obligations to respect, protect and fulfil each contain elements of obligation of conduct and obligation of result'.[17] There is thus a clear relationship between this 'conduct/result' framework of duties and the tripartite typology. We will not consider this categorization of duties in any detail. This is primarily because it is not always clear what difference (if any) there is between obligations of conduct and of result.[18] However, despite the fact that our analysis does not expressly address the framework of obligations of conduct and obligations of result, it is important to point out that the obligations generated by ICESCR range from those relating to processes that have to be taken with regard to ESR decision-making to those that relate to the enjoyment of the rights themselves.

15 Asbjørn Eide 'Realization of Social and Economic Rights and the Minimum Threshold Approach' (1989) 10(2) *Human Rights Law Journal* 35, 40.

16 Ibid 38.

17 'The Maastricht Guidelines on Violations of Economic, Social and Cultural Rights' (1998) 20 *Human Rights Quarterly* 691, paragraph 7.

18 For example, states have an obligation to eliminate the occurrence of hunger – this is an obligation of result. However, in some instances the elimination of hunger requires states to do nothing more than to refrain from certain actions. See Asbjørn Eide 'Realization of Social and Economic Rights and the Minimum Threshold Approach' (1989) 10(2) *Human Rights Law Journal* 35, 38. Refraining from doing something would seem to be more an obligation of conduct. Similarly the duty to respect ESR is an obligation of conduct. Continued, uninterrupted enjoyment of ESR could, however, also be construed as an obligation of result.

An in-depth analysis of the legal obligations imposed by Article 2(1) ICESCR[19]

Article 2(1) states that each state party to the present Covenant

> *undertakes to take steps*, [. . .], especially economic and technical, *to the maximum of its available resources*, with a view to achieving *progressively* the full realization of the rights recognized in the present Covenant by *all appropriate means*, including particularly the *adoption of legislative measures.* (Emphasis added)

It is worth reiterating, that while full realization of the right may be achieved progressively, the duty to start moving towards that goal as swiftly as possible is of immediate effect.[20]

Article 2(1) ICESCR particularly mentions the adoption of legislative measures for the fulfilment of the rights. In many instances, legislation will be indispensable to giving effect to the rights under ICESCR.[21] However, adopting relevant legislation does not exhaust the state's obligations. The precise mode of implementation of ICESCR is left to the state parties' discretion. The decisive question is whether the measures and procedures adopted achieve results that are consistent with the full discharge of Covenant obligations.[22] Notably, General Comment No. 9 on the Domestic Application of the Covenant requires states to do whatever it takes to make ICESCR applicable domestically.

As highlighted in Chapter 1, the budget is generally adopted by parliament in the form of legislation.[23] Shultz has argued that no legislative measure carries more weight in the realization of ESR than the public budget.[24] The Maastricht guidelines point out that the failure to reform or repeal legislation that is inconsistent with ICESCR is a violation of the state's obligations.[25] Alston and Quinn argue that Article 2(1) would require legislative action to be taken where existing legislation is in violation of the obligations assumed under the

19 Much of this section is drawn from Aoife Nolan and Mira Dutschke, 'Article 2(1) ICESCR and States Parties' Obligations: Whither the Budget?' [2010] *European Human Rights Law Review* 280.

20 ComESCR, *General Comment No. 3, The Nature of States Parties Obligations* UN Doc E/1991/23 annex III at 86 (1990) paragraph 2.

21 Ibid, paragraph 3.

22 ComESCR, *General Comment No. 9, The Domestic Application of the Covenant* UN Doc E/C.12/1998/24 (1998) paragraph 5.

23 Diane Elson, *Budgeting for Women's Rights: Monitoring Government Budgets for Compliance with CEDAW* (UNIFEM 2006) 125.

24 Jim Shultz, *Promises to Keep: Using Public Budgets as a Tool to Advance Economic, Social and Cultural Rights* (Fundar 2002) 31.

25 'The Maastricht Guidelines on Violations of Economic, Social and Cultural Rights' (1998) 20 *Human Rights Quarterly* 691, 697.

treaty.[26] If, therefore, allocations in the budget are not adequate in terms of ensuring the satisfaction of duties imposed by ICESCR, this would have to be corrected. At the domestic level, states have a duty to use all appropriate means to rectify the shortcomings.[27] The state is responsible for establishing mechanisms and institutions to correct violations.[28] The specific inclusion of 'economic and technical means' in Article 2(1) warrants measures adjusting the flow of economic resources towards the realization of the rights in ICESCR.

That said, the rights in ICESCR do not always create direct, extensive claims on the public budget. If, for example, it is more effective in the context of a specific country to satisfy the right to shelter through the implementation of a regulatory framework rather than by allocating funding, then that is in line with the human rights obligation as well.[29]

Progressive realization

The duty to 'achieve progressively' refers to the achievement of the full scope and content of the right.[30] This recognizes the reality that the full realization of ESR may not be possible immediately. There is thus a margin of discretion accorded to states with regard to the progress of realization. This is necessary due to, among other things, limitations in terms of the resources that are realistically available to different states. In other words, the duty of 'progressive realization' assumes that expectations and obligations of states are not uniform or universal but rather that they are relative to the levels of development and the resources available.[31] The state bears the burden of proof to show that actual progress in the enjoyment of rights has been made and is, therefore, under a duty to report on its current performance and the extent to which it is moving forward expeditiously and effectively towards full realization.[32]

26 Philip Alston and Gerard Quinn, 'The Nature and Scope of the States Parties' Obligations under the International Covenant on Economic, Social and Cultural Rights' (1987) 9 *Human Rights Quarterly* 156, 167.

27 'The Maastricht Guidelines on Violations of Economic, Social and Cultural Rights' (1998) 20 *Human Rights Quarterly* 691.

28 Ibid 698–9.

29 Andrew Norton and Diane Elson, *What's behind the Budget? Politics, Rights and Accountability in the Budget Project* (Overseas Development Institute 2002) 20.

30 Audrey Chapman, 'A "Violations Approach" for Monitoring the International Covenant on Economic, Social and Cultural Rights' (1996) 18 *Human Rights Quarterly* 23, 38.

31 Ibid 31.

32 Victor Dankwa, Cees Flinteman and Scott Leckie. 'Commentary on the Maastricht Guidelines on Violations of Economic, Social and Cultural Rights' (1998) 20 *Human Rights Quarterly* 705, 716.

The obligation of progressive achievement does not simply require an increase in resources. Beyond that, it entails an increasingly effective use of the resources available, which must be optimally prioritized to fulfil the rights in ICESCR.[33] This includes the need to ensure for everyone the satisfaction of subsistence requirements, as well as the provision of essential services, on an equitable basis.[34] The duty to progressively realize the rights in relation to social security, for example, has been interpreted to mean that there is a duty to *expand access* and a duty to *improve the implementation*.[35] This means there is a duty to make social assistance accessible not only to a larger *number* of people but also to a wider *range* of people as resources become available.[36]

One example of such an argument being made in a litigation context was the South Africa *Mahlangu* case. Here, the complainants asked the High Court to direct the state to extend the age threshold for the child support grant from under the age of fourteen to eighteen. If successful, 2.6 million children would have become eligible for the grant.[37] The claimants' arguments centred on the duty to progressively realize ESR and to make the right available to a larger group or range of people as resources become available over time. Ultimately, the state announced plans to extend the grant to all children under eighteen before the Court handed down judgment.

Some jurisdictions have entrenched the duty to progressively realize aspects of ESR in their Constitutions. The Transitional Provisions of the 2008 Constitution of Ecuador entrenches the duty to progressively allocate resources towards the national health system in Article 20. Article 20 states that the general health budget destined for the financing of the health system will be increased annually by a percentage not inferior to 0.5 per cent of the GDP. The provision goes on to say that this increase shall continue until it reaches at least four per cent of the GDP. In relation to education, the Constitution obliges the state to assign public resources from the General Budget in a progressive manner for the initial basic education and bachelor's degrees. It stipulates an annual increase of at least 0.5 per cent of the GDP until it reaches a minimum of six per cent. The Constitution of Colombia states in Article 48 that social security is a mandatory public service, the coverage of which will be extended gradually.[38]

33 Asbjørn Eide, 'Economic and Social Rights' in Janusz Symonides (ed) *Human Rights: Concepts and Standards* (Ashgate 2000) 126.

34 Ibid.

35 Sandra Liebenberg, 'The Right to Social Assistance: the Implications of *Grootboom* for Policy Reform in South Africa' (2001) 17 *South African Journal of Human Rights* 232, 241.

36 Ibid 241.

37 See *Florence Mahlangu v Minister of Social Development and Minister of Finance* (unreported) cited in Katherine Hall and Paula Proudlock *Litigating for a Better Deal*, Children's Institute Annual Report 2008 available at www.ci.org.za/depts/ci/pubs/pdf/general/annual/report08/litigating.pdf (accessed 7 April 2009).

38 Aoife Nolan and Mira Dutschke, 'Article 2(1) ICESCR and States Parties' Obligations: Wither the Budget' [2010] *European Human Rights Law Review* 280, 281.

Measuring the extent of progressive realization requires information on the extent to which obligations are realized in relation to specific groups.[39] Collecting the relevant data is therefore an inherent process requirement or obligation of conduct. Because this obligation measures performance over time, the data has to be collected in a manner that allows identification of progress made towards implementation.[40] Performance standards relative to the context of the country have to be set up to enable the realization of this duty to be measured.[41] The requirement to collect data and other similar process requirements are essential steps that enable a principled policymaking process.[42] Consequently, the content of the duty to realize progressively is not just about the positive actions that have to be taken but also about the process through which decisions regarding those actions are taken. Effectiveness, participation, accountability and equality are identified principles that are aspects of the duty to progressively realize ESR.[43]

The duty to realize rights progressively is by its very nature flexible and context-dependent. It has also been understood to mean a duty to optimize ESR so far as legally and factually possible.[44] The obligation embodies the realization that there are a large number of competing ESR demands on the state. Fredman refers to these competing demands as 'competing principles' and argues that, if there are no pertinent competing principles, a particular right may have to be fulfilled immediately as opposed to progressively.[45] In other words, in the absence of legitimately competing rights or principles the aspects of ESR obligations might be immediate.[46] However, as will be discussed below and in Chapter 4, even when competing priorities, rights and principles justify the progressive realization of a right there are certain aspects of the related obligations that are of immediate application, and it can be argued that the immediate obligations should be prioritized to a certain extent within the budgetary allocations.

39 Judith V. Welling, 'International Indicators and Economic, Social and Cultural' (2008) 30 *Human Rights Quarterly* 933, 949.

40 Maria Green, 'What We Talk About When We Talk About Indicators: Current Approaches to Human Rights Measurement' (2001) 23 *Human Rights Quarterly* 1062, 1084.

41 Audrey R. Chapman and Sage Russell, 'Introduction' in Audrey R. Chapman and Sage Russell (eds) *Core Obligations: Building a Framework for Economic, Social and Cultural Rights* (Intersentia 2002) 5.

42 Craig Scott and Philip Alston, 'Adjudicating Constitutional Priorities in a Transnational Context: A Comment on *Soobramoney's* Legacy and *Grootboom's* Promise' (2000) 16 *South African Journal on Human Rights* 206, 254.

43 Sandra Fredman, *Human Rights Transformed – Positive Rights and Positive Duties* (Oxford UP 2008) 83.

44 Ibid 80.

45 Ibid 80.

46 Ibid 81.

However, this should not distract from the fact that there are instances where the state must increase a particular allocation of resources to comply with ICESCR. The ComESCR has, for example, called on Colombia to improve the supply of housing and allocate resources to provide the entire population with drinking water and sewerage services.[47]

The duty not to take retrogressive measures

As stated above, the obligation of progressive realization implies that retrogressive measures are incompatible with ICESCR. The ComESCR states that any deliberately retrogressive measure requires the most careful consideration.[48] They would need to be fully justified by reference to the totality of the rights provided for in ICESCR and in the context of the full use of the maximum available resources.[49] The ComESCR has not specified exactly what constitutes a 'deliberate retrogressive measure' but General Comment No. 4 provides some guidance, stating that, 'a general decline of living and housing conditions, *directly attributable* to policy and legislative decisions by State Parties, and in the absence of accompanying compensatory measures, would be inconsistent with the obligations under the Covenant.'[50]

A deliberate retrogressive measure therefore means any measure that implies a step back in the level of protection accorded to the rights in ICESCR as a consequence of an intentional decision by the state.[51] This includes unjustified reduction in public expenditures devoted to implementation of ESR in the absence of adequate compensatory measures aimed to protect the injured individuals.[52] This provision is especially important during times of crisis where states must do all they can to avert retrogression in the realization of ESR.[53] It has been argued that a lack of counter-cyclical policies in times of crisis often end up reducing employment and other hard-fought-for ESR-related gains. If a government chooses not to use available resources for this purpose, questions about progressive realization of ESR have to be posed.[54]

47 ComESCR, *Conclusions and Recommendations of the Committee on Economic, Social and Cultural Rights, Columbia* UN Doc E/C.12/1995/18 at 41 (1996) paragraph 200(c); ComESCR, *Conclusions and Recommendations of the Committee on Economic, Social and Cultural Rights, Columbia* UN Doc E/C.12/1/Add.74 (2001) paragraph 121.

48 ComESCR, *General Comment No. 3, The Nature of States Parties Obligations* paragraph 9.

49 Ibid, paragraph 2.

50 ComESCR, *General Comment No. 4, The Right to Adequate Housing* UN Doc E/1992 /23 annex III at 114 (1991) paragraph 59, emphasis added.

51 María Magdalena Sepúlveda Carmona, *The Nature of the Obligations under the International Covenant on Economic, Social and Cultural Rights* (Intersentia 2003) 323.

52 Ibid 324.

53 *Bringing Human Rights to Bear in Times of Crisis: A Human Rights Analysis of Government Response to the Economic Crisis. Submission to the high-Level Segment 13th session of the UNHRC on the global economic and financial crises* (2010) 4.

54 Ibid 5.

In a 2012 letter to states' parties, the Chairperson of the ComESCR outlined the conditions that 'any proposed policy change or adjustment' in response to the crises has to meet. First, the policy must be temporary, covering only the period of the crisis; second, the policy must be necessary and proportionate, in the sense that the adoption of any other policy, or a failure to act, would be more detrimental to economic, social and cultural rights; third, the policy must not be discriminatory and must comprise all possible measures, including tax measures, to support social transfers and mitigate inequalities that can grow in times of crisis and to ensure that the rights of disadvantaged and marginalized individuals and groups are not disproportionately affected; and, finally, the policy should identify the minimum core content of rights, or a social protection floor, as developed by the International Labour Organization, and ensure the protection of this core content at all times.[55]

The ComESCR has commented on retrogressive measures on a number of occasions,[56] albeit that the Committee frequently does not apply the label of 'retrogressive measures' to measures that it appears to be criticizing as such.[57] In relation to Colombia, the ComESCR expressed its concern about the fact that housing and health care subsidies had been reduced substantially.[58] Colombia was advised to increase housing subsidies and allocate a higher percentage of its GDP to the health sector.[59] The ComESCR also noted with concern Algeria's steady decline in state expenditure on the health care system, as well as the plan confirmed by the delegation to eliminate subsidies for medicines.[60] Even though this was not specifically labelled a retrogressive measure, it effectively amounts to one because the state is taking steps backwards in relation to ESR realization. In relation to Senegal, the ComESCR commented on the budgetary cutbacks in the educational sector, noting that they will have serious social and economic consequences for the future of the country.[61]

55 Committee on Economic, Social and Cultural Rights, 'Letter from CESCR Chairperson to States Parties in the context of the economic and financial crisis', CESCR/48th/SP/MAB/SW, 16 May 2012, 2 www2.ohchr.org/english/bodies/cescr/docs/LetterCESCRtoSP16.05.12.pdf (accessed 26 August 2013).

56 It should be noted that a challenge with analyzing ComESCR general comments in relation to non-retrogression is that they generally do not specify the circumstances in which the reductions took place.

57 Aoife Nolan, 'Putting ESR-Based Budget Analysis into Practice: Addressing the Conceptual Challenges' in Aoife Nolan, Rory O'Connell and Colin Harvey (eds) *Human Rights and Public Finance* (Hart 2013).

58 ComESCR, *Conclusions and Recommendations of the Committee on Economic, Social and Cultural Rights, Columbia* UN Doc E/C.12/1/Add.74 (2001) paragraphs 21 and 26 respectively.

59 Ibid, paragraphs 42 and 47 respectively.

60 ComESCR, *Conclusions and recommendations of the Committee on Economic, Social and Cultural Rights, Algeria,* UN Doc E/C.12/1/Add.71 (2001) paragraph 20.

61 ComESCR, *Conclusions and Recommendations of the Committee on Economic, Social and Cultural Rights, Senegal,* UN Doc E/C.12/1993/18 (1994) paragraph 7.

The ComESCR also commented on the successive restrictions on social security benefits introduced by Canada – noting with concern that there had been a dramatic drop in the proportion of unemployed workers receiving benefits – to half of the previous coverage.[62] The ComESCR criticized the new programme, stating that fewer low-income families were eligible to receive any benefits at all.[63] In the last example, the ComESCR specified that the measure constituted a restriction of existing enjoyment of an ESR. This could therefore fall both under the duty to respect existing access (that is the duty to avoid interference with existing access) and the prohibition on deliberate retrogressive measures. However, since the ComESCR specifically mentioned paragraph 9 of General Comment No. 3 it fits better under the latter obligation. Importantly, from the perspective of the post-2008 economic crisis context, the ComESCR's 2012 Concluding Observations about Iceland criticized cuts made by that state to its budgets for public health care and the public education system and explicitly recommended that the budgets in these areas be increased.[64]

Retrogressive measures have also been considered in national contexts. The UK case of *ex parte Tandy*[65] concerned a retrogressive measure taken by the UK Education Authority in respect of special needs education that was ultimately rejected by the House of Lords. The Education Authority in this case reduced the number of hours of home tuition provided for under the Education Act of 1996 to a child suffering from myaligic encephalomyelitis (ME) from five to three hours per week. It had been reported that the budget for the local authority providing the special needs education had been cut from £100 000 to £25 000. The child's parents were told that the decision to cut the hours was motivated entirely by these budgetary cutbacks.[66] The House of Lords discussed how the respondent county council's available resources were determined.[67] It found that even though the council, through the local education authority, had applied for a higher allocation of resources they effectively experienced a budget cut of seventy-five per cent with regard to home tuition.[68] The court appreciated the dilemma faced by the council

62 ComESCR, *Conclusions and Recommendations of the Committee on Economic, Social and Cultural Rights, Canada,* UN Doc E/C/12/1/Add.31 (1998) paragraph 20.

63 Ibid. For other post-2008 examples, see ComESCR, *Concluding Observations*: *Spain*, UN Doc E/C.12/ESP/CO/5 (2012); ComESCR, *Concluding Observations: New Zealand*, UN Doc E/C.12/NZL/CO/ (2012).

64 ComESCR, *Concluding Observations: Iceland*, UN Doc E/C.12/ISL/CO/4 (2012), paragraph 6.

65 *R v East Sussex ex parte Tandy* [1998] AC 714.

66 Ibid 734.

67 The Education Committee required £8.499 million and received £7.24 million. Together with overspending from the previous year of £1.85 million, the Education Committee had to cut back expenditure by £3.085 million. See Ibid 744.

68 Ibid 744.

but maintained that the shortage of resources in terms of Section 298 of the Education Act was not a legitimate consideration in determining what constitutes 'suitable education'.[69] The court did consider that it might be impossible for the council to perform its statutory duties in light of the acute budget cuts they experienced. It suggested, however, that resource constraints may be a defence for a failure to perform a statutory duty, but could not be relied upon to preclude a duty from arising. If there was more than one way to provide 'suitable education' the authority was entitled to make a choice. The court also suggested that the local authority could divert funding from other education applications that are merely discretionary to discharge statutory duties.[70]

A different judicial approach was adopted towards retrogressive budget cuts in the Canadian case *Newfoundland (Treasury Board) v NAPE*.[71] In this case, the Canadian Supreme Court scrutinized the constitutionality of an Act that cancelled the commencement of promised pay equity payments to female hospital workers, due to a fiscal crisis. The effect of the legislation was to erase the obligation the province had for approximately $24 million. The Court acknowledged the fact that the province was experiencing a fiscal crisis due in part to a reduction of anticipated federal transfer payments by $130 million. Over forty-five per cent of Newfoundland government spending is financed through federal equalization payments or federally established program financing.[72] The government successfully justified the promised pay cuts using the constitutional limitations clause.[73] The Court stated that budgetary considerations cannot normally be invoked as a freestanding pressing and substantial objective for the limitations clause of the Charter[74] but it was possible if principles to be protected are considered sufficiently important.[75] Courts would always be extremely sceptical about arguments to limit Charter rights due to budget constraints because there are always budgetary implications. In the present case, the Government successfully invoked the limitations clause, the Court noting that the cut in promised pay constituted ten per cent of the budgetary deficit.[76]

This case provides a clear example of a budgetary retrogressive measure because it constituted a deliberate step backwards in achieving equality of an ESR right, namely the right to fair pay. The ComESCR states that retrogressive measures require the most careful consideration in light of all the ESR

69 Ibid 747.
70 Ibid 749.
71 2004 SCC 66.
72 Binnie J for the Court paragraph 59.
73 Binnie J for the Court paragraph 85.
74 Binnie J for the Court paragraph 64.
75 Binnie J for the Court paragraph 71.
76 Binnie J for the Court paragraph 75.

obligations faced by the state. In *NAPE* the Court considered that the required budget cuts could have been made elsewhere in light of the fiscal crisis and found that equality expenditure could not necessarily rank above other social expenditure such as hospital beds or school rooms.[77] The Court in this case considered that various pressing ESR-related needs existed before finding a justifiable limitation of equality rights, thereby allowing a retrogressive measure. (It cannot be presumed, however, that the ComESCR would have reached the same conclusion.)

Maximum available resources

The duty to allocate the maximum of available resources also leaves the state a margin of discretion in relation to the quantum of resources to be used towards the realization of the rights in ICESCR. The ComESCR, however, retains the authority to decide whether the state party has fulfilled its obligations. A state does not have absolute discretion in the allocation of funding and the speed and progress of realization; if it did, an international treaty would be redundant.[78] The drafters of ICESCR therefore felt that 'resources' must refer to real resources of the country and not only to the budget appropriations.[79]

Alston and Quinn argue that,

> implicit in this formulation is the assumption that governmental allocations, as reflected in the national budget are not automatically to be taken as authoritative in determining whether the maximum of available resources has been devoted to the satisfaction of the requisite rights. Rather, it may be appropriate to probe beyond those allocations and take account of the countries' 'real' resources.[80]

This does not mean that a state must use all of its resources on meeting ESR, but rather that it must use the maximum amount of resources that can be expended for a particular purpose without sacrificing other, essential services.[81] This entails that, even though progressive realization and the use of maximum of available resources are two distinct concepts, the progress of realization expected of states is directly related to the resources that are available. Implicit in this duty is a process requirement, that a state may be requested to show

77 Binnie J for the Court paragraph 95.

78 Philip Alston and Gerard Quinn 'The Nature and Scope of the States Parties' Obligations under the International Covenant on Economic, Social and Cultural Rights' (1987) 9 *Human Rights Quarterly* 156, 178.

79 Ibid 178.

80 Ibid.

81 Ibid.

that adequate consideration has been given to all the possible resources available to satisfy each of ICESCR requirements, even if the effort to give effect to full realization is not immediately possible. A failure to do so would be a failure to meet its obligation of conduct to ensure a principled policymaking process.[82]

The authors of *Dignity Counts* highlight that, 'while analyzing both proposed and actual spending is useful, just looking at the budget does not tell you how effectively or efficiently the money is being spent, or whether the resources allocated are reaching their intended purpose'.[83] This is significant given that, as highlighted in Chapter 2 and elsewhere, 'the obligation to use the "maximum available resources" also implies the duty to use the resources allocated in an effective and efficient manner and the prohibition of the diversion of resources devoted to Covenant-related issues'.[84] This obligation also renders the non-expenditure of resources allocated to ESR-related activities due to inefficient administration or corruption impermissible in terms of the Covenant.[85]

Another point that has been emphasized in the context of maximum available resources, is that of sufficiency or adequacy; namely whether the resources allocated and spent by the state are sufficient/adequate to fully satisfy ESR requirements.[86] Benchmarks may be established by national or international institutions.[87] In terms of establishing benchmarks for spending on ESR, a national example is provided by Brazil. Article 212 of the Brazilian Constitution requires that the maintenance and development of education shall never receive less than eighteen per cent from the Union and twenty-five per cent of tax revenues including transfers from the states, Federal Districts and the municipalities.

82 Ibid 180.

83 Helena Hofbauer, Ann Blyberg and Warren Krafchik, *Dignity Counts: A Guide to Using Budget Analysis to Advance Human Rights* (Fundar, IBP, IHRIP 2004) 36.

84 María Magdalena Sepúlveda Carmona, *The Nature of the Obligations under the International Covenant on Economic, Social and Cultural Rights* (Intersentia 2003) 315. See also Ann Blyberg, *Notes from an International Budget Project roundtable discussion on the Obligation to use 'Maximum of Available Resources'* (International Human Rights Internship Programme 2008), 1.

85 Sepúlveda, ibid 317; Blyberg, ibid.

86 See, e.g., Radhika Balakrishnan and others, *Maximum Available Resources and Human Rights: Analytical Report* (Centre for Women's Global Leadership, Rutgers – the State University of New Jersey 2011) 5–6.

87 It should be borne in mind, however, that benchmarks (including constitutional benchmarks) set by states have to be scrutinized in terms of their human rights compliance. They are also used to compare the state's performance in relation to international human rights indicators. Eitan Felner, 'A New Frontier in Economic and Social Rights Advocacy? Turning Quantitative Data into a Tool for Human Rights Accountability' (2008) 9 *SUR International Journal on Human Rights* 109, 115.

As discussed in Chapter 2, attention must also be paid to how budgets change over time and to the spending on ESR as a percentage of the overall budget and overall national wealth. If government spending on the realization of ESR is dropping relative to GDP or other government expenditures, this will be a strong indication that there are available resources but that a particular right has not been prioritized.

The Maastricht Guidelines on Violations of ESR set out that reduction or diversion of specific public expenditure is a violation of ICESCR if this results in the non-enjoyment of the right and is not accompanied by adequate measures to redress that effect.[88] Doubt has been expressed whether the ComESCR can effectively challenge the allocation of resources by states.[89] Certainly, it has historically been reluctant to do so.[90] There are, however, some examples of the ComESCR making recommendations that address the employment of maximum available resources. For example, the ComESCR has criticized Canada for spending only 1.3 per cent of government expenditures on social housing.[91]

Another issue identified by *Dignity Counts* is that of efficiency of spending.[92] This requirement is more difficult to assess but strong arguments can be made that where a sum has been allocated to ESR realization and is subsequently not used, that government is not giving effect to its obligations.[93] Efficiency refers to the allocated funds being spent as efficiently as possible through government getting the best quality goods for a programme at the lowest

88 'The Maastricht Guidelines on Violations of Economic, Social and Cultural Rights' (1998) 20 *Human Rights Quarterly* 691, 697. See also Audrey R. Chapman 'Violations Approach for Monitoring the International Covenant on Economic, Social and Cultural Rights' (1996) 18 *Human Rights Quarterly* 23, 23.

89 Robert Robertson, 'Measuring State Compliance with the Obligation to Devote the "Maximum of Available Resources" to Realizing Economic, Social and Cultural Rights' (1994) 16 *Human Rights Quarterly* 693, 703. The author gives examples of how the Committee has skirted the issue of how many resources should be made available.

90 See Aoife Nolan, 'Putting ESR-Based Budget Analysis into Practice: Addressing the Conceptual Challenges' in Aoife Nolan, Rory O'Connell and Colin Harvey (eds) *Human Rights and Public Finance* (Hart 2013).

91 ComESCR, *Conclusions and Recommendations of the ComESCR, Canada* UN Doc E/C.12/1993/5 (1993) as cited in Robert Robertson, 'Measuring State Compliance with the Obligation to Devote the "Maximum of Available Resources" to Realizing Economic, Social and Cultural Rights' (1994) 16 *Human Rights Quarterly* 693, 703.

92 Helena Hofbauer, Ann Blyberg and Warren Krafchik, *Dignity Counts: A Guide to Using Budget Analysis to Advance Human Rights* (Fundar, IBP, IHRIP (2004) 37. *Dignity Counts* does not specifically refer to this as efficiency of spending, but they demonstrate that the Health Ministry had significantly underspent its budget while Tourism and Defence had significantly overspent. This is what is referred to as 'efficiency' by Sandra Fredman, *Human Rights Transformed – Positive Rights and Positive Duties* (Oxford UP 2008) 82.

93 Fredman ibid 82.

possible cost.[94] The obligation to use the 'maximum of available resources' also implies a prohibition against diverting resources from ESR related issues to non-ESR related issues.[95] The principal indicator employed by the ComESCR is a comparative analysis of the financial resources spent by the state in Covenant-related expenditures and non-related items.[96] For example, in response to the Korean periodic report, the ComESCR noted the high level of defence expenditures in contrast with the shrinking budget for key areas of economic, social and cultural rights.[97] The ComESCR also came down harshly on Colombia in 1995 when it recommended that the Colombian government should combat the practice of non-utilization of budget items earmarked for social expenditure in the state's overall budget, and ensure that such appropriations are used for the purposes for which they were budgeted.[98] Also interesting in this regard is Article 48 of the Colombian Constitution, which states that resources allocated for social security may not be used for any other purpose.

A final issue addressed in *Dignity Counts* is that of equity. According to that source, if spending is inequitable between genders, classes, regions or other distinctions, the government would be in breach of its duty. The problem with this requirement is that 'equity' is not defined in *Dignity Counts* and the concept seems to be used interchangeably with 'equality'. It is, therefore, unclear as to whether the concept of 'equity' corresponds to the concept of 'equality' under international human rights law. ComESCR has used the concept of equity in relation to the right to health. Equity (like equality and non-discrimination) is concerned with ensuring that adequate resources are allocated to health systems so that poor people have access to equal health facilities, goods and services.[99] Equity is mentioned in relation to economic affordability for everyone.[100] General Comment No. 14 also refers to 'gender equity'[101] and

94 Ann Blyberg, *Notes from an International Budget Project roundtable discussion on The obligation to use 'Maximum of Available Resources* (International Human Rights Internship Programme 2008) 4.

95 María Magdalena Sepúlveda Carmona, *The Nature of the Obligations under the International Covenant on Economic, Social and Cultural Rights* (Intersentia 2003) 315. See also Blyberg, Ibid 1, who recommends this as an indicator for the assessment if the duty to 'maximum of available resources' has been satisfied.

96 Sepúlveda, ibid 316–17.

97 ComESCR, *Conclusions and Recommendations of the Committee on Economic, Social and Cultural Rights, Republic of Korea* UN Doc E/C.12/1/Add.59 (2001) paragraph 9.

98 ComESCR, *Conclusions and Recommendations of the Committee on Economic, Social and Cultural Rights, Columbia* UN Doc E/C.12/1995/18 at 41 (1996) paragraph 200(b).

99 Gillian MacNaughton 'Untangling Equality and Non-discrimination to Promote the Right to Health Care for All' (2009) 11 *Health and Human Rights Journal* 47, 54.

100 ComESCR *General Comment No. 14, on the Right to the Highest Attainable Standard of Health*, E/C.12/2000/4 (2000) paragraph 12 (b).

101 Ibid, paragraph 16.

the 'equitable distribution' of health facilities throughout the country.[102] More broadly, one of the core requirements of Article 12 is that there should be an 'equitable distribution of all health facilities, goods and services'.[103] There seems to be considerable overlap between equity and the principles of equality and non-discrimination. This is so especially when prohibited grounds of discrimination include economic and social situation, property, place of residence and, of course, sex.[104] Non-discrimination on grounds of economic status, social situation and property are linked with the ComESCR understanding of equity, which 'demands that poorer households should not be disproportionately burdened with health expenses as compared to richer households.'[105]

In terms of domestic human rights law jurisprudence, a clear example of the equality approach to the problem of maximum available resources was in the South African Constitutional Court case of *Khosa v Minister of Social Development.*[106] In this case, discrimination in relation to a particular ESR – the right to social security of non-nationals – was considered. The Court found a violation of the equality clause under the Constitution. It then proceeded to estimate what the costs would be for inclusion of the affected group excluded from the scheme and found that it was minimal when compared to the overall expenditure of that department.[107] Equality in accessing a public service was also the issue in the Canadian case of *Eldridge.*[108] In this case, failure to provide sign language interpretation where it is necessary was considered a *prima facia* violation of the equality rights of deaf people. The Court held that the Government had not shown that the extension to other services would unduly strain the fiscal resources of the state.[109] In this case, the Supreme Court of Canada also considered what the cost would be of including the affected group of people and compared it to the overall cost of the department of health.[110]

It is true that the full realization of ESR requires the allocation of resources. However, inadequate administration of social assistance programmes is often caused by poor management practices and lack of capacity to spend the resources that are made available.[111] This is relevant to the fact that the term

102 Ibid, paragraph 36.
103 Ibid, paragraph 43 (e) and paragraph 52.
104 ComESCR, *General Comment No. 20, Non-Discrimination in Economic, Social and Cultural Rights,* UN Doc E/C.12/GC/20 (2009).
105 ComESCR, *General Comment No. 14, on the Right to the Highest Attainable Standard of Health*, paragraph 12 (b).
106 2004 6 BCLR 569 (CC).
107 See Mokgoro J., paragraph 60.
108 *Eldridge v British Colombia* (*Attorney General*) [1997] 3 SCR 624.
109 Ibid, paragraph 10.
110 Ibid, paragraph 87.
111 Sandra Liebenberg, 'The Right to Social Assistance: the Implications of *Grootboom* for Policy Reform in South Africa' (2001) 17 *South African Journal of Human Rights*, 232, 247.

'resources' does not just refer to financial resources alone.[112] The phrase 'maximum available resources' includes *all* resources available, such as information, technical, organizational, human, natural and administrative resources.[113] Taken in this broad sense, the duty to allocate the 'maximum of available resources' includes the resources necessary to ensure smooth administration of the programme.

While ESR-based budget analysis work is, by definition, focused on the budget, this does not necessarily limit the scope of practitioners' inquiries to financial resources alone. The use of non-financial resources still has to be provided for and funded. For example, the use of human resources requires allocation of money for salaries. A key question is how budget allocations towards non-financial resources can be tracked through the national budget.

Immediate obligations imposed by Article 2(1)

The full scope of ESR in ICESCR is subject to progressive realization and the resources that are available according to Article 2(1), discussed above. As stated earlier this does not mean that all obligations have to be realized progressively: certain obligations are to be realized immediately. The ComESCR identifies aspects of rights that are 'capable of immediate implementation',[114] ie elements that are justiciable irrespective of the resource situation.[115] We will discuss several of these obligations in more detail in Chapter 4. This section will focus on those immediate obligations that have been explicitly linked to Article 2(1) by the ComESCR.

112 Robert Robertson, 'Measuring State Compliance with the Obligation to Devote the "Maximum of Available Resources" to Realizing Economic, Social and Cultural Rights' (1994) 16 *Human Rights Quarterly*, 693, 695.

113 Geraldine van Bueren, 'Alleviating Poverty through the Constitutional Court' (1999) 15 *South African Journal of Human Rights*, 52, 61.

114 For example, ComESCR, *General Comment No. 3, The Nature of States Parties Obligations* paragraph 5 lists these rights as being articles 3 (Equal right of men and women to the enjoyment of all the rights set forth in ICESCR), 7 (a) (i) (Fair wages and equal remuneration for work of equal value without distinction of any kind, in particular women being guaranteed conditions of work not inferior to those enjoyed by men, with equal pay for equal work), 8 (The rights of trade unions), 10 (3) (Special measures of protection and assistance should be taken on behalf of all children and young persons without any discrimination for reasons of parentage or other conditions.), 13 (2) (a) (Primary education shall be compulsory and available free to all), (3) (Private schools) and (4) (The establishment of educational institutions) and 15 (3) (The States Parties to the present Covenant undertake to respect the freedom indispensable for scientific research and creative activity).

115 Ida Koch, 'The Justiciability of Indivisible Rights' (2003) 72 *Nordic Journal of International Law* 3, 18.

Obligation 'To Take Steps'

Article 2(1) requires states 'to take steps' towards the full realization of ESR. The ComESCR has stated that while full realization is to happen 'progressively' the duty to start moving towards full realization is neither progressive nor subject to available resources.[116] This phrase implies at the very least a duty to design strategies and programmes to achieve to the full realization of ESR.[117] Steps taken must be concrete, targeted and deliberate.[118]

Fredman argues that this requires the state to set out a clear and detailed plan setting both goals and time tables and subject to continuous monitoring.[119] The Committee emphasizes that such steps should be deliberate, concrete and targeted as clearly as possible towards meeting the obligations recognized in the Covenant.[120] Thus, Article 2(1) furnishes right-holders with an entitlement to state action to create the legal or administrative norms necessary to make ESR provisions available, progressively.[121]

Minimum core

The ComESCR has identified the obligation of the state to give effect to the minimum essential level of each right.[122] It has been argued that this minimum essential level of realization is the beginning of the progressive realization of ICESCR provisions.[123] Put differently, the core content of rights should be seen as a bottom or floor from which states should endeavour to go up.[124] The concept of a minimum core is therefore relevant to the notion of progressive realization, and thus is inextricably linked to Article 2(1). The minimum core obligation is defined as follows:

> The Committee is of the view that a minimum core obligation to ensure the satisfaction of, at the very least, minimum essential levels of each of the rights is incumbent upon every State party. Thus, for example, a

116 See, for example, ComESCR, *General Comment No. 14, The Right to the Highest Attainable Standard of Health*, paragraph 30.
117 ComESCR, *General Comment No. 3, The Nature of States Parties Obligations*, paragraph 11.
118 ComESCR, *General Comment No. 3, The Nature of States Parties Obligations* UN Doc E/1991/23 annex III at 86 (1990) paragraph 2.
119 Sandra Fredman, *Human Rights Transformed – Positive Rights and Positive Duties* (Oxford UP 2008) 83.
120 *General Comment No. 3*, paragraph 2.
121 Sandra Fredman, *Human Rights Transformed – Positive Rights and Positive Duties* (Oxford UP 2008) 88.
122 ComESCR, *General Comment No. 3, The Nature of States Parties Obligations*, paragraph 10.
123 Audrey R. Chapman and Sage Russell, 'Introduction' in Audrey R. Chapman and Sage Russell (eds) *Core Obligations: Building a Framework for Economic, Social and Cultural Rights* (Intersentia 2002) 15.
124 Ibid 16.

> State party in which any significant number of individuals is deprived of essential foodstuffs, of essential primary health care, of basic shelter and housing, or of the most basic forms of education is, *prima facie*, failing to discharge its obligations under the Covenant. If the Covenant were to be read in such a way as not to establish such a minimum core obligation, it would be largely deprived of its *raison d'être*. [. . .] [I]t must be noted that any assessment as to whether a State has discharged its minimum core obligation must also take account of resource constraints applying within the country concerned. [. . .] In order for a State party to be able to attribute its failure to meet at least its minimum core obligations to a lack of available resources it must demonstrate that every effort has been made to use all resources that are at its disposition in an effort to satisfy, as a matter of priority, those minimum obligations.[125]

The rights-specific minimum core obligations are spelled out in some of the General Comments, although it is important to note from a budget analysis practitioner perspective that the ComESCR has defined the minimum core more clearly *vis-a-vis* some ESR, than it has with regard to others.[126]

In relation to the right to education, for example, the ComESCR stated that the core obligation includes the provision of primary education.[127] With regard to the highest attainable standard of health, the ComESCR has stated that at the very minimum the core obligations in relation to the right to the highest attainable standard of health are: a minimum essential food and freedom from hunger; basic shelter, housing and sanitation, and an adequate supply of water; and essential drugs.[128] Of comparable importance are reproductive, maternal (pre-natal as well as post-natal) and child health care; immunization; prevention, treatment and control of diseases; and education and access to information and appropriate training for health personnel.[129] Note that this General Comment includes other, more procedural aspects under core obligations.[130] For reasons of clarity, these aspects will be discussed under

125 ComESCR, *General Comment No. 3, The Nature of States Parties Obligations*, paragraph 10.

126 For example, the minimum core of the right to food is defined comprehensively by *General Comment 12* on the right to adequate food as consisting of the 'minimum essential food which is sufficient, nutritionally adequate and safe, to ensure their freedom from hunger'. (ComESCR *General Comment No. 12: The Right to Adequate Food* UN Doc E/C.12/1999/5 (1999) paragraph 14). In relation to the right to adequate housing, the minimum core for housing has not been explicitly defined in *General Comment No. 4* (on the right to adequate housing) or in other General Comments.

127 ComESCR, *General Comment No. 13, The Right to Education* UN Doc E/C.12/1999/10 (1999) 57.

128 ComESCR, *General Comment No. 14, The Right to the Highest Attainable Standard of Health*, paragraph 43.

129 Ibid, paragraph 44.

130 Ibid.

'other immediate obligations' below, as they refer to process requirements inherent in the core obligations imposed by these rights.

The duty to ensure access to a social security scheme (which is part of the core obligations imposed by that right) requires that everyone be enabled to acquire at least essential health care, basic shelter and housing, water and sanitation, foodstuffs, and the most basic forms of education.[131] In addition, if a state party cannot provide this minimum level for all risks and contingencies within the maximum of resources available, the ComESCR recommends that the state party, after a wide process of consultation, select a core group of social risks and contingencies.[132] States must also ensure that the right of access to such schemes on a non-discriminatory basis, especially for disadvantaged and marginalized individuals and groups.[133] Part of the minimum core is also respect of existing social security schemes;[134] the adoption and implementation of a national social security strategy and plan of action, as well as the duty to monitor the extent of the realization of the right to social security.[135] We will return to the question of process obligations imposed by ESR in Chapter 4.

In relation to the right to food, the ComESCR states that violations of ICESCR occur when a state fails to ensure the satisfaction of at the very least the minimum essential level required to be free from hunger.[136] Two observations flow from this: first, it is clear that the full realization of the right to food is more than a mere freedom from hunger.[137] Second, the General Comment says that when the state fails to ensure the satisfaction of the minimum essential level of the right because of alleged resource constraints, 'the State has to demonstrate that every effort has been made to use all the resources at its disposal in an effort to satisfy, as a matter of priority, those minimum obligations'.[138]

The obligation to 'make every effort' to ensure minimum core entitlements seems to place these obligations at a higher resource priority than the duty to progressively realize the full scope of the right, which is found in Article

131 ComESCR, *General Comment No. 19, The Right to Social Security*, paragraph 59(b).

132 Ibid.

133 Ibid.

134 Ibid, paragraph 59(c).

135 Ibid, paragraph 59(f).

136 ComESCR, *General Comment No. 12, The Right to Adequate Food*, UN Doc E/C.12/1999/5 (1999) paragraph 17.

137 The right to adequate food is realized when everyone has access at all times to adequate food or means for its procurement. The right to adequate food shall not be interpreted in a narrow or restrictive sense which equates it with a minimum package of calories, proteins and other nutrients. See Ibid, paragraph 6.

138 Ibid, paragraph 17.

2(1). Thus a failure to satisfy the basic needs and minimum standards for a dignified human existence would *prima facia* amount to a breach of the state's obligations. The state bears an increased justificatory burden to demonstrate that every effort has been made to satisfy the minimum obligations as a priority.[139] This could be argued to imply that core obligations should have a calculated priority in resource allocation. In other words, the minimum core obligation would require the state to ascertain the extent to which the minimum needs are not met and the resources required to give effect to the minimum core obligations.[140] Bilchitz argues that the minimum core protects basic survival interests and that these interests have a relative priority over the full scope of the right.[141] If this is accepted then these should be reflected in the allocation of resources.[142] In support of this argument, it is worth pointing out that the ComESCR describes the minimum core obligation as non-derogable in number of places.[143] Importantly the minimum core standard applies to everyone within the state. *General Comment No. 3* specifically states that if 'any significant number of individuals is deprived' of the minimum core content then the state is in breach of its obligations.

Variations on the minimum core content concept have been applied by German, Swiss, Brazilian, Argentine and Colombian Courts in their jurisprudence, although only a few will be mentioned here.[144]

139 Sandra Liebenberg, 'The International Covenant on Economic, Social and Cultural Rights and its Implementation for South Africa' (1995) 11 *South African Journal on Human Rights* 359, 367.

140 See ComESCR, *General Comment No. 12, The Right to Adequate Food*, UN Doc E/C.12/1999/5 (1999) paragraph 11 '[W]here resources are demonstrably inadequate the obligation remains for a state party to strive to ensure the widest possible enjoyment [. . .]. Moreover the obligation to monitor the extent or realization, or more especially of the non-realization [. . .] are in no way eliminated as a result of resources constraints.'

141 David Bilchitz, 'Towards a Reasonable Approach to the Minimum Core: Laying the Foundations for Future Socio-Economic Rights Jurisprudence' (2003) 19 *South African Journal on Human Rights* 1, 15.

142 Robert Robertson, 'Measuring State Compliance with the Obligation to Devote the "Maximum of Available Resources" to Realizing Economic, Social and Cultural Rights' (1994) 16 *Human Rights Quarterly*, 693, 702.

143 ComESCR, *General Comment No. 14, on the Right to the Highest Attainable Standard of Health*, paragraph 47; ComESCR, *General Comment No. 15, The Right to Water* (Article 11 and 12) UN Doc E/C.12/2002/11 (2002) paragraph 40.

144 Alicia E. Yamin and Oscar Parra-Vera, 'How do Courts Set Health Policy? The Question of the Colombian Constitutional Court' (2009) 6 (2) *PLoS Medicine*; International Commission of Jurists, *Courts and the Legal Enforcement of Economic, Social and Cultural Rights* (International Commission of Jurists 2008) 24. The *Limbuela* case referred to in Chapter 1 could be interpreted as the UK courts striving to protect the minimum core of the right to an adequate standard of living.

A concept similar to the minimum core obligation was the subject of the German Constitutional Court's *Hartz IV* case.[145] Here the Court scrutinized the process by which the legislature set the level of unemployment and welfare assistance. The German Basic Law guarantees an 'Existenzminimum', which is similar to the concept of the minimum core.[146] In the *Hartz IV* case the Court found that the manner in which the country's welfare laws were recalculated during the reform process did not meet constitutional muster. Importantly, the Court found that the methods used to calculate and evaluate the income and consumption levels of low-income households was not legitimate. Further, the Court found that some expenditure line items had been reduced without a legitimate, statistical evaluation.

Importantly, the Court highlighted that in relation to children the lawmakers had avoided any substantive evaluation of child specific rights and/or needs. The lawmakers were therefore ordered to recalculate the level of benefits using sound statistical evidence of the monetary resources needed for a basic, dignified existence.[147]

Saiz has highlighted that the minimum core standard is significant in relation to a budget analysis exercise in a regressive economic climate for a number of reasons. The minimum core provides a series of very specific entitlements and principles in relation to each right. These should form the framework of any rescue or stimulus packages or any other responses to the crisis.[148] Governments have an immediate obligation to prioritize the achievement for everyone of certain minimum levels of enjoyment that are essential to survival and a life in dignity.[149] So, for example, efforts and resources must be directed as an immediate priority to the maintenance and strengthening of programmes aimed at ensuring that children complete basic education, or that women do not die in childbirth.[150] Meeting these core obligations should, under certain circumstances, trump other policy considerations.[151] In the context of the recession and the economic crisis, this obligation could imply ring-fencing

145 *Hartz IV case* BverfG,1BvL 1/09 9.2.2010 Absatz-Nr (1–220) available at www.bundesverfassungsgericht.de/entscheidungen/ls20100209_1bvl000109.html (accessed 15 September 2010). For an English translation of this case see www.bundesverfassungsgericht.de/en/decisions/ls20100209_1bvl000109en.html (accessed 3 June 2013).

146 Aoife Nolan and Mira Dutschke, 'Article 2(1) ICESCR and States Parties' Obligations: Wither the Budget' (2001) 3 *European Human Rights Law Review* 280, 288.

147 As well as *Hartz IV,* see the more recent *Asylum case*, 1 BvL 10/10, 18 July 2012, translation available at www.bundesverfassungsgericht.de/en/decisions/ls20120718_1bvl001010en.html (accessed 8 June 2013).

148 Ignacio Saiz, 'Rights in Recession? Challenges for Economic and Social Rights Enforcement in Times of Crisis' (2009) 1 *Journal of Human Rights in Practice* 277, 282.

149 Ibid 282.

150 Ibid 282.

151 Ibid 282.

budgets to ensure that essential goods and services are universally available and accessible. It could also be achieved by taking steps to remove barriers, which might prevent poor and disadvantaged groups from achieving minimum levels of rights enjoyment.[152]

As highlighted briefly in Chapter 2, there are also a number of issues that arise when considering the extent of the state's minimum core obligation.[153] First, there is considerable debate over what the minimum core is or should be.[154] Is it exclusively an obligation of result or does it also incorporate obligations of conduct? The quotation from *General Comment No. 3* set out above presents the minimum core as an obligation of result. However, later comments of the ComESCR suggest that it incorporates elements of 'conduct'.[155] It will be seen in Chapter 4 that various process requirements are part of what the ComESCR has termed 'core obligations'.[156] Second, the ComESCR's discussion of the minimum core obligations imposed by various ESR is very limited, meaning that the full scope of that obligation is not fully clear in all contexts and should be subject to further inquiry. A key question is whether the minimum core is a universal, absolute measure or one that is relative, varying from state to state or over time. Lastly, there is some debate whether the minimum core right is a common right for all contracting parties irrespective of their stage of development. Obviously if this was the case, developing countries would have difficulties complying with the standard. It would also mean that the minimum core level would be of limited practical importance in developed states. Koch argues that the notion of progressive realization urges us to consider the possibility of developing national minimum standards according to the resource situation in the country in question. She

152 Ibid 283.

153 See, for example, discussions described in Aoife Nolan, 'A Report of Discussions and Outcomes at the Economic, Social and Cultural Rights Litigation Strategy Workshop' in Malcolm Langford and Bret Thiele (eds) *Road to a Remedy: Current Issues in Litigation of Economic, Social and Cultural Rights* (University of New South Wales Press 2005).

154 See generally Katherine Young, 'The Minimum Core of Economic and Social Rights: A Concept in Search of Content' (2008) 33 *Yale Journal on International Law* 113.

155 See, for example, ComESCR, *General Comment No. 14, The Right to the Highest Attainable Standard of Health*, paragraph 43 (f), where the Committee stated that the minimum core obligation imposed by the right to the highest attainable standard of health requires states 'To adopt and implement a national public health strategy and plan of action, on the basis of epidemiological evidence, addressing the health concerns of the whole population; the strategy and plan of action shall be devised, and periodically reviewed, on the basis of a participatory and transparent process; they shall include methods, such as right to health indicators and benchmarks, by which progress can be closely monitored; the process by which the strategy and plan of action are devised, as well as their content, shall give particular attention to all vulnerable or marginalized groups.'

156 Ibid, paragraph 43; ComESCR, *General Comment No. 12, The Right to Adequate Food*, paragraphs 7–20, ComESCR, *General Comment No. 13, The Right to Education*, paragraph 57.

considers the duty to take steps 'to the maximum of available resources' to mean that the minimum core obligation varies according to the resources available in the country.[157] On the other hand, Costa argues that, while the progressive obligations vary from state to state, the core content obligations are not subject to progressive realization and are not contingent on state resources, and should therefore not vary from state to state.[158]

Conclusion

So far, we have set out what (in the sense of which broad categorizations of obligations) may be measured in the context of ESR-based budget analysis. Crucially in terms of the framework employed later in this book, we have spelt out in detail the key budget-related obligations imposed by Article 2(1) ICESR. As is expressly recognized in the section 'Different frameworks for defining the legal obligations imposed by ESR' of this chapter, there are other frameworks that may be employed as ESR-based by budget analysis practitioners in their work. We turn to these in Chapter 4.

157 Ida Koch, 'The Justiciability of Indivisible Rights' (2003) 72 *Nordic Journal of International Law* 3, 20.

158 Fernanda Doz Costa, 'Poverty and Human Rights: From Rhetoric to Legal Obligations-A Critical Account of Conceptual Framework' (2008) 9 *SUR International Journal on Human Rights* 81, 88.

4 A human rights framework

Part 2: An analysis of the tripartite typology and the obligations of non-discrimination and process

Introduction

This chapter builds on Chapter 3's consideration of the international ESR framework from a budget analysis perspective. Focussing on key obligations imposed by ESR identified by the Committee on Economic, Social and Cultural Rights, the chapter examines the tripartite typology of obligations according to which state's ESR duties are categorized in terms of the obligation(s) to respect, protect and fulfil rights. Having outlined the budget-related aspects of those obligations, the chapter considers some of the key challenges posed by the use of the typology from a budget analysis practitioner perspective. The final set of obligations considered are immediate obligations imposed by ESR that were not previously addressed in Chapter 3, particularly the prohibition on non-discrimination and process requirements. The chapter concludes with a discussion of the overlaps between the different analytical frameworks applied to ESR in both this chapter and the previous one.

The 'Tripartite Typology'

The notion of the various obligations engendered by rights was first pinpointed by Henry Shue in his 1980 work, *Basic Rights: Subsistence, Affluence and US Foreign Policy*.[1] Shue suggested that every basic right, as well as most other moral rights, could be analyzed using a very simple tripartite typology of interdependent duties of avoidance, protection and aid.[2] Variations on Shue's typology of duties were later offered by several commentators, with the

1 Henry Shue, *Basic Rights: Subsistence, Affluence, and US Foreign Policy* (Princeton UP 1980). The following paragraph is taken from Aoife Nolan, 'Addressing Economic and Social Rights Violations by Non-State Actors through the Role of the State: A Comparison of Regional Approaches to the "Obligation to Protect"' (2009) 9 *Human Rights Law Review* 225.

2 Henry Shue, 'The Interdependence of Duties', in Philip Alston and Katerina Tomasevski (eds) *The Right to Food* (Martinus Nijhoff Publishers 1984).

terminology of 'respect, protect and fulfil' being first employed by the Special Rapporteur to the UN Sub-Commission on Prevention of Discrimination and Protection of Minorities, Asbjørn Eide, in his 1987 Report on the *Right to Adequate Food as a Human Right*.[3] The Committee on Economic, Social and Cultural Rights subsequently adopted and employed the tripartite typology of the obligations to 'respect, protect and fulfil' as its interpretive framework for analyzing the rights contained in ICESCR.[4]

As discussed in Chapter 1, the separation of civil and political on the one hand and social, economic and cultural rights on the other has received harsh criticism from many writers.[5] The advantage of the tripartite typology is that it can be applied to all rights and therefore supports the interdependence and integrated nature of economic and social rights and civil and political rights. The alleged 'positive' versus 'negative' divide was previously used to argue for a weaker status of ESR on the basis that, unlike their civil and political counterparts, they required positive state action and the positive allocation of resources. The typology reflects, however, that it is not rights themselves, but rather the obligations imposed by rights, that are negative or positive in nature. Indeed, an advantage of basing an analysis on the tripartite level of obligations is that it illustrates the equal nature of all human rights, the interdependencies of all duties and the scope of the state's duties.[6] Furthermore, the classification is useful for the present purposes because each 'layer' of obligations attracts relatively specific and identifiable budget obligations. This tripartite approach

3 For more on the evolution of, and variations on, this typology, see Ida Koch 'Dichotomies, Trichotomies or Waves of Duties?' (2005) 5 *Human Rights Law Review* 81 and Matthew Craven, *The International Covenant on Economic, Social and Cultural Rights – A Perspective on its Development* (Oxford UP 1995) 109–10.

4 ComESCR first adopted the tripartite typology in ComESCR, *General Comment No, 12 The Right to Adequate Food*, UN Doc E/C.12/1999/5 (1999) paragraph 15; ComESCR, *General Comment No. 13, The Right to Education*, UN Doc E/C.12/1999/10 (1999) paragraphs 46–7 and 50; ComESCR, *General Comment No. 14, The Right to the Highest Attainable Standard of Health*, UN Doc E/C.12/2000/4 (2000) paragraphs 33–7; ComESCR, *General Comment No. 15, The Right to Water*, UN Doc E/C.12/2002/11 (2002) paragraphs 20–9; ComESCR, *General Comment No. 19, The Right to Social Security*, UN Doc E/C.12/GC/19 (2007) paragraphs 43–50. It should perhaps be noted that the European Committee on Social Rights has not explicitly incorporated the tripartite typology.

5 See generally *The Vienna Declaration and Programme of Action* (1993) paragraph 1–5; also Nicholas Haysom 'Constitutionalism, Majoritarian Democracy and Socio-economic rights' (1992) 8 *South African Journal of Human Rights* 451, 460; 'The Limburg Principles on the Implementation of the International Covenant on Economic, Social and Cultural Rights' (1987) 9 *Human Rights Quarterly* 122 UN Doc E/CN.4/1987/17, Annex. paragraph 3; Victor Dankwa, Cees Flinterman and Scott Leckie. 'Commentary on the Maastricht Guidelines on Violations of Economic, Social and Cultural Rights' (1998) 20 *Human Rights Quarterly* 705, 711.

6 María Magdalena Sepúlveda Carmona, *The Nature of the Obligations under the International Covenant on Economic, Social and Cultural Rights* (Intersentia 2003) 170.

does not exhaust ways of analyzing government obligations and should be supplemented with other methods, but it does further the indivisibility and interrelatedness of all human rights.[7]

The obligation to respect

The obligation to respect has been applied to the rights in both ICESCR and the International Covenant on Civil and Political Rights (ICCPR). Under international human rights law, the obligation to respect requires states to abstain from interfering with an individual's freedom, but also includes the duty to take positive actions necessary to ensure the rights.[8] In terms of ICESCR the obligation to respect requires states to refrain from interfering with the enjoyment of economic, social and cultural rights.[9] This duty entails respect for an individual's freedom to take the necessary actions and use the necessary resources – alone or in association with other people – to satisfy ESR needs.[10]

The ComESCR deliberately extended this obligation to encompass *existing* access to public services and resources. This naturally led to more positive action being required from states towards the satisfaction of this duty.[11] Koch argues that the ComESCR's interpretation requires states to uphold the existing supply and to guarantee all individuals equal access to continued enjoyment of the right; the obligation to respect may therefore attract positive and resource-demanding duties.[12] However, the budgetary obligations may not appear directly in the substantive provisions in question. The legal basis for effecting expenditure may well be hidden in the institutional framework required to implement the rights including education of government officials.[13]

In addition, budgetary obligations can arise from the judicial intervention ensuring compliance with the obligation to respect. These resource allocations can be either preventative or restorative in protecting against action that

7 Ida Koch, 'Dichotomies, Trichotomies or Waves of Duties?' (2005) 5 *Human Rights Law Review* 81, 87.

8 María Magdalena Sepúlveda Carmona, *The Nature of the Obligations under the International Covenant on Economic, Social and Cultural Rights* (Intersentia 2003) 136.

9 'The Maastricht Guidelines on Violations of Economic, Social and Cultural Rights', paragraph 6.

10 Asbjørn Eide, 'Economic and Social Rights' in Janusz Symonides (ed) *Human Rights: Concepts and Standards* (Ashgate/UNESCO 2000) 127.

11 This is most apparent perhaps ComESCR, *General Comment No. 15, The Right to Water*, where the ComESCR specifically deviates from the 'negative' wording in relation to the obligation to respect and speaks about 'protection' during armed conflicts, emergency situations and national disasters. This point is discussed further below.

12 Ida Koch 'Dichotomies, Trichotomies or Waves of Duties?' (2005) 5 *Human Rights Law Review* 81, 89.

13 Ida Koch 'The Justiciability of Indivisible Rights' (2003) 72 *Nordic Journal of International Law* 3, 13.

threatens the *status quo*.[14] Restorative jurisprudence in relation to failures to respect existing enjoyment of ESR may therefore also require the allocation of appropriate resources.

The decision of *SERAC v Nigeria*[15] is a case in point. The African Commission on Human and Peoples' Rights was confronted with a range of alleged violations of the African Charter on Human and Peoples' Rights, including the forced eviction and destruction of housing in several Ogoni villages by state security forces working in concert with the state-owned Nigerian National Petroleum Company.[16] The African Commission recognized the state's obligation to respect the free use of resources at the disposal of individuals or groups for the purpose of rights-related needs.[17] With regard to the right to shelter, the Commission observed that the state has an obligation to respect housing rights. This means it has to abstain from carrying out or sponsoring any practice that impedes individual access to the resources most appropriate to satisfy housing needs.[18] The Commission found that this obligation had been violated[19] and appealed to the government of Nigeria to ensure adequate 'compensation' to the victims, including 'relief and resettlement assistance to victims of government sponsored raids, and undertaking a comprehensive clean-up of lands and rivers damaged by oil operations'.[20] The restitution directed by the Commission is relevant here because it is the manifestation of positive, resource dependent obligations in relation to the obligation to *respect* existing enjoyment of rights.[21]

The obligation to respect deals with existing access or enjoyment of a right and therefore affords protection against interference with the status quo.[22] To be effective in that endeavour, it has to be of immediate application. The ComESCR has stated that reference to progressive achievement based on the availability of resources will rarely be relevant in relation the duty to refrain from forced evictions (an element of the obligation to respect the right to adequate housing).[23]

14 International Commission of Jurists, *Courts and the Legal Enforcement of Economic, Social and Cultural Rights* (International Commission of Jurists 2008) 42.
15 Communication Number 155/ *SERAC v Nigeria* 1996.
16 Malcolm Langford and Aoife Nolan, *Litigating Economic, Social and Cultural Rights: A Legal Practitioners' Guide* (COHRE Centre for Housing Rights and Evictions 2006) 81.
17 Communication Number 155/ *SERAC v Nigeria* 1996, paragraph 45.
18 Ibid, paragraph 61. Note that the African Charter on Human and People's Rights does not include an explicit right to adequate housing. The right was read in by the Commission based on the right to property (Article 14) and the right to protection of the family (Article 18(1)).
19 Ibid, paragraph 62.
20 Ibid, see order.
21 Ibid, see order.
22 Malcolm Langford and Aoife Nolan, *Litigating Economic, Social and Cultural Rights: A Legal Practitioners' Guide* (COHRE Centre for Housing Rights and Evictions 2006) 79.
23 ComESCR, *General Comment No. 7, Forced Evictions, and the Right to Adequate Housing*, UN Doc E/1998/22 (1997) paragraph 8.

Even though the obligation to respect is arguably not qualified by references to resources, giving effect to this duty by maintaining access to ESR benefits can, in certain instances, require the allocation of additional resources. In relation to the right to water, for example, the ComESCR states that during times of armed conflict, states have to protect objects indispensable for survival of the civilian population.[24] This includes drinking water installations and supplies and irrigation works, as well as the natural environment in general.[25] This example reiterates that ensuring the continuation of existing enjoyment and access to rights can have positive resources implications.

This is especially relevant in changing economic climates. In particular, the ComESCR specifically states that vulnerable members of society must be protected in times of severe resource constraints, whether caused by a process of adjustment, of economic recession, or by other factors.[26] In some instances, therefore, states will have to take positive action and allocate resources to ensure that existing access of ESR is continued in relation to those groups in society whose enjoyment of rights are most at risk, thereby adhering to their (the state's) obligation to *respect* ESR.

Courtis describes an instance in which the Argentina Supreme Court ordered government to readjust pension levels in line with the changing economic climate.[27] The majority decision of the Court stresses the links between pension levels and the rights to food, housing, education and health, or the right to an adequate standard of living for retired workers. The Court considered the progressive development of human rights, and held that the availability of resources cannot be employed as an argument to deny or restrict recognized rights.[28] On face value, this case could be considered to concern primarily the obligation of progressive realization. It is mentioned here, however, because it also deals with a situation of existing enjoyment of recognized rights. In particular, Courtis says that the Court claimed in this case that the availability of resources cannot be employed as an argument to deny or restrict recognized rights.[29] This case therefore also suggests that the obligation to *respect* is not subject to the availability of resources.

There is an area of potential overlap here. When existing enjoyment of a right is limited, there may be a violation of both the obligation to respect and the obligation not to take any retrogressive measures. The ComESCR has stated that evictions, for instance, should not result in rendering individuals

24 ComESCR, *General Comment No. 15, The Right to Water*, paragraph 22.

25 Ibid.

26 ComESCR, *General Comment No. 3, The Nature of States Parties Obligations*, paragraph 12.

27 Christian Courtis, 'Argentina: Some Promising Signs' in Malcolm Langford (ed) *Social Rights Jurisprudence: Emerging Trends in International and Comparative Law* (Cambridge UP 2008) 156.

28 Ibid 156.

29 Ibid 156.

homeless.[30] Take the example of the state adopting a 'city beautification' policy and ordering the eviction of occupants of areas and buildings targeted for redevelopment. If the state fails to provide adequate alternative housing, the policy could constitute a retrogressive measure because it involves the state taking a step backwards in the realization of ESR. The eviction and resultant homelessness, on the other hand, would be a manifestation of a failure to respect existing enjoyment. It should be noted that the relationship between retrogressive measures and the obligation to respect has not been fully explored by the ComESCR or other commentators. In light of the ComESCR's concentration on 'state interference' in its discussions of the obligation to respect, we conclude that the difference between the obligation to respect and the obligation not to take retrogressive measures essentially relates to the situation where a step backwards by the state (retrogression) does not interfere with the current enjoyment of the right (the obligation to respect). For example, a promise of funding that is subsequently withdrawn before it was actually allocated may constitute a retrogressive measure, but not a violation of the obligation to respect.

The obligation to protect

In international law human rights duties are primarily held by states.[31] However, the obligation to protect requires states to protect right-holders ESR enjoyment from non-state actor interference.

In practical terms, the obligation to protect requires states, for example, to ensure that privatization of the health sector does not constitute a threat to health facilities, goods and services; or to control marketing of medical equipment and ensure that medical practitioners and other health professionals meet appropriate standards of education, skill and ethical codes of conduct.[32]

30 ComESCR, *General Comment No. 7, Forced Evictions, and the Right to Adequate Housing*, paragraph 17.

31 Private duties can nonetheless arise from the language of particular treaties even though they are not expressly mentioned in the text. Jordan Paust, 'The Other Side of Right: Private Duties Under Human Rights Law' (1992) 5 *Harvard Human Rights Journal* 51, 55. There are examples to be drawn from a range of human rights treaties. ICESCR – for the present purposes the most important – recognizes individual responsibility, stating that '[t]he individual, having duties to other individuals and to the community to which he belongs, is under a responsibility to strive for the promotion and observance of the rights recognized in the [. . .] Covenant'. Similarly Article 5 ICESCR includes third parties by stating that nothing in the Charter implies that a 'person or group has the right to engage in any activity or to perform any act aimed at the destruction of any of the rights or freedoms recognized herein, or at their limitation to a greater extent than is provided for in the [. . .] Covenant'.

32 ComESCR, *General Comment No. 14, The Right to the Highest Attainable Standard of Health*, paragraph 35. ComESCR, *General Comment No. 15, The Right to Water*, paragraph 24.

an operator but has simply failed to put an end to the alleged violations in its capacity as regulator'.[44] Such an approach is consistent with enforcing the obligation to protect. Nolan argues that even though the European Committee does not apply the tripartite typology or explicitly use the language of the 'obligation to protect' in its decision-making, it requires states to prevent, punish and remedy violations committed by third parties.[45]

An interesting issue regarding the obligation to protect is that of privatization, which has also been mentioned by the ComESCR[46] and has recently received attention by the Special Rapporteur on the Right to Adequate Housing as a Component of the Right to an Adequate Standard of Living.[47] Chirwa has argued that implementation of cost recovery measures and the removal of subsidies, which go hand-in-hand with privatization, may threaten human rights – especially of the poor. State interventions in ESR delivery are critical to increasing or sustaining access by poor communities.[48] The UN High Commissioner for Human Rights has warned that overemphasis on commercial objectives at the expense of social objectives is one of the ways in which privatization can undermine the enjoyment of ESR.[49] As highlighted above, the obligation to protect places the obligation firmly with the state to ensure that privatization does not interfere with the enjoyment of ESR.[50] In this regard, the United Kingdom's *Water Industry Act* (as amended in 1999) is of interest. It empowers a minister to require subsidies to be provided by private suppliers to certain vulnerable groups, on the basis of age, ill-health, disability of financial circumstances.[51] Maintaining access to the enjoyment of ESR through the provision of state assistance, including, for example, the allocation of adequate resources to subsidies, or requiring such of private service deliverers, can therefore be argued to be an aspect of the obligation to protect.

44 Ibid, paragraph 14.

45 Aoife Nolan, 'Addressing Economic and Social Rights Violations by Non-State Actors through the Role of the State: A Comparison of Regional Approaches to the "Obligation to Protect"' (2009) 9 *Human Rights Law Review* 225, 251.

46 ComESCR, *General Comment No. 16, The Equal Rights of Men and Women to the Enjoyment of all Economic, Social and Cultural Rights*, paragraph 20.

47 Raquel Rolnik, *Report of the Special Rapporteur on Adequate Housing as a Component of the Right to an Adequate Standard of Living, and the Right to Non-discrimination in this Context: Promotion and Protection of All Human Rights, Civil, Political, Economic, Social and Cultural Rights, including the Right to Development*, A/HRC/10/7 (2009) 23–30.

48 Danwood Chirwa, 'Privatization of Water in Southern Africa: A Human Rights Perspective' (2004) 4 *African Human Rights Law Journal* 218, 228.

49 UN High Commissioner for Human Rights, *Economic, social and cultural rights: Liberalization of trade in services and human rights. Report of the High Commissioner,* E/CN 4/Sub 2/2002/9 25 June 2002 as summarized by Chirwa ibid 229–30.

50 Chirwa, ibid 233.

51 Malcolm Langford and others, *Legal Resources for the Right to Water: International and National Standards* (COHRE 2003) 54.

COHRE describes a case related to the disconnection of water supplied by a privately owned company in Argentina: *Quevedo Miguel Angel y otros c/Aguas Cordobesas S.A. Amparo*.[52] The complainants sued the water service company arguing that the disconnection was illegal, that the company failed to comply with its regulatory obligation to provide 50 daily litres of water regardless as to whether payment was provided, and that even that minimum supply obligation was too low. The judge refused to hold that the power of the company to cut or restrict the supply of water on the grounds of non-payment was illegal, but recognized that the contractual obligation to provide a minimum of 50 litres of water in all circumstances was clearly insufficient for a standard family and therefore required the company to provide a minimum of 200 litres per household. The judge found that the provincial state had an obligation to ensure the existence of adequate and efficient public utilities services and to effectively regulate and control them. The court ordered the Company to provide free water to those who were unable to pay for it. Interestingly enough this did not preclude the possibility of the company reaching an agreement with the responsible state authorities to be compensated for the costs of meeting this obligation.[53] This case illustrates that the budgetary implications for the state in the context of a failure to protect ESR may include compensation to private parties by the state, to ensure protection of ESR.

Growing awareness of the increasing role of non-state actors in relation to both the delivery of ESR-related goods and services and the violation of such rights means that states should provide an environment that facilitates the discharge of such human rights responsibilities by third parties. It follows that there may be situations where a failure to realize ESR as required by Article 2(1) would give rise to violations by states as a result of states' failure to take appropriate measures to regulate and control third parties.[54] If the state has delegated the realization of an ESR policy or programme, the state remains responsible to the full extent of their ICESCR obligations. Similarly, it has been argued that it is clear from the work of the ComESCR that even when a state has privatized some public services it remains responsible for the satisfaction of a minimum essential level of each right. Privatization therefore does not relieve states of their Article 2(1) obligations, in particular towards the most vulnerable and disadvantaged groups in society.[55]

52 Juez Sustituta de Primera Instancia y 51 Nominación en lo Civil y Comercial de la Ciudad de Córdoba (Civil and Commercial First Instance Court). April 8, 2002. The discussion below is based on COHRE's account of the case in Langford and others, ibid 113.

53 Langford and others, ibid 114.

54 Manisuli Ssenjoyonjo, 'The Applicability of International Human Rights Law to Non-State Actors: What Relevance to Economic, Social and Cultural Rights?' (2008) 12 *International Journal of Human Rights* 725, 737.

55 María Magdalena Sepúlveda Carmona, *The Nature of the Obligations under the International Covenant on Economic, Social and Cultural Rights* (Intersentia 2003) 367.

The obligation to protect is also particularly relevant in the context of the recession and the current restrictive economic climate. It has been argued that the causes of the financial crisis can be traced back to the sub-prime mortgage crisis, the loose monetary policy and low interest rates, combined with a resistance to regulation and excessive risk-taking of the banks as well as the explosion of the credit/debt between 2002 and 2007.[56] The conduct of banks, private institutions, has therefore had a large influence – if not a leading role – in the recent economic crisis, which has and will continue to have a devastating impact on the enjoyment of ESR worldwide. It can therefore be argued that the failure to control and regulate the banking sector was one of the causes of the crisis. Yet despite this, there has been little effort to integrate the key human rights principles of accountability and transparency into government policy responses.[57] Massive public funding was made available to recapitalize the banks, including taking partial or full government ownership. Yet the massive resources devoted to rescuing the financial sector have far exceeded the resources devoted to the fiscal stimulus or social protection programmes needed to restore the economy and rescue people's jobs and standard of living.[58] From a human rights perspective, government has an obligation to protect ESR, which in this situation would include regulation, control and oversight of the financial industry to guard against excessive risk-taking and speculation.[59]

The obligation to fulfil

The obligation to fulfil tends to be the most resource-dependent (and demanding) of the duties imposed by ESR and is often the one that raises the most questions as regards its precise delineation. It has been argued that the more resource-demanding the obligations become, the less detail is used in describing them.[60] Many ESR, however, have to be vaguely defined at the fulfilment level (and, indeed at other levels) because ESR-related needs are likely to vary significantly from state party to state party. In this they are

56 *Bringing Human Rights to Bear in Times of Crisis: A Human Rights Analysis of Government Response to the Economic Crisis Submission to the High – Level Segment. 13th session of the UNHRC on the Global Economic and Financial Crises*, (2010) 11. Raquel Rolnik, *Report of the Special Rapporteur on Adequate Housing as a Component of the Right to an Adequate Standard of Living, and the Right to Non-discrimination in this Context: Promotion and Protection of All Human Rights, Civil, Political, Economic, Social and Cultural Rights, including the Right to Development*, UN Doc A/HRC/10/7 (2009) paragraph 6.

57 *Bringing Human Rights to Bear in Times of Crisis: A Human Rights Analysis of Government Response to the Economic Crisis*, ibid 11.

58 Ibid 11.

59 Ibid 13.

60 Ida Koch 'The Justiciability of Indivisible Rights' (2003) 72 *Nordic Journal of International Law* 3, 12.

little different from civil and political rights. Indeed, there are strong arguments in favour of open-textured framing of all human rights and related obligations, so that states are able to respond adequately to individual circumstances and historical developments in concretizing their meaning over time.[61]

This complexity makes monitoring the obligation to fulfil quite challenging. To overcome this, the ComESCR sought to frame the obligation to fulfil in such a way as to avoid it becoming meaningless rhetoric. The Committee did so by identifying that the violation of the obligation to fulfil occurs through the failure to take all the necessary steps to ensure the realization of the rights.[62] Examples of failures to fulfil include both immediate and progressive obligations. In terms of immediate obligations, the ComESCR has warned against the failure to adopt or implement a national health policy or a failure to identify indicators and benchmarks as well as the failure to monitor the realization of the rights.[63] These are obligations that are generally identified as immediate obligations and independent of the resources that are available.

The obligation to fulfil implies that state parties are under a duty to do whatever it takes to overcome obstacles for the full enjoyment of the right in question.[64] The state also has to ensure that in fulfilling Covenant rights it complies with the whole range of obligations generated by ICESCR – namely that the ESR are progressively realized using the maximum of available resources and that the fulfilment of ESR is prioritized in accordance with the various obligations imposed by ICESCR.

Examples of right to health violations involving the obligation to fulfil would be: the failure to adopt or implement a national health policy; insufficient expenditure or misallocation of public resources; the failure to monitor the realization of the right to health, for example by identifying right to health indicators and benchmarks; and the failure to take measures to reduce the inequitable distribution of health facilities, goods and services.[65] Phrased in positive terms, the obligation to fulfil requires states by implication to adopt appropriate, administrative, budgetary, promotional and other measures towards the full realization of ESR.

61 Aoife Nolan, Bruce Porter and Malcolm Langford, 'The Justiciability of Social and Economic Rights: An Udpated Appraisal (2007) 15 *Centre for Human Rights and Global Justice*, Working Paper 9.

62 ComESCR, *General Comment No. 14, on the Right to the Highest Attainable Standard of Health*, paragraph 52

63 Ibid.

64 Ida Koch 'The Justiciability of Indivisible Rights' (2003) 72 *Nordic Journal of International Law* 3, 15.

65 ComESCR, *General Comment No. 14, on the Right to the Highest Attainable Standard of Health*, paragraph 52.

The obligation to fulfil has been divided into the obligations to facilitate and provide,[66] and, in some cases, the obligation to promote.[67] Generally, when access to rights is limited or non-existent, the obligation to fulfil requires the state to be a proactive agent capable of bringing about an increase in access to a range of ESR rights. This level of obligation therefore obliges the state to identify problem situations and provide relief, as well as the creation of conditions that allow and enable rights-holders to manage their own access to the goods and services protected by rights.[68] The obligation to fulfil requires the implementation of measures to modify discriminatory patterns that result in the disadvantage of vulnerable groups.[69] It was shown above that the obligations to respect and protect involve state expenditures. However, at this tertiary level of obligation, state expenditures are at the core and the very essence of the individual rights.[70] There are a variety of ways in which the obligation to fulfil can be violated, including through insufficient expenditure or a misallocation of public resources that results in the non-enjoyment of the right and the failure to take measures to reduce the inequitable distribution of wealth.[71]

The ComESCR has applied various aspects of the obligation to fulfil. In relation to the right to food it states that the obligation to fulfil (facilitate) requires pro-active engagement in activities intended to strengthen people's access to and utilization of resources and means to ensure their livelihoods.[72] It should also enable people to ensure the realization of ESR themselves.[73]

66 ComESCR, *General Comment No. 12, The Right to Adequate Food*, paragraph 15.

67 See, for example, footnote 23 of ComESCR, *General Comment No. 14, The Right to the Highest Attainable Standard of Health* where the Committee explained that '[a]ccording to general comments No. 12 and 13, the obligation to fulfil incorporates an obligation to *facilitate* and an obligation to *provide*. In the present general comment, the obligation to fulfil also incorporates an obligation to *promote* because of the critical importance of health promotion in the work of WHO and elsewhere.' The obligation to fulfil has also been interpreted to include the obligation to promote in the context of the right to water in ComESCR, *General Comment No. 15, The Right to Water*, paragraph 25. See also ComESCR, *General Comment No. 13, The Right to Education*, paragraph 50, where the obligation to fulfil is divided into the obligations to facilitate and provide; ComESCR, *General Comment No. 19, The right to Social Security*, paragraphs 47–50, where the obligation to fulfil is divided into the obligations to facilitate, promote and provide.

68 International Commission of Jurists, *Courts and the Legal Enforcement of Economic, Social and Cultural Rights* (International Commission of Jurists 2008) 48.

69 Ibid 49.

70 María Magdalena Sepúlveda Carmona, *The Nature of the Obligations under the International Covenant on Economic, Social and Cultural Rights* (Intersentia 2003) 164.

71 Ibid 199. Sepulveda refers to ComESCR, *General Comment No. 14, The Right to the Highest Attainable Standard of Health*, paragraph 41. Note that the General Comment refers to 'inequitable distribution of health facilities' as opposed to 'inequitable distribution of wealth'.

72 ComESCR, *General Comment No. 12, The Right to Adequate Food*, paragraph 15.

73 Ibid.

This includes the duty to assess the current situation of the country and to repeat such assessments at brief intervals.[74] In relation to the right to education and the obligation to fulfil (facilitate), the state has to take positive measures to ensure that education is culturally appropriate and of good quality.[75] These aspects of the obligation to fulfil (facilitate) are necessary because they lay the foundation required for full realization to take place progressively. Assessment should identify people that are in need and should identify ways and means to remedy the situation. Continuous reassessment must be done to ascertain if the adopted measures are indeed successful.[76] The obligation to fulfil (facilitate) also requires assistance to those that are close to or below the poverty line, in order to enable them to make better use of their entitlements. This includes services to assist people to improve their productivity or credit arrangements that do not threaten participants with dangerous indebtedness.[77] Technical and vocational training programmes to improve the capacity of persons to earn their own living would also fall under this layer of obligation. Facilitating access may involve the allocation of subsidies and price regulations.[78] Again, such measures require the allocation of financial, human and other resources.

In *General Comment No. 14* on the highest attainable standard of health, the obligation to fulfil is divided according to the obligations to facilitate, provide, and to promote the right to health.[79] The obligation to fulfil (promote) includes research and provision of information; ensuring that health services are culturally appropriate and that health care staff are trained to recognize and respond to the specific needs of vulnerable or marginalized groups; the dissemination of appropriate information and moreover supporting people in making informed choices about their health.[80] In relation to the right to water, the obligation to fulfil (promote) includes the obligation to ensure that there is appropriate education concerning the hygienic use of water, protection of water sources and methods to minimize water wastage.[81] These examples of obligations associated with the obligation to promote include process requirements as part of the obligation to fulfil.[82] They are relevant here

74 Asbjørn Eide, 'Economic and Social Rights' in Janusz Symonides (ed) *Human Rights: Concepts and Standards* (Ashgate/UNESCO 2000) 138.
75 ComESCR, *General Comment No. 13, The Right to Education*, paragraph 50.
76 Asbjørn Eide, 'Economic and Social Rights' in Janusz Symonides (ed) *Human Rights: Concepts and Standards* (Ashgate/UNESCO 2000) 138.
77 Ibid 139.
78 Ibid 138.
79 ComESCR, *General Comment No. 14, The Right to the Highest Attainable Standard of Health*, paragraph 37.
80 Ibid.
81 ComESCR, *General Comment No. 15, The Right to Water*, paragraph 25.
82 See 'Other Immediate Obligations' below, where these types of requirements are discussed in more detail. Many of these initiatives can be pursued with minimal resource allocation and are therefore also discussed under immediate obligations.

because these process requirements also have budgetary implications – they require the state to expend funds, to create and maintain institutions necessary to promoting acceptance of the right.[83] Training of health staff, for example, will require the allocation of financial resources.

Finally, whenever an individual or group is unable, for reasons beyond their control, to enjoy a particular right by the means at their disposal, states have the obligation to fulfil (provide) that right directly.[84] In relation to the right to water, the ComESCR states that the obligation to fulfil (provide) includes measures that ensure equitable access to water. This includes adopting pricing policies for free and low-cost water, to ensure that poor people are not disproportionately burdened with water expenses.[85] To this end, states should develop plans and strategies to give effect to the right.[86] It is clear that, in order to be implementable, such a strategic plan has to be budgeted for. In relation to the right to education, the ComESCR has stated that the obligation to fulfil (provide) includes the obligation to design and provide resources for curricula that reflect the contemporary needs of students. It also inter alia includes building classrooms, training teachers and paying them domestically competitive salaries.[87] Again, giving effect to these duties will require the allocation of resources. The state's obligation to provide directly can range from a minimum safety net to a full comprehensive welfare model as in the Nordic countries.[88]

There are certain groups of people that are entitled to special measures. For instance, international human rights law recognizes that children will frequently be unable to take care of their own ESR-related needs. They also bear no responsibility for their parents' failure to provide for them.[89] Similarly, individuals deprived of their freedom (detained persons in prison and other institutions) cannot by their own means ensure the satisfaction of their basic needs. Asylum seekers, refugees and displaced persons generally do not have the same opportunity as others to achieve an adequate standard of living on

83 María Magdalena Sepúlveda Carmona, *The Nature of the Obligations under the International Covenant on Economic, Social and Cultural Rights* (Intersentia 2003) 164.

84 ComESCR, *General Comment No, 12 The Right to Adequate Food*, paragraph 15.

85 ComESCR, *General Comment No. 15, The Right to Water*, paragraph 27.

86 Ibid, paragraph 26.

87 ComESCR, *General Comment No. 13, The right to Education*, paragraph 50.

88 Asbjørn Eide, 'Economic and Social Rights' in Janusz Symonides (ed) *Human Rights: Concepts and Standards* (Ashgate/UNESCO 2000) 140.

89 See Article 10(3) of ICESCR: 'Special measures of protection and assistance should be taken on behalf of all children and young people without any discrimination for reasons of parentage or other conditions. Children and young people should be protected from economic and social exploitation. Their employment in work harmful to their morals or health or dangerous to life or likely to hamper their normal development should be punishable by law. States should also set age limits below which the paid employment of child labour should be prohibited and punishable by law.'

their own, and therefore require direct provision to a larger extent than the rest of the population, until conditions are established in which they can obtain their own entitlements.[90]

Thus, the obligation to fulfil may also include an obligation to prioritize allocation for those more vulnerable groups. It should be noted that vulnerability has to be considered in the national context. One likely response by governments towards claims regarding the obligation to fulfil (provide) is that they lack the resources to do so. The obligation to fulfil thus has to be read in the context of the resources that are available to the state. The ComESCR has made specific recommendations that could be classified under the obligation to fulfil ESR with regard to the allocation of resources. An example of the ComESCR's jurisprudence highlighting the resource implications entailed by the obligation to fulfil is the ComESCR urging of Algeria to allot a large share of the national budget surplus to the struggle against poverty.[91]

Challenges in using the tripartite typology

There are some obstacles to using the tripartite typology to analyze the budget-related obligations imposed by ICESCR. For instance, the ComESCR's employment of this typology post-dated its consideration of the right to adequate housing in its *General Comments No. 4* and 7. It is, therefore, more challenging to employ this analytical framework in the context of the right to adequate housing than it would be in relation to, for example, the right to health, in which context the ComESCR made explicit use of the tripartite typology in its delineation of state obligations.

Second, because the framework is different to, and not derived from, the actual text in ICESCR, the prioritization and translation of norms from the Covenant into the tripartite typology can be challenging. Welling has argued that it is not immediately evident from the tripartite framework which obligations under the Covenant must be implemented immediately and which must be implemented progressively, as the resources become available.[92] According to the ComESCR, '[s]ome measures [. . .] are of a more immediate nature, while other measures are more of a long-term character, to achieve progressively the full realization of [ESR]'.[93] (In practice, as discussed

90 Asbjørn Eide, 'Economic and Social Rights' in Janusz Symonides (ed) *Human Rights: Concepts and Standards* (Ashgate/UNESCO 2000) 140.

91 ComESCR, *Conclusions and recommendations of the Committee on Economic, Social and Cultural Rights, Algeria*, UN Doc E/C.12/1/Add.71 (2001) paragraph 34. Increases in spending to health care and education were specifically mentioned at paragraph 40.

92 Judith Welling, 'International Indicators and Economic, Social and Cultural' (2008) 30 *Human Rights Quarterly* 933, 953.

93 ComESCR, *General Comment No. 12 The Right to Adequate Food*, paragraph 16.

above it has become clear that the obligations to respect and protect are immediate in nature, while the obligation to fulfil includes both immediate and progressive obligations.[94])

A third challenge is that the lines between the different obligations in the tripartite typology have necessarily become blurred to some extent. Consider the evolution of the obligation to respect. In a situation where the state is providing health care in a non-discriminatory manner, the obligation to respect will be fulfilled if the state simply continues providing the service. The obligation to fulfil will refer in that situation to the duty to improve on the existing services progressively. If a state is, however, providing a health care service on a discriminatory basis, then there might be a violation of the obligation to respect. A correction of such a violation will require the state to take positive action to extend the existing health services to all on a non-discriminatory basis. It is at this point that it becomes difficult to distinguish between action taken in terms of the obligation to respect and action taken to comply with the obligation to fulfil.[95] Similarly, the obligation to protect and the obligation to fulfil may require similar actions depending only on whether the violating institution is a public or a private one.[96]

Another challenge is posed by the subdivision of the obligation to fulfil into three specific aspects. The incorporation of three sublevels (facilitate, provide and promote) gives the impression that in order to keep the terminology 'tripartite' the obligation to fulfil has taken on an extremely wide scope. Since these separate obligations are different to each other, it has been argued that they may possibly be better categorized as independent categories.[97]

In particular, the obligation to promote could fall under any of the three key obligations that constitute the tripartite typology. When states take measures to comply with one level of their obligation to protect, these measures

94 See for example the ComESCR, *General Comment No. 15, The Right to Water (Article 11 and 12)*: the obligation to respect requires states to 'refrain from interfering with the enjoyment of the right to water' paragraph 21. Similarly at paragraph 23 the ComESCR states that '[t]he obligation to *protect* requires State parties to prevent third parties from interfering in any way with the enjoyment of the right to water'. Respecting someone's right implies that people already have access and enjoyment of that right. Similarly what is at stake with regards to the obligation to protect is the protection of an already existing (but now threatened) position. See Ida Koch 'The Justiciability of Indivisible Rights' (2003) 72 *Nordic Journal of International Law* 3, 14. It should be noted, however, that simply because a duty is of immediate application it does not mean that giving effect to the duty will not require any resources.

95 Ida Koch, 'Dichotomies, Trichotomies or Waves of Duties?' (2005) 5 *Human Rights Law Review* 81, 89.

96 Ibid 90.

97 María Magdalena Sepúlveda Carmona, *The Nature of the Obligations under the International Covenant on Economic, Social and Cultural Rights* (Intersentia 2003) 208.

might at the same time serve to comply with the obligation to promote. Consider the obligation to protect the right to adequate housing. This duty may also be fulfilled if states promote the rights of tenants, by providing adequate information on their rights *vis-à-vis* their landlords for example. In the same vein, attempts to protect the right to the highest attainable standard of health may also involve a promotion of consumer's rights. Promotional activities are only one way that states have to comply with their duties but it is possible to say that the requirement to promote is not just an ancillary obligation and that it has in fact taken on its own independent character. It could also mean that all human rights should include this type of a duty. Human rights supervisory bodies stress the importance of the promotion of human rights and seem to impose the obligation to promote by requiring states to encourage citizens to respect and protect human rights through education, training and public information.[98] One challenge of the tripartite typology is therefore to avoid seeing the obligation to promote as an ancillary obligation.

It is important to note that the tripartite typology was not supposed to become a frozen abstraction replacing the notion of positive versus negative rights. Rather, it was designed as an analytical tool to define what was needed to enable people to be secure against predictable infringements of their rights.[99]

It is clear that the tripartite typology has definite strengths. It should, however, not be applied exclusively. Not only do the various elements overlap with each other, but as is described below the various elements of the tripartite typology also overlap with other approaches. Instead of applying the tripartite approach rigidly and in isolation from other frameworks, it should rather be supplemented with the other approaches described in Chapter 3 and below, when determining the state's ESR-related obligations.

Other immediate obligations

In Chapter 3 we discussed some of the key immediate obligations under Article 2(1). However, these are certainly not the only immediate obligations imposed by ESR.[100] In its *General Comment No. 3*, the ComESCR identified various articles in ICESCR that are of immediate application, including the right to equality between men and women (Article 3), and the right to special measures

98 Ibid 166.

99 Ida Koch, 'The Justiciability of Indivisible Rights' (2003) 72 *Nordic Journal of International Law* 3, 10–11.

100 While this section is headed 'other immediate obligations', Article 2(1) clearly still has a key role to play in relation to many of the obligations discussed here, whether in terms of constituting their basis or establishing the context within which they are to apply.

of protection to young people and children (Article 10(3)).[101] The ComESCR has emphasized that non-discrimination is an immediate and cross-cutting obligation in the Covenant,[102] and the duty to ensure non-discrimination requires measures to prevent discrimination as well as, in some cases, the adoption of special measures to attenuate or suppress conditions that perpetuate discrimination.[103]

In many instances, immediate obligations in relation to particular rights have been spelled out by the ComESCR. For instance, in the context of the right to adequate housing, the duty to monitor the housing situation is of immediate effect.[104] Furthermore, a strategy should immediately be put in place that identifies the resources available to the state, is subject to effective coordination and is based on participatory practices.[105]

101 The other rights are fair wages and equal remuneration for work of equal value without distinction of any kind (Article 7(a)(1)); the right to form trade unions (Article 8); the right to free and compulsory primary education to all (Article 13(2)(a)); the right of parents and legal guardians to choose schools other than those established by the public authorities and the liberty of individuals and bodies to establish and direct educational institutions (Article 13(4)). It is interesting to note that these examples include obligations to respect, protect, and fulfil.

102 ComESCR, *General Comment No. 20, Non-Discrimination in Economic, Social and Cultural Rights*, paragraph 7.

103 See ComESCR, ibid, paragraphs 7–9.

104 ComESCR, *General Comment No. 4, The Right to Adequate Housing*, paragraph 13. See also the ComESCR, *Consideration of Reports Submitted By States Parties under Article 16 and 17 of the Covenant*, UN Doc E/C.12/GBR/CO/5 (2009): 'In relation to the right to an adequate right to housing the Reporting Guidelines request the following information: Indication of a national survey on homelessness and inadequate housing, in particular the number of individuals and families who are homeless or inadequately housed and without access to basic infrastructures and services such as water, heating, waste disposal, sanitation, and electricity, as well as the number of persons living in over-crowded or structurally unsafe housing. (a) The measures taken to ensure access to adequate and affordable housing with legal security of tenure for everyone, irrespective of income or access to economic resources; (b) The impact of social housing measures, such as the provision of low-cost social housing units for disadvantaged and marginalized individuals and families, in particular in rural and deprived urban areas, whether there are waiting lists for obtaining such housing and the average length of waiting time; (c) Measures taken to make housing accessible and habitable for persons with special housing needs, such as families with children, older persons and persons with disabilities. They also request indications regarding the measures in place to protect against buildings on polluted sites or in immediate proximity of pollution sources that threaten the health of inhabitants. Further they request indications whether there are any disadvantaged and marginalized individuals and groups, such as ethnic minorities, who are particularly affected by forced evictions and the measures taken to ensure that no form of discrimination is involved whenever evictions take place. They also want to know the number of persons and families evicted within the last five years and the legal provisions defining the circumstances in which evictions may take place and the rights of tenants to security of tenure and protection from eviction.'

105 Ibid, paragraphs 12–13.

We have already discussed the core obligations imposed by ESR in some detail in Chapter 3. From a process perspective, however, it is important to reiterate that, in many instances, immediate obligations in relation to particular rights have been delineated by the ComESCR in the context of the 'core obligations' imposed by ESR.[106] For example, the core content of the right to the highest attainable standard of health includes further processes worth mentioning here. Proper assessments of the extent of need, as well as a process of participation, are two obvious examples.[107] Since these process requirements are necessary in the development of a strategy, they have to happen immediately. Another argument for their immediate application is the fact that satisfaction of these process requirements is likely to lead to a more principled policymaking process.[108]

The right to participate specifically in relation to ESR is also mentioned by the Office of the High Commissioner for Human Rights who states that the institutional framework for implementing ESR should include mechanisms

106 The Committee has adopted the approach of delineating the 'core obligations' imposed by ESR in a number of its General Comments since 2000. (See ComESCR, *General Comments 14, 15, 17–19* and *21*). As Young observes, these include 'a template of "core obligations" that straddle different rights, duties of positive provision, and wider institutional strategies' (Katherine Young, 'The Minimum Core of Economic and Social Rights: A Concept in Search of Content' (2008) 33 *Yale Journal of International Law* 113, 152.). These core obligations include – but are not limited to – the minimum core entitlement(s) outlined by the Committee in its earlier statements on the 'minimum core', which are focussed on in Chapter 3. For the sake of ease, we have chosen to deal with process obligations here rather than in the context of Chapter 3. However, it would be possible to argue that some of the General Comments certainly appear to include process requirements within the 'minimum core' obligations imposed by ESR. (See, e.g., the language in *General Comment No. 19*, para 59).

107 ComESCR, *General Comment No. 14, The Right to the Highest Attainable Standard of Health*. These process elements are derived from paragraph 43(f) Ibid: 'To adopt and implement a national public health strategy and plan of action, on the basis of epidemiological evidence, addressing the health concerns of the whole population; the strategy and plan of action shall be devised, and periodically reviewed, on the basis of a participatory and transparent process; they shall include methods, such as right to health indicators and benchmarks, by which progress can be closely monitored; the process by which the strategy and plan of action are devised, as well as their content, shall give particular attention to all vulnerable or marginalized groups.'

108 A. Blyberg gives examples of process-related indicators relevant for budget analysis, for example: 'Has the government established structures and processes to facilitate civil society participation in commenting on/proposing/effecting modifications in revenue at the national and local levels?' and 'Has the government established structures and processes to facilitate civil society access to information on revenue in national and local budgets?' in 'Government Human Rights Obligations and Budget Work' (2008) unpublished on file with the authors. See also Philip Alston and Gerard Quinn, 'The Nature and Scope of the States Parties' Obligations under the International Covenant on Economic, Social and Cultural Rights' (1987) 9 *Human Rights Quarterly* 156, 181.

that ensure the participation of relevant stakeholders, ensure access to information and transparency, establish accountability mechanisms, respect due process in decision-making, and provide remedies in case of violations.[109] Failure to include mechanisms to satisfy these procedural requirements may also amount to violations of international obligations.[110] The ComESCR has reiterated that the human rights framework includes the right of those affected by key decisions to participate in the decision-making processes. It adds that, according to the experience of the ComESCR, policies or programmes formulated without the active and informed participation of those affected are most unlikely to be effective.[111]

From a human rights perspective, the right to information is particularly important in the context of the recession. Without the right to information and the right to participate, democratic debate around the precise details of many of the economic rescue packages is not possible.[112] Some economists have argued that the opaque and complicated nature of the bail outs may not be entirely unintentional, asserting that governments moved money around quickly so the public would not understand that this was an elaborate way to subsidize the banks and transfer money to the rich.[113]

These process requirements are relevant to a budgetary analysis because resources have to be allocated for them to be put into effect. Developing an implementation strategy, monitoring the realization of ESR and the establishment of participatory processes all entail costs, and should hence be reflected in the budget.

Overlaps

Before concluding our discussion of the budget-related obligations imposed by ESR under ICESCR, it is important to acknowledge that there are considerable overlaps between the various approaches to categorizing ESR

109 OHCHR *Report of the High Commissioner for Human Rights on Implementation of Economic, Social and Cultural Rights*, E/2009/90 (2009) paragraph 33. See also Henry Steiner 'Political Participation as a Human Right' (1988) 1 *Human Rights Yearbook* 77, 93 who argues that article 25(b) of the International Covenant on Civil and Political Rights firmly establishes that the right to partake in public affairs includes something more than merely the right to vote.

110 Economic and Social Council, *Report of the High Commissioner for Human Rights on Implementation of Economic, Social and Cultural Rights*, E/2009/90 (2009) paragraph 33.

111 ComESCR, *Substantive Issues Arising in the Implementation of the International Covenant on Economic, Social and Cultural Rights; Poverty and the International Covenant on Economic, Social and Cultural Rights*, E/C.12/2001/10 (2001) paragraph 12.

112 *Bringing Human Rights to Bear in Times of Crisis: A Human Rights Analysis of Government Response to the Economic Crisis Submission to the High–Level Segment 13th session of the UNHRC on the Global Economic and Financial Crises* (2010) 13.

113 Ibid.

obligations that are described above in both this chapter and Chapter 3. First, there is overlap and interaction between the tripartite typology above and various immediate duties. The obligations to respect and to protect were argued to be immediate. Additionally, immediate duties such as the duty not to discriminate and the various process requirements described above apply to each level of obligation to respect, protect and fulfil. The obligation to fulfil overlaps with the obligation to provide a minimum core. In addition to that, there are elements of the obligation to fulfil that are of a progressive nature – such as the full realization of ESR and hence coincide with the progression realisation duty imposed by Article 2(1).

There are also striking similarities between the obligation to respect and the obligation to refrain from retrogressive measures, both of which are immediate obligations. It was shown above, however, that the obligation to respect can require more than simply refraining from retrogressive measures. Furthermore, as has already been made clear, retrogressive measures do not necessarily equate to a violation of the obligation to respect.

The correspondence between, and common concerns of, the different frameworks can be demonstrated by looking to the housing context. As argued earlier, a certain, calculated priority ought to be accorded by states to give effect to immediate obligations in the overall context of progressive realization of the full scope and content of the right. If the state has a duty to consult with occupiers, for example, in an eviction situation, funding for that process must be made available in order to make it successful. If this is to give effect to certain aspects of the right to adequate housing, it has to happen immediately, rather than progressively. This duty of consultation is an immediate, process-related obligation under the Article 2(1) analogy, but may also be classified as giving effect to the obligation to respect, in the sense that it deals with the existing access to an ESR. The pertinent point is that both frameworks can be applied to analyze the same situation and will frequently result in a similar priority being afforded to particular obligations.

Conclusion

In developing a human rights-based framework applicable to budgetary decisions, this chapter and Chapter 3 constitute an important step towards linking ESR obligations with budgets. This is fundamental to efforts to ascertain whether resource allocation and expenditures by the state satisfy the human rights obligations generated by ICESCR.

A key finding of our analysis is that the implementation of nearly all ESR obligations may require the allocation of resources, whether financial or otherwise in nature. It thus underlines the crucial relationship between budget decisions and the realization of ESR. As such, it complements and supports existing work involving the application of a human rights-based approach to budget decisions.

The first part of this book has examined the global dimension, studying best practice and considering in depth the principles in ICESCR. In the second part of this book, we examine how these principles can be applied in practice in the local context. We will now turn to our two Northern Ireland-based case studies.

Part Two

5 Mental health

Introduction

The right to the highest attainable standard of physical and mental health is a fundamental human right, underpinning the exercise of other human rights. Every human being is entitled to the enjoyment of the highest attainable standard of health conducive to living a life in dignity.[1] The Committee on Economic Social and Cultural Rights (ComESCR) has stressed that even in times of financial stress, the right to health in particular of 'the vulnerable members of society must be protected by the adoption of relatively low-cost targeted programmes'.[2]

This chapter focuses on the right to mental health, as set out in Article 12 International Covenant on Economic Social and Cultural Rights (ICESCR).

The right to mental health is interdependent and interconnected with the full enjoyment of a wide range of other basic rights. To mention only the obvious, mental health problems can affect the right to life due to possible suicide risks, the right to personal liberty due to the risk of detention, the right to a private and family life, the right to work and many other basic rights. According to the World Health Organization (WHO), mental health is defined as a state of well-being in which every individual realizes his or her own potential, can cope with the normal stresses of life, can work productively and fruitfully, and is able to make a contribution to her or his community.[3]

While the right to mental health is thus a vital, interdependent part of the human rights corpus, it may not receive adequate attention and funding. The WHO estimates that mental and behavioural disorders account for twelve per cent of the global burden of disease.[4] In 2001, the WHO stated that the mental

1 ComESCR, *General Comment No. 14 on the Right to the Highest Attainable Standard of Health*, E/C.12/2000/4 (2000) paragraph 1.

2 ComESCR, ibid 18.

3 www.who.int/features/factfiles/mental_health/en (accessed 22 May 2013).

4 WHO uses the term 'Global Burden of Disease' to analyze a comprehensive and comparable assessment of mortality and loss of health due to diseases, injuries and risk factors for all

health budgets for the majority of countries constitute less than one per cent of their total health expenditure.[5] The relationship between disease burden and disease spending is therefore disproportionate.[6]

Mental health is a topic of considerable importance in Northern Ireland. As we will discuss later in the chapter, the legacy of the conflict and problems of disadvantage mean that there is greater mental health need in Northern Ireland than in the rest of the UK.

This chapter identifies some of the international law obligations and illustrates their application by reference to aspects of the mental health budget in Northern Ireland up to December 2011. As such, it applies the human rights-based budget analysis framework developed in Chapters 3 and 4 to mental health service delivery in Northern Ireland.

The chapter first sets out the content of the right to the highest attainable standard of health care, focusing on mental health. The chapter then presents information on the funding of selected aspects of the Northern Ireland health service and in particular mental health services. Subsequent sections identify some of the key ICESCR obligations relating to mental health. The first of these are the interrelated principles of equality, non-discrimination and equity. Following that, there is a discussion of obligations encompassed by Article 2(1) ICESCR as they apply to mental health. The chapter concludes with a review of some of the procedural obligations imposed by ICESCR. In setting out the obligations, the chapter refers back to examples from the funding of mental health services in Northern Ireland, with particular reference to the shift from institutionalization to community care, provision of services for children and adolescents, and the budgetary process.

The right to the highest attainable standard of mental health

Introduction

This section sets out the content of the right to the highest attainable standard of mental health.[7] The right to 'the highest attainable standard of physical

regions of the world. The overall burden of disease is assessed using the disability-adjusted life year (DALY), a time-based measure that combines years of life lost due to premature mortality and years of life lost due to time lived in states of less than full health. See www.who.int/healthinfo/global_burden_disease/en (accessed 10 August 2010). This technical term is not to be misunderstood as referring to people affected by diseases as a 'burden'.

5 WHO, *The World Health Report 2001: New Understanding, New Hope* (2001) 3 available at www.who.int/whr/2001/en (accessed 27 October 2010).

6 WHO ibid and Alicia Yamin, Eric Rosenthal, 'Out of the Shadows: Using Human Rights Approaches to Secure Dignity and Well-being for People with Mental Disabilities' (2005) 2(4) *PLoS Med* 296.

7 Mental health overall can be approached from a variety of perspectives including that of mental disability. The International Convention on the Protection and Promotion of the Rights of Persons with Disabilities (CRPD) clearly includes mental health issues. The

and mental health' is not confined to the right to health care. On the contrary, Article 12 ICESCR acknowledges that the right to health embraces a wide range of socio-economic factors that promote conditions in which people can lead a healthy life, and extends to the underlying determinants of health, such as food and nutrition, housing, access to safe and potable water and adequate sanitation, safe and healthy working conditions, and a healthy environment.[8] This wider definition of health also takes into account socially-related concerns such as violence and armed conflict.[9] The right to the highest attainable standard of health takes into account both the individual's biological and social-economic preconditions as well as the state's available resources.[10] The right thus refers to the enjoyment of a variety of facilities, goods and services, as well as conditions necessary for the realization of the highest attainable standard of health.[11]

The following paragraphs set out the scope and content of the right to mental health.[12] It should be noted, however, this chapter only looks at the budgeting for mental health-specific services and facilities and thus does not discuss issues relevant to the underlying determinants of health and mental health more generally.

In setting out the scope and content of the right, attention is paid below to the adoption of the Declaration of Alma-Ata. The section then turns to Article 12 ICESCR and the accompanying *General Comment 14* on the right to health, as well as other interpretive sources such as the work of the UN Special Rapporteurs on the right to the highest attainable standard of health.

issue of mental health and its relationship to discrimination against persons with a disability is undoubtedly a complex one. A partial or limited reference to a broader notion of mental disability would therefore not do justice to the broad and inclusive concept of disability. Article 12 ICESCR, and mental health as a health issue, is therefore the main point of the chapter's analysis.

8 ComESCR, *General Comment No. 14, The Right to the Highest Attainable Standard of Health*, paragraph 4. See also *Free Legal Assistance Group and Others v Zaire*, Comm. No. 25/89, 47/90, 56/91, 100/93 (2005), African Commission on Human and Peoples' Rights at paragraph 47.

9 ComESCR, ibid, paragraph 10. It should be acknowledged that many issues relevant to good health are outside the control of the state; for this reason the WHO definition of the right to health, which is 'a complete state of physical, mental and social well-being' was not considered appropriate for the legal definition of the right to the highest attainable standard of health. See Lawrence O. Gostin, 'The Human Right to Health: A Right to the Highest Attainable Standard of Health' (2001) 31 *Hastings Center Report* 29, 29.

10 ComESCR, *General Comment No.14 The Right to the Highest Attainable Standard of Health*, paragraph 9.

11 ComESCR, ibid.

12 The definition of the right to the highest attainable standard of health has to take into consideration the historical developments in the World Health Organization and its relationship with the United Nations and the ComESCR and their respective, developing understandings of the various concepts. For a detailed historical analysis of the divergence between 'public health' and 'the right to health' see Benjamin Meier, 'The World Health Organization, the Evolution of Human Rights, and the Failure to Achieve Health for All' in John Harrington, Maria Stuttaford (eds), *Global Health and Human Rights: Legal and Philosophical Perspectives* (Routledge 2010).

The Declaration of Alma-Ata on primary health care

The 1978 Declaration of Alma-Ata on primary health care has been hailed as the most comprehensive attempt to develop a single policy framework, spelling out the policy shift that culminated in the adoption of the Declaration.[13] In the early 1970s, arguments for a shift in emphasis in developing countries started emerging, favouring cost-effective interventions over-expensive high-technology medicine.[14] These preferences were echoed in the global North and were instrumental in defining the Primary Health Care approach (PHC).[15]

This Declaration of Alma-Ata was adopted in 1978 and was agreed by Ministers of Health from around the globe.[16] Many of the principles addressed in this Declaration today form part and parcel of the right to the highest attainable standard of health discussed in more detail below.[17] It also spells out what the concept of Primary Health Care referred to when the Declaration was adopted.[18] The main themes of the Declaration are: the importance of prioritizing those who are most in need (Green has defined this as equity, a component of the right to health);[19] the need for community participation;[20] the need for a multi-sectoral approach to health problems;[21] the need to ensure the adoption and use of appropriate technology;[22] and emphasis on health promotion activities.[23] The need for effective planning; the importance of integrated referral systems; the critical role of suitably trained human resources; and, finally, the importance of international cooperation have also been

13 Anthony Green, *An Introduction to Health Planning for Developing Health Systems* (Oxford UP 2007) 55.

14 Green, ibid 62.

15 Green, ibid 55.

16 Paul Hunt, *Report of the Special Rapporteur on the Right of Everyone to the Enjoyment of the Highest Attainable Standard of Physical and Mental Health*, UN Doc A/HRC/7/11 (2008) paragraph 21.

17 Hunt, ibid, paragraph 22.

18 Anthony Green, *An Introduction to Health Planning for Developing Health Systems* (3rd edition Oxford UP 2007) 63. Declaration of Alma-Ata, International Conference on Primary Health Care, Alma-Ata, USSR (1978) available at www.who.int/publications/almaata_declaration_en.pdf, principle 7. Green points out at 64 that the term 'primary health care' may have been unfortunate because it already had connotations in many countries including the UK to refer to the first level of care.

19 Declaration of Alma-Ata, ibid, principle 2. Green, ibid 63, 64–8; Paul Hunt, *Report of the Special Rapporteur on the right of everyone to the enjoyment of the highest attainable standard of physical and mental health* UN Doc A/HRC/7/11 (2008) paragraph 22(a).

20 Declaration of Alma-Ata, ibid, principles 4 and 6. Green, ibid 63, 69–70; Hunt, ibid, paragraph 22(b). Participation is discussed in more detail below.

21 Declaration of Alma-Ata, ibid, principle 7. Green, ibid 63, 73–4; Hunt, ibid, paragraph 22(c).

22 Declaration of Alma-Ata, ibid, principle 6. Green, ibid 63, 74–5.

23 Declaration of Alma-Ata, ibid, principle 7.2. Green, ibid 63, 75–6; Hunt, ibid, paragraph 22(f).

considered central to Alma-Ata by the Special Rapporteur on the Right to the Highest Attainable Standard of Health.[24] Notably, the Alma-Ata Declaration was referred to repeatedly by the Committee on Economic, Social and Cultural Rights in its *General Comment No. 14*, with that body stating in particular that, 'read in conjunction with more contemporary instruments, such as the Programme of Action of the International Conference on Population and Development,[25] the Alma-Ata Declaration provides compelling guidance on the core obligations arising from Article 12'.[26] We will return to Article 12 and *General Comment No. 14* below.

Mental health as a topic is largely absent from the Declaration of Alma-Ata other than an acknowledgment 'that health, which is a state of complete physical, mental and social wellbeing, and not merely the absence of disease or infirmity, is a fundamental human right'.[27] Indeed, mental health only made it on to the health agenda after the Declaration was adopted.[28] None the less, seeing that mental health is a crucial aspect of the right to health, the basic principles underlying the Declaration, such as the importance of the Primary Health Care (PHC) approach as well as the focus on community-based interventions can and should be applied to the understanding of the right to the highest attainable standard of *mental* health. The WHO strongly advocates the position that mental health should be integrated as an essential element in the primary health care level.[29]

During the 1980s and 1990s there was a global shift towards 'vertical (or selective) biomedical interventions' that downplayed the focus on PHC and the principles of Alma-Ata.[30] This shift was in the context of severe pressure on health budgets as explained by a WHO report:

> The financial optimism of the 1970s was soon dispelled in many parts of the world by a combination of high oil prices, low tax revenues and

24 Hunt, ibid, paragraph 22.

25 United Nations, *Report of the International Conference on Population and Development*, Cairo, 5–13 September 1994 United Nations publication, Sales No. E.95.XIII.18, chapter I, resolution 1, annex, chaps. VII and VIII.

26 ComESCR, *General Comment No. 14 on the Right to the Highest Attainable Standard of Health*, paragraph 43.

27 Declaration of Alma-Ata, International Conference on Primary Health Care, principle 1.

28 Paul Hunt, *Report of the Special Rapporteur on the Right of Everyone to the Enjoyment of the Highest Attainable Standard of Physical and Mental Health*, UN Doc A/HRC/7/11 (2008) paragraph 24.

29 WHO, *The World Health Report 2001: New Understanding, New Hope* (2001) available at www.who.int/whr/2001/en, page 55 (accessed 5 November 2013).

30 Paul Hunt, *Report of the Special Rapporteur on the Right of Everyone to the Enjoyment of the Highest Attainable Standard of Physical and Mental Health*, UN Doc A/HRC/7/11 (2008) paragraph 27. Hunt explains that 'vertical' programmes focus on 'one or more diseases or health conditions' and are to be distinguished from integrated or comprehensive approaches: Hunt at paragraph 56.

> economic adjustment. Countries seeking to finance essential health care were faced with two difficult prescriptions: focus public spending on interventions that are both cost-effective and have public good characteristics (the message of the World Development Report 1993), and boost financing through charging users for services. Whilst many governments started to levy fees, most recognized the political impossibility of focusing spending on a few essential interventions alone.[31]

Such 'structural adjustment' programmes driven by the underlying neoliberal economics led to reduced health budgets.[32] As a result the 'poor were deterred from receiving treatment and the user fees yielded limited income'.[33] With human and financial resources being pulled into the vertical, biomedical focussed programmes, pressures on the under-resourced health systems was increased – sometimes to the point of collapse.[34]

According to WHO and echoed by Special Rapporteur Paul Hunt, attempts to reform the health care system in this crisis were guided by 'efficiency' – focusing above all on doing more for less.[35]

From a human rights perspective efficiency (in terms of providing more health care and health care-related services for less resources) should not be the sole indicator of the success of a health strategy. With that in mind the next section outlines the scope of the ICESCR right to the highest attainable standard of health, with a focus on mental health.

Essential elements of the right to mental health

Article 12(1) sets out the general principle of the right to highest attainable standard of physical and mental health. Article 12(2) identifies several specific

31 WHO, *Everybody's Business: Strengthening Health Systems to Improve Health Outcomes* (2007) 9 available at www.who.int/healthsystems/strategy/everybodys_business.pdf (accessed 10 August 2010).

32 *Report of the Special Rapporteur on the Right of Everyone to the Enjoyment of the Highest Attainable Standard of Physical and Mental Health*, UN Doc A/HRC/7/11 (2008) paragraph 27.

33 WHO, *Everybody's Business: Strengthening Health Systems to Improve Health Outcomes* (2007) 9 taken from www.who.int/healthsystems/strategy/everybodys_business.pdf (accessed 10 August 2010). See also Hunt (ibid) paragraph 27.

34 Hunt, ibid, paragraph 27.

35 Hunt, ibid, paragraph 29. WHO, *Everybody's Business: Strengthening Health Systems to Improve Health Outcomes* (2007) 9 available www.who.int/healthsystems/strategy/everybodys_business.pdf (accessed 10 August 2010). Green defines technical efficiency in relation to the financing of health systems as optimizing the relationship between inputs and outputs of a particular services: Antony Green, *An Introduction to Health Planning for Developing Health Systems*, 132. He also talks about allocative efficiency which aims to balance the allocation of resources to shifting health problems, demographic changes, or migration patterns at 134.

correlative obligations. Article 12(2)(a) requires states to tackle stillbirth rate and infant mortality and to promote the healthy development of the child. Article 12(2)(b) addresses environmental and industrial hygiene;[36] Article 12(2)(c) focuses on the prevention treatment and control of diseases[37] while 12(2)(d) concerns medical services and attention. Article 12(2)(d) spells out the right to health facilities, goods and services. This includes medical service and attention in the event of both physical and mental sickness.[38] The ComESCR states that this right includes the provision of equal and timely access to basic preventive, curative, rehabilitative services and health education in relation to both physical and mental health, as well as regular screening programmes.[39] It also expresses a preference for community-level care, where this is possible, and specifically mentions 'appropriate mental health treatment and care'.[40]

The right to mental health therefore extends well beyond a minimalist understanding of the right to life-saving treatment, even if it does not include a right to be healthy. As with other ICESCR rights, the right to the highest attainable standard of health has a number of essential elements – the precise application of which depends on the local context.[41] The normative content of the right to the highest attainable standard of health includes the availability, accessibility, acceptability and quality of health care services and facilities.[42]

Availability requires functioning public health and health care facilities, goods, services and programmes to be available in sufficient quantity.[43] It must

36 Article 12(2)(b) embraces the prevention of alcohol abuse and the use of tobacco, drugs and other harmful substances. ComESCR, *General Comment No. 14 on the Right to the Highest Attainable Standard of Health*, paragraph 15. WHO factsheet no. 220, 'Mental Health: Strengthening Mental Health Promotion' (2007) available at www.who.int/mediacentre/factsheets/fs220/en/print.html (accessed 4 August 2010) explains that mental health is determined by socio-economic and environmental factors. The clearest evidence is associated with indicators of poverty including poor income. Mental health is also linked to behaviour. Substance abuse, depression and anxiety are more prevalent and more difficult to cope with in conditions of high unemployment and stressful work conditions, for example. WHO has specifically linked limited education, human rights violations, gender discrimination and poor income to mental issues.

37 Article 12(2)(c) refers to the establishment of prevention and education programmes for behaviour-related health concerns and the promotion of social determinants of good health, including education, economic development and gender equity. ComESCR, *General Comment No. 14 The Right to the Highest Attainable Standard of Health*, paragraph 16.

38 ComESCR, *General Comment No. 14, The Right to the Highest Attainable Standard of Health*, paragraph 17.

39 ComESCR, ibid, paragraph 17.

40 ComESCR, ibid, paragraph 17.

41 ComESCR, ibid, paragraph 12.

42 ComESCR, ibid.

43 ComESCR, ibid, paragraph 12(a). See also paragraph 16.

be assumed that this includes public mental health as well as mental health care facilities, goods services and programmes. These facilities, goods, services and programmes include the underlying determinants of health, hospitals, clinics, health-related buildings and essential drugs as defined by WHO.[44] Accessibility must be based on equity and non-discrimination[45] and is discussed in more detail below. Acceptability of health facilities, goods and services refers to the requirement of sensitivity to cultural differences, gender-specific needs, and life-cycle requirements.[46] This means that mental health services must be acceptable to people of all age groups and characteristics and must respond to their specific mental health care needs. Finally, health facilities, goods and services must also be scientifically and medically appropriate and of good quality.[47]

The obligations of government therefore go beyond the provision of psychiatric medication to a broad array of services necessary to maintain mental health including primary, secondary, community-based mental health services as well as hospital-based treatment and services.[48] Since these measures require more a reallocation or redistribution of resources than new resources per se, the Special Rapporteur has argued that the downsizing of psychiatric hospitals and the extension of community care can be achieved even with very minimal resource allocations.[49] The UN Principles for the Protection of Persons with Mental Illness and the Improvement of Mental Health Care (the MI Principles) state that all persons have the right to 'the best available mental health care, which shall be part of the health and social care system.'[50] The Special Rapporteur spelt out some of the entitlements stemming from the right to the highest attainable standard of mental health, which indicate what the full realization of this particular aspect of the right to health might include.[51]

> A full package of community-based mental health and support services conducive to health, dignity, and inclusion, including medication, psychotherapy, ambulatory services, hospital care for acute admissions, residential facilities, rehabilitation for persons with psychiatric disabilities

44 ComESCR, ibid, paragraph 12(a).
45 ComESCR, ibid, paragraph 12(b)(i) and (iii).
46 ComESCR, ibid, paragraph 12(c).
47 ComESCR, ibid, paragraph 12(d).
48 Lawrence O Gostin, 'Beyond Moral Claims: A Human Rights Approach in Mental Health' (2001) 10 *Cambridge Quarterly of Healthcare Ethics* 264, 272.
49 Paul Hunt, *Report of the Special Rapporteur on the Right of Everyone to the Highest Attainable Standard of Physical and Mental Health*, E/CN.4/2005 51 (2005) paragraph 35.
50 United Nations, 'Principles for the Protection of Persons with Mental Illness and the Improvement of Mental Health Care', *General Assembly resolution 46/119* (1991) Principle 1.
51 Paul Hunt, *Report of the Special Rapporteur on the Right of Everyone to the Highest Attainable Standard of Physical and Mental Health*, UN Doc E/CN.4/ 2005/ 51 (2005) paragraph 43.

> programmes to maximize the independence and skills of persons with intellectual disabilities, supported housing and employment, income support, inclusive and appropriate education for children with intellectual disabilities and respite care for families looking after a person with a mental disability 24 hours a day. In this way, unnecessary institutionalization can be avoided.[52]

Having introduced the normative content of the right to mental health, we will now present information on the funding of mental health in Northern Ireland.

Mental health in Northern Ireland

Introduction

This section outlines the context to mental health in Northern Ireland. It begins with a review of the historical development of mental health law and policy, and the changing funding environment. It then outlines the key changes in the administration of health in Northern Ireland following the 1998 Belfast/Good Friday Agreement and highlights the important Review of Mental Health and Learning Disability (the 'Bamford Report'). Finally, it considers the impact on mental health of the global economic crisis, which developed in 2007, and the subsequent Spending Review and Budgetary process during 2010 and early 2011.

Historical context

Following the establishment of Northern Ireland in 1921 the development of mental health services was stifled by 'extreme financial restraint'.[53] However, these limitations eased with the creation of a National Health Service (NHS) in 1948. The 'parity principle', which meant that the standard of provision was to be equal throughout the UK, was important in ensuring adequate funding in less-prosperous regions such as Northern Ireland.[54] The legal basis of post-war mental health provision was largely provided by the Health Services Act (NI) 1948, which placed a duty on the Ministry of Health and Local Government to promote 'services designed to secure improvement in the physical and mental health'[55] of the population and the Mental Health Act (NI) 1948, which included an emphasis on mental health promotion rather

52 Ibid, paragraph 43.

53 Pauline Prior, *Mental Health and Politics in Northern Ireland* (Avebury 1993) 72.

54 Ibid 72.

55 Cited in ibid 56.

than treatment.[56] Increased resources supported an expansion of both inpatient and outpatient mental health services between 1949 and 1961.[57]

A Royal Commission on Mental Illness and Mental Deficiency 1954–7 envisaged a radical shift from hospital towards community-based treatment.[58] The subsequent Mental Health Act (NI) 1961 did not, however, provide a 'clear mandate to local authorities to develop either preventative or rehabilitative services'[59] and in contrast to the corresponding English legislation 'the Northern Ireland bill proposed no extra powers or funding to local welfare authorities to develop community services'.[60] Community-based services were consequently slow to develop.[61]

Public administration in Northern Ireland was radically altered by the conflict, which emerged in the late 1960s. During direct rule, public expenditure on health and social services in Northern Ireland increased and was approximately thirty per cent higher per capita than in England and Wales.[62]

However, following the election of the UK Conservative government in 1979 the pressure to limit health and social services expenditure increased. Northern Ireland was initially protected from the scale of public expenditure cuts that occurred in Britain but, by the 1990s, mental health services were 'subject to the same constraints as those in other parts of the United Kingdom'.[63] The regional health strategy for 1987–92 planned for resources to remain constant in real terms.[64] Financial pressures helped to prompt a renewed focus on community-based services, which were seen as less costly than hospital provision.[65] Despite this, levels of institutionalization remained very high: in Northern Ireland 222 persons per million were in long-stay hospitals as compared with 15 in England and Wales.[66] In addition to introducing a very different financial environment, this period also saw a shift in the role of Health and Social Services Boards, from one of providing services to commissioning them from the private and voluntary sectors.[67] The 1980s also saw the adoption of the 1986 Mental Health (NI) Order, which remains the main legal instrument regarding mental health in Northern Ireland.

56 Ibid 56.
57 Ibid 79.
58 Ibid 88.
59 Ibid 93.
60 Ibid 89.
61 Ibid 93.
62 Ibid 122.
63 Ibid 141.
64 Ibid 122.
65 Ibid 136.
66 Deirdre Heenan, 'Mental Health Policy in Northern Ireland: The Nature and of Extent of User Involvement' (2009) 8 *Social Policy and Society* 451, 455.
67 Pauline Prior, *Mental Health and Politics in Northern Ireland* (Avebury 1993) 125.

Post-1998 developments

Northern Ireland's system of governance has been radically altered following the Belfast/Good Friday Agreement 1998. As mentioned in Chapter 1, a number of public functions, including health, were devolved to the Northern Ireland Assembly, which operated intermittently and was suspended over the entire period from October 2002 to May 2007. Upon its reinstatement, Michael McGimpsey of the Ulster Unionist Party was nominated Minister for the Department for Health, Social Services and Public Safety (DHSSPS). In May 2011 he was replaced by Edwin Poots of the Democratic Unionist Party.

Over much of the period in which the Assembly was suspended, two major reviews were carried out into health administration[68] and mental health provision respectively. The latter most directly concerns us. The 'Bamford' Review of Mental Health and Learning Disability was commissioned by the DSHSSPS in 2002 and concluded its work in 2007. It examined a range of aspects of mental health provision[69] and appeared to signal a new era for the provision of mental health services. As part of the Bamford review, one of its papers commented that 'Resources dedicated to mental health are often inadequate and inequitable compared to those available to other parts of the public sector, and this is reflected in poor access, neglect and discrimination.'[70]

The DHSSPS is in the process of developing a legal basis for the recommendations of the Bamford Review. It has consulted on an equality impact assessment for a single piece of legislation to cover issues of mental health and capacity,[71] as recommended in the Bamford Report,[72] with a view to bringing in modernizing legislation. The Northern Irish legislative framework is based on the Mental Health (NI) Order 1986, while other parts of the UK have updated their legislation more recently.[73]

However, this question of reforming the provision of mental health services and ensuring a sound financial basis for mental health services arises in the difficult economic environment.

68 Following a Review of Public Administration (RPA) carried out between 2002–05, nineteen area-based trusts were centralized into five and four Health and Social Care Boards were merged into one. The RPA also saw the Health Promotion Agency replaced by the Public Health Agency. For more information on the RPA see www.northernireland.gov.uk/index/work-of-the-executive/review-of-public-administration-short-version.htm (accessed 26 August 2013).

69 Terms of reference are available on the Review website: www.dhsspsni.gov.uk/bamford.htm (accessed 26 August 2013).

70 The Bamford Review of Mental Health and Learning Disability (Northern Ireland), *Mental Health Improvement and Well-being – A Personal, Public and Political Issue* (2006) 121.

71 Available at www.dhsspsni.gov.uk/showconsultations?txtid=43469 (accessed 5 November 2013).

72 Bamford Review of Mental Health and Learning Disability (Northern Ireland) (2007) *A Comprehensive Legislative Framework*.

73 Mental Health (Care and Treatment) (Scotland) Act 2003; Mental Health Act 2007.

The economic crisis and the NI budget 2011

As explained in Chapter 1, the NI Executive had to respond to decisions of the Conservative-Liberal Democrat government to reduce public expenditure drastically in 2010. Faced with the implications of the 2010 Spending Review – which in Northern Ireland, according to the Department of Finance and Personnel, would amount to an eight per cent decrease in current expenditure and a forty per cent decrease in capital expenditure in real terms over the four years[74] – the NI Executive announced the Draft Budget 2011–15 on 15 December 2010,[75] with the departments expected to produce more detailed departmental budgets before Christmas 2010. In the event, the Department of Health published its draft budget for consultation in the second week of January 2011.[76] Given the deadlines on finalizing a budget set out in the Northern Ireland Act 1998, this meant there was a deadline of 16 February to respond to this consultation. A revised budget was published by the Department of Finance and Personnel on 7 March 2011[77] and approved by the NI Assembly on 9 March, though the Minister for Health was one of the negative votes.[78]

The Draft Budget 2011–15 indicated that the Health Budget would be protected as regards the 'health-related element' of that Department's budget – about seventy-seven per cent of the Department's spend; however, the part of the Department's budget associated with personnel services would be subject to cuts.[79] The Draft Budget proposed that the allocation for DHSSPS

Table 5.1 Three biggest departments: Current expenditure in millions with per cent increase/decrease in brackets.[80]

Department	*2010–11*	*2011–12*	*2012–13*	*2013–14*	*2014–15*
DHSSPS	4,302.9	4,348.1 (+1)	4,427.7 (+1.8)	4,543.2 (+2.6)	4,629.2 (+1.9)
Education	1,914.8	1,852.2 (–3.3)	1,857.3 (+.3)	1,861.6 (+.2)	1,847.7 (–.7)
Justice	1,223.7	1,213.1 (–.9)	1,189 (–2)	1,166.7 (–1.9)	1,176.4 (+.8)
Executive Total	10,316.1	10,242.9 (–.7)	10,311.9 (+.7)	10,369.6 (+.6)	10,440.4 (+.7)

74 DFP, Revised Budget 2011–15, paragraph 3.18 available at www.northernireland.gov.uk/revised_budget_-_website_version.pdf (accessed on 4 May 2011).

75 The Draft budget is available at www.northernireland.gov.uk/budget2010 (accessed 14 March 2011).

76 Available at www.dhsspsni.gov.uk/draftbudgetconsultation2011.pdf (accessed on 14 March 2011).

77 Available at www.northernireland.gov.uk/budget2010 (accessed 14 March 2011).

78 Official Record for the NI Assembly, 9 March 2011, available at http://archive.niassembly.gov.uk/record/reports2010/110309.htm (accessed 20 May 2013).

79 Paragraph 3, 42–4.

80 Draft Budget 2011–15, 31.

Table 5.2 Health and the two biggest departments: Capital expenditure in millions.[81]

Department	*2010–11*	*2011–12*	*2012–13*	*2013–14*	*2114–15*
DHSSPS	201.7	214.8	278.8	184.9	163.3
Regional development	556.2	438.3	425.3	540.9	558.8
DSD	269.6	150.3	120.6	99	190.3
Executive Total	1,488.1	1,183.9	1,124.9	1,078.6	1,373.8

current expenditure would be very modestly increased (in unadjusted figures) over the course of the four-year budget.

The Draft Budget 2011–15 proposed a significant reduction, however, in the capital expenditure for DHSSPS.

These are the overall figures for the selected Departments. The central issue therefore was what would appear in the Departmental proposals and specifically what would appear regarding mental health. The DHSSPS Consultation Paper noted that the figures above represented a real decrease in both current and capital expenditure (presumably allowing for inflation).[82] It anticipated that the shortfall would amount to fifteen per cent by 2014–15. The Consultation Paper stressed that there would be cuts in real terms in the short term and beyond.[83] The Paper does not give many details and makes almost no mention of mental health, apart from one reference to fulfilling contractual requirements regarding a mental health crisis unit.[84] One might expect that the impact on people with mental health problems would be highlighted in accompanying Section 75 (see Chapter 1) statutory equality duty publications. A 'full high level impact assessment' was promised in the Consultation Paper, but none was published before the finalization of the budget; the Department decided to postpone this in light of the new figures in the revised Budget.[85] The Department published an Equality Action plan for consultation, which did refer to programmes to promote mental health; somewhat worryingly though it described several of these as dependent on resources that were 'uncertain' after 2011.[86]

81 Draft Budget 2011–15, 32.

82 DHSSPS *Consultation Paper on the Draft Budget 2011–15: Settlement and Proposals*; there are no page or paragraph numbers in this nine-page document.

83 Seventh page.

84 Eighth page.

85 Freedom of Information Request. DHSSPS 2011–0044, 4 April 2011.

86 Draft Equality Action Plan for DHSSPS, available at www.dhsspsni.gov.uk/dhssps_draft_equality_action_plan.pdf. See page 28 (investment in community services), page 29 (resettlement from hospitals) (accessed 20 May 2013).

Table 5.3 Three biggest departments: Current expenditure in millions with per cent increase/decrease in brackets.[87]

Department	*2010–11*	*2011–12*	*2012–13*	*2013–14*	*2014–15*	*% over*
DHSSPS	4,302.9	4,383.1 (+1.9)	4,447.6 (+1.5)	4,569.2 (+2.7)	4,659.4 (+2)	+8.3
Education	1,914.8	1,894.6 (−1.1)	1,876.1 (−1)	1,887.7 (+.6)	1,874.5 (−.7)	−2.1
Justice	1,223.7	1,213.1 (−.9)	1,189 (−2)	1,166.7 (−1.9)	1,176.4 (+.8)	−3.9
Total	10,316.1	10,329.1 (+.1)	10,353.4 (+.2)	10,431.9 (+.4)	10,519.9 (+.8)	+2

The Department of Finance published a revised budget on 7 March 2011. The revised document promised more monies for DHSSPS: an extra £91 million for current expenditure and £29 million for capital expenditure over the four years of the budget.[88]

The Revised Budget included some specific comments from DHSSPS on mental health: specifically, mental health promotion would be a focus and the Bamford Action Plan for Mental Health and Learning Disability would continue to be implemented.[89] The Revised Budget also included a breakdown of how DHSSPS would spend its budget. This indicated broadly that Hospital and Community Health (the biggest heading for current expenditure) would increase every year between 1.3 and 3.4 per cent. Funding for the Family Health Service would increase between 1.8 and 5.2 per cent every year.

87 Revised Budget 2011–15, Table 3.1.

88 Revised Budget 2011–15, paragraph 3.50.

89 Again there are no page numbers but the relevant section reads:

The continued implementation of the Bamford Action Plan for Mental Health and Learning Disability will see more early intervention, the development of community services to support independent living; further reduction in long-stay hospital populations; and improvements in prison mental health and children and young people's provision. The Department will also need to make further progress in implementation of the Autism Action Plan, the Dementia Strategy and the Physical Disability Strategy. A new Mental Capacity (Health, Welfare and Finance) Bill will be brought to the Assembly in 2012–13 and improvements in the quality and effectiveness of social work services, including their accessibility, availability and responsiveness will be progressed through the implementation of the first social work strategy in NI.

The Bamford Action Plan is available at www.dhsspsni.gov.uk/bamford_action_plan_2009–2011.pdf (accessed 19 May 2011).

The budget for mental health

Introduction

This section identifies the evidence for the claim that Northern Ireland has greater mental health needs than the rest of the UK. It compares patterns of expenditure across UK regions, in an attempt to ascertain if there are any regional disparities between Northern Ireland and Britain. We present the figures on health expenditure in Northern Ireland and provide more details about expenditure on mental health in Northern Ireland.

Mental health need in Northern Ireland

Research has indicated that the prevalence of mental illness – and therefore the need for services and institutions providing mental health services – is higher in Northern Ireland than in any other region of the UK. The mental health system during the period prior to the twenty-first century has been identified as suffering from 'poorly resourced services relative to other areas of the UK, and the added burden of living in a divided society characterized by high levels of poverty, unemployment and social deprivation . . . The prolonged civil conflict in Northern Ireland has cast a long shadow . . .'[90] The Bamford review and other research and advocacy organizations have highlighted the fact that Northern Ireland as a region has higher mental health-related need than the rest of the UK but that it receives comparatively less funding than the rest of the UK.[91] The Participation and Practice of Rights Project has noted that, for example, 11.8 per cent of the total NHS budget in England and Wales is allocated to mental health, but the equivalent figure in Northern Ireland is only 8.4 per cent, despite the greater mental health needs in Northern Ireland.[92] Numerous reports have argued that the prevalence of mental illness in Northern Ireland is high relative to other UK regions and to the Republic of Ireland.[93] A 2002 government review of Health and Social

90 Deirdre Heenan, 'Mental Health Policy in Northern Ireland: The Nature and of Extent of User Involvement' (2009) 8 *Social Policy and Society* 451, 451.

91 The Bamford Review of Mental Health and Learning Disability (Northern Ireland) *Mental Health Improvement and Well-being – A Personal, Public and Political Issue* (2006) pages i, 7, 9.

92 See Participation and the Practice of Rights Project, *2009 Submission to the UN ComESCR*, Belfast Northern Ireland available at www2.ohchr.org/english/bodies/cescr/docs/ngos/Participation_and_Practice_of_Rights_Project_UK_CESCR42.pdf (accessed 23 September 2010) at 13.

93 Dermot O'Reilly and Siobháin Browne, *Health and Health Service Use in Northern Ireland: Social Variations* (2001) 74. Available at www.dhsspsni.gov.uk/health_service_use_ni.pdf (accessed 26 August 2013); Dermot O'Reilly and Mark Stevenson, 'Mental Health in Northern Ireland: Have "the Troubles" Made it Worse?' (2003) 57 *Journal of Epidemiology and Community Health* 488.

Care needs found that the level of mental illness was twenty-five per cent higher in Northern Ireland than in England.[94] This is a reflection of the general trend that health needs are greater in Northern Ireland than in England.[95]

The conflict is one possible factor in explaining the higher prevalence of mental health problems in Northern Ireland. A number of studies have found a connection between experience of 'the Troubles' and mental illness. An analysis of the 1997 *Northern Ireland Health and Wellbeing Survey* concluded that 'It is probable that [the] mental health of the population in Northern Ireland has been significantly affected by the Troubles'.[96] The 2001 *Northern Ireland Health and Social Well Being Survey* found that eighteen per cent of people who reported that they were 'not very much' affected by the Troubles felt depressed, compared to thirty-four per cent of those who stated that they were affected 'a lot' by the Troubles.[97] Research indicates that suicide rates are highest among persons who grew up during the conflict.[98]

Another possible factor is the socio-economic condition of Northern Ireland. A comparison of twelve developed countries has identified a causal relationship between the level of income inequality in a society and rates of mental illness.[99] The *Northern Ireland Health and Social Well Being Survey* (2001) found a correlation between mental illness and economic status[100] as well as a number of other factors. Although it is difficult to compare income inequality in the UK regions over time, due to the absence of consistent data,[101] research

94 DHSSPS, DFP, OFMDFM, *Overview of the Health and Social Care Needs and Effectiveness Review* (2002) 13.

95 This was the conclusion of the Appleby Report, which suggested a reasonable estimate of the difference at seven per cent. The Appleby Report also noted that there needed to be mechanisms to deal with the Barnett formula's inability to accommodate this need differential, 51–4. Appleby Report, *Independent Review of Health and Social Care Services in Northern Ireland* (2005) available at www.dhsspsni.gov.uk/appleby-report.pdf (accessed 26 August 2013).

96 Dermot O'Reilly and Mark Stevenson, 'Mental Health in Northern Ireland: Have "the Troubles" Made it Worse?' (2003) 57 *Journal of Epidemiology and Community Health* 488.

97 NISRA, *Health and Well Being Survey* (2001) Available at www.csu.nisra.gov.uk/survey.asp49.htm (accessed 26 August 2013).

98 Michael W. Tomlinson, 'War, Peace and Suicide: The Case of Northern Ireland' (2012) 27 (4) *International Sociology* 464–82.

99 Richard Wilkinson and Kate Pickett, *The Spirit Level: Why More Equal Societies Almost Always Do Better* (Allen Lane 2009) 66–7. For a critique see Christopher Snowdon, *The Spirit Level Delusion: Fact-Checking the Left's New Theory of Everything* (Democracy Institute 2010). For a defence by the authors see www.equalitytrust.org.uk/resources/response-to-questions (accessed 26 August 2013).

100 Sixteen per cent of employed people were 'depressed' compared to thirty per cent of unemployed people.

101 Tania Burchardt and Holly Holder, 'Inequality and the Devolved Administrations: Scotland, Wales and Northern Ireland' in John Hills, Tom Sefton and Kitty Stewart (eds), *Towards A More Equal Society? Poverty Inequality and Policy since 1997* (Policy Press 2009) 262.

has confirmed that Northern Ireland is characterized by 'considerably higher levels of income inequality than Britain'.[102]

Health expenditure

Between 2004–05 and 2009–10, there had been an average yearly increase of 3.7 per cent in total health expenditure in Northern Ireland (Figure 5.1).

Looking at health spending in Northern Ireland alone, however, only paints half the picture. To contextualize this data the spending in Northern Ireland has to be compared to other regional expenditure.

Figure 5.2 below shows how Northern Irish expenditure translates into per capita expenditure in this region. While there has not been a continual annual increase in per capita health expenditure, the average yearly increase in Northern Ireland over this period was 3.3 per cent. Figure 5.2 also compares per capita health expenditure in Northern Ireland with a simple average of per capita health expenditure in Britain.

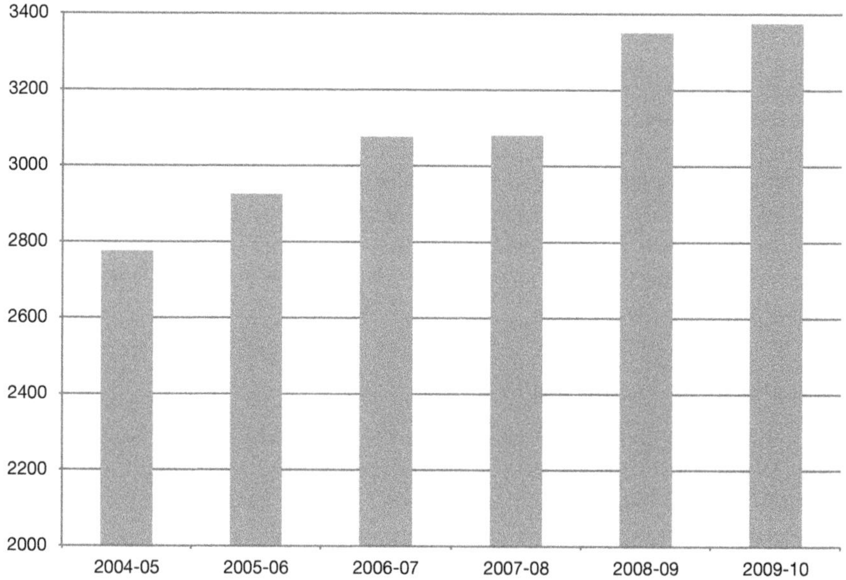

Figure 5.1 Health expenditure in Northern Ireland in £m (2009–10 values).[103]
Source: PESA Table 10.4.

102 Paddy Hillyard and others, *Bare Necessities: Poverty and Social Exclusion in Northern Ireland* (Democratic Dialogue 2003) 44.

103 Note that the figure for 2009–10 is an estimate.

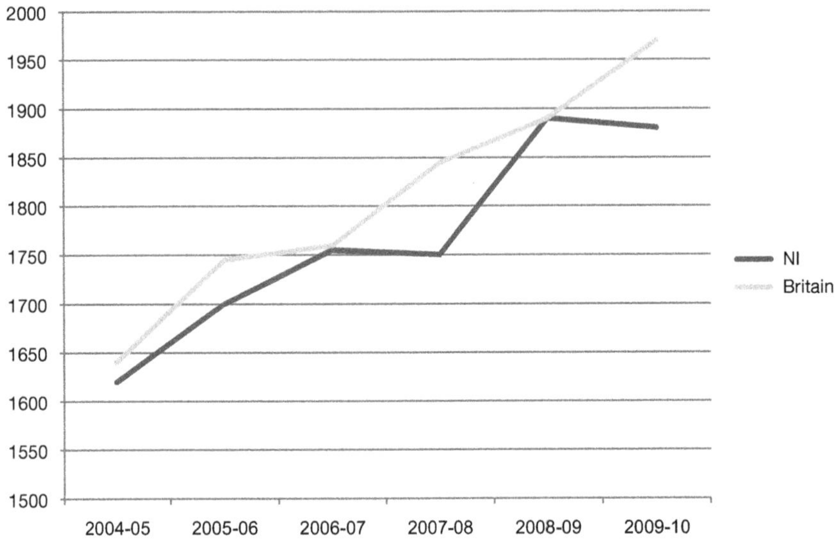

Figure 5.2 Real per capita health expenditure by UK region in £ (2009–10 prices).[104]
Source: PESA Tables 10.5, 10.6, 10.7, 10.8.

Figure 5.2 above shows that, with the exception of 2008–09, per capita health spending has been lower in Northern Ireland than in Britain. According to a 2002 study commissioned by the Northern Ireland Executive, due to a range of factors such as demographics, mortality, deprivation and community tensions, Northern Ireland ideally requires a 16.5 per cent *higher* per capita spend on health overall than in England; another independent review suggests a figure of seven per cent.[105]

Expenditure on mental health

The table below shows that spending on the Mental Health Programme of Care (POC) declined from 8.0 per cent of total Health and Social Care (HSC) expenditure in 2004/05 to 7.3 per cent in 2007/08. However, it increased in subsequent years, rising to 8.2 per cent in 2009/10 in Northern Ireland. According to the table below the share of mental health funding proportionate to overall health funding has remained quite steady, despite a severe drop in overall health funding between 2008 and 2010. Table 5.1 presents information

104 Note that the figures for 2009/10 are estimates.
105 John Appleby, *Independent Review of Health and Social Care Service in Northern Ireland* (2005) 42.

Table 5.4 Expenditure of HSC Trusts on mental health: Key statistics (2009–10 prices).

Year	*2004/ 05*	*2005/ 06*	*2006/ 07*	*2007/ 008*	*2008/ 09*	*2009/ 10*	*2010/ 11*
Mental Health Expenditure (£m)	195.3	202.3	204.7	205.5	226.0	234.9	223.3
Annual Increase (%)	–	4.0	1.3	0.4	10.5	4.0	–4.9
Share of Expenditure (%)	8.0	7.8	7.6	7.3	7.5	8.2	Not available
Per Capita (£)	114.18	117.29	117.54	116.80	127.36	131.31	123.92
Per Capita Annual Increase (%)	–	2.7	0.2	–0.6	9.0	3.1	–5.6

Source: DHSSPS FOI 27/08/2010.

on the expenditure of HSC Trusts on the mental health POC in Northern Ireland for the period from 2004/05 to 2010/11. It shows that real-term growth in mental health spending was substantial in 2008/09 (10.5 per cent) and strong in 2005/06 and 2009/10 (both 4.0 per cent). The increase was minor in 2006/07 (1.3 per cent) and marginal in 2007/08 (0.4 per cent).

Looking at expenditure on a per capita basis, Table 5.4 shows that in 2004/05, HSC Trusts spent approximately £114 on mental health for each person in Northern Ireland. According to the 2010 McKinsey Report, once allowance is made for the higher levels of need in Northern Ireland, then 'we [Northern Ireland] spend less than half of England's per capita spend on supporting people with mental health problems and learning disabilities.'[106] Per capita mental health spending declined slightly in 2007/08 (by 0.6 per cent) but, positively, increased significantly in the following year (9.0 per cent).

Community care

During our research, the importance of the shift from institutional care to community care was regularly highlighted. This indeed is critical to best practice as identified by WHO and other international experts and organizations (see above 'The Declaration of Alma-Ata on Primary Health Care').

106 McKinsey Report: *Reshaping the System: Implications for Northern Ireland's Health and Social Care Services of the 2010 Spending Review*, available at www.dhsspsni.gov.uk/index/mckinsey report.htm, 14 (accessed 20 May 2013).

Therefore, we decided to look more closely at the funding for community care in Northern Ireland.

The value of community care was acknowledged by the Royal Commission on Mental Illness and Mental Deficiency 1954–7 and Northern Ireland subsequently underwent a process of deinstitutionalization. The number of mental health patients resident in hospitals fell from 6,486 in 1961 to 1,500 by the mid-1990s.[107] However, continuing demand for psychiatric beds has raised concern in a number of quarters about the extent to which hospital provision has been reduced.[108] In addition, this reduction in hospital provision was not accompanied by a corresponding expansion of community-based care. It was not until the late 1980s that significant movement towards community care took place in Northern Ireland.[109] The Northern Ireland *Regional Strategy for Health and Social Services* (1987–92) planned an annual redeployment of at least one per cent of revenue spending from hospitals to community-based services.[110] Nevertheless, a 2002 needs assessment suggested that a shortfall in community provision remained:

> A number of initiatives introduced in GB [Great Britain] to support community mental health and to provide a better quality of life for service users have not been replicated here. The gap in services is estimated at £26m . . . Lack of investment in community mental health has resulted in a higher proportion of people remaining in long-stay hospitals than necessary.[111]

The level of inpatient beds in Northern Ireland is significantly higher than in other parts of the UK (6.4 per 1,000 persons compared to 4.5 in Scotland, 3.4 in Wales and 3.2 in England[112]). According to the Bamford Review, this 'reflects a lack of alternative provision, the result of deficiencies in the current and previous strategies, lack of investment and resources . . .'[113]

This report commented that 'the model of care in Northern Ireland is accepted to be too reliant on inpatient care'[114] and added that:

107 Pauline Prior, 'Mental Health Policy in Northern Ireland' in James Campbell and Roger Manktelow *Mental Health Social Work in Ireland: Comparative Issues in Policy and Practice* (Ashgate 1998) 33.
108 Prior, ibid 34.
109 Ibid 36.
110 Ibid 31.
111 DHSSPS, DFP and OFMDFM, *Overview of the Health and Social Care Needs and Effectiveness Review* (2002) 83.
112 DHSSPS, DFP and OFMDFM, *Overview of the Health and Social Care Needs and Effectiveness Review* (2002) 13–14.
113 *Bamford Review Strategic Framework for Adult Mental Health Services* (2005) 25.
114 *Bamford Review Strategic Framework for Adult Mental Health Services* (2005) 139.

> The present balance of resource spend is approximately 60% on hospital services and 40% on community services. The recommended developments in community services should be reflected in a reversal of this balance of expenditure within 10 years of implementation of the Strategic Framework.[115]

In order to review progress towards community care, this analysis examines overall DHSSPS expenditure and the expenditure of HSC Trusts. It is important to note that neither of these sources reconcile with the sixty per cent (community-based care) vs forty per cent (hospital-based care) ratio identified by the Bamford review (which did not detail how this figure was arrived at).[116] Nevertheless, these sources provide consistent measures, which allow progress towards community care to be tracked over time. Looking first at DHSSPS spending, Table 5.5 shows that between 2005/06 and 2008/09 the proportion of expenditure on community-based services increased from twenty-seven per cent to thirty-five per cent.

Turning to the expenditure of HSC Trusts, Table 5.6 shows the share of community and hospital expenditure between 2005/06 and 2008/09. In 2005/06, community care represented twenty-eight per cent of HSC expenditure on mental health. By 2007/08, this had increased to thirty-three per cent. However, community care fell to thirty-two per cent of mental health

Table 5.5 DHSSPS balance of mental health expenditure 2005/06–08/09.

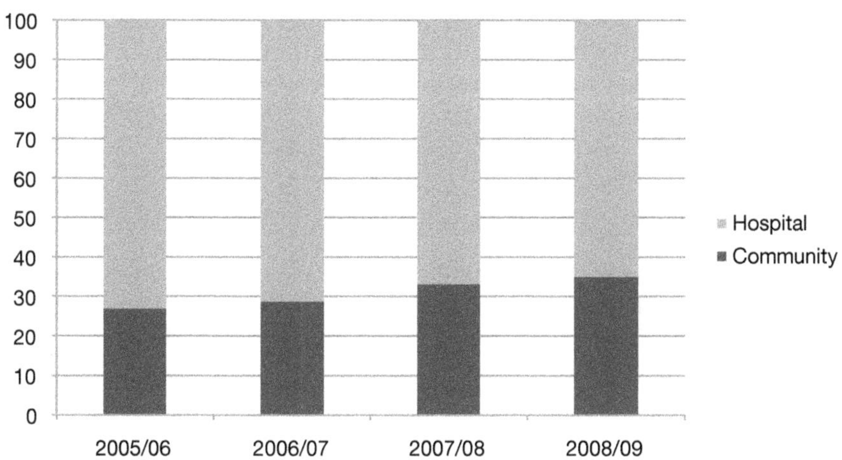

Source: DHSSPS Strategic Resourcing Framework 2006/07, 2007/08 and 2008/09.

115 *Bamford Review Strategic Framework for Adult Mental Health Services* (2005) 45.
116 Ibid.

Table 5.6 HSC Trusts balance of mental health expenditure 2005/06–08/09.

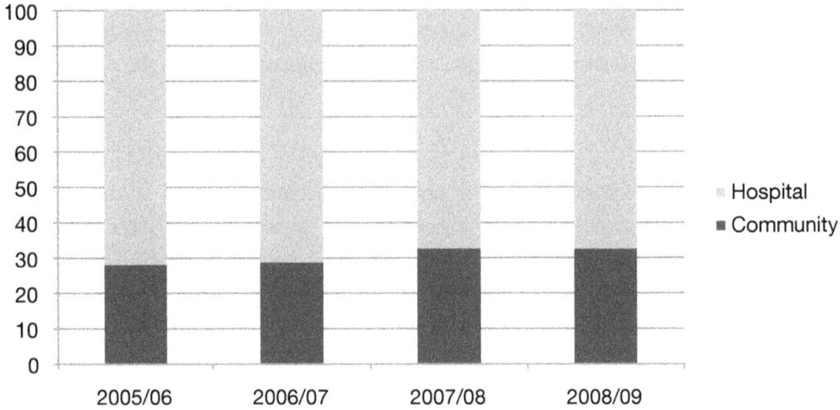

Source: Communication with DHSSPS.

expenditure in the following year (2008/09) due to a proportionally larger rise in expenditure on hospital provision.

Both graphs indicate a progressive increase of community-based investment.

Human rights obligations and mental health

Introduction

Having discussed the content of the right to health and presented the context relating to the funding of health and mental health in Northern Ireland, this section and the following ones identify some of the key ICESCR obligations as they relate to mental health. Each section relates the obligation under consideration to the data on the funding of mental health.

Equity, equality and non-discrimination

The principles of equality and non-discrimination are central to the human rights paradigm. These two concepts, which are closely related, have often been conflated in international law.[117] In addition, particularly with regard to the highest attainable standard of health, the ComESCR also refers to

117 Gillian MacNaughton, 'Untangling Equality and Non-discrimination to promote the Right to Health Care for All' (2009) 11 *Health and Human Rights Journal* 47, 47. MacNaugthon argues that this potentially reduces the impact of these principles on addressing social inequalities. *Report of the Special Rapporteur on the Right of Everyone to the Enjoyment of the Highest Attainable Standard of Physical and Mental Health*, UN Doc A/HRC/7/11 (2008), paragraph 42 refers to equality and non-discrimination as 'twin human rights principles' which mean that outreach and other programmes must be in place to ensure that disadvantaged groups enjoy the same access as those that are more advantaged.

equity, which is discussed later.[118] Paul Hunt notes that equality and non-discrimination[119] are akin to the health concept of equity.[120]

Eliminating discrimination requires paying 'sufficient attention to groups of individuals which suffer historical or persistent prejudice rather than merely comparing the treatment of individuals in similar situations'.[121] This may entail temporary or even permanent special measures, that is to say measures designed to redress problems of the unequal enjoyment of rights in practice; such special measures would recognize that special attention should be paid to the needs of disadvantaged and vulnerable groups.[122]

Discrimination against people with mental illnesses can act as a barrier to persons seeking social support, diagnosis and treatment.[123] Discrimination, like other human rights violations, therefore can have serious adverse impacts on a person's mental and physical health.[124] Discrimination against persons with mental illnesses can take many forms.[125] The right to equality obliges

118 ComESCR, *General Comment No. 14, The Right to the Highest Attainable Standard of Health*, paragraph 12 (b).

119 According to the ComESCR 'discrimination constitutes any distinction, exclusion, restriction or preference or other differential treatment that is directly or indirectly based on the prohibited grounds [. . .] and which has the intention or effect of nullifying or impairing the recognition, enjoyment or exercise, on an equal footing, of Covenant rights'. See the ComESCR, *General Comment No. 20, Non-Discrimination in Economic, Social and Cultural Rights*, UN Doc E/C.12/GC/20 (2009) at paragraph 7. For a similar definition see Article 1, ICERD, Article 1, CEDAW and Article 2, CRPD; Human Rights Committee, *General Comment No. 18, Non-discrimination*, UN Doc HRI/GEN/1/Rev.6 at 146 (2003) paragraphs 6 and 7.

120 *Report of the Special Rapporteur on the Right of Everyone to the Enjoyment of the Highest Attainable Standard of Physical and Mental Health*, UN Doc A/HRC/7/11 (2008) paragraph 43.

121 ComESCR, *General Comment No. 20, Non-Discrimination in Economic, Social and Cultural Rights*, paragraph 8 (b): talking about elimination of both formal and substantive discrimination.

122 ComESCR, ibid, paragraph 9. Examples of permanent special measures include interpretation services for linguistic minorities and reasonable accommodation of the needs of people with sensory impairments.

123 Paul Hunt and Judith Mesquita, 'Mental Disabilities and the Human Right to the Highest Attainable Standard of Health' (2006) 28 *Human Rights Quarterly* 332, 349. See also Pauline Prior, 'Removing Children from Care of Adults with Diagnosed Mental Illnesses – a Clash of Human Rights' in (2003) 6 *European Journal of Social Work* 179, 189.

124 Lawrence O. Gostin, 'Beyond Moral Claims: A Human Rights Approach in Mental Health' (2001) 10 *Cambridge Quarterly of Healthcare Ethics* 264, 265.

125 For example, if public health insurance does not cover mental illness, the right of people suffering these kinds of conditions as a group is violated; see Alicia Yamin, Eric Rosenthal, 'Out of the Shadows: Using Human Rights Approaches to Secure Dignity and Well-being for People with Mental Disabilities' (2005) 2 (4) *PLoS Med* 297 citing Mental Disability Rights International (2004) *Human Rights and Mental Health in Peru*; Paul Hunt and Judith Mesquita, 'Mental Disabilities and the Human Right to the Highest Attainable Standard of Health' (2006) 28 *Human Rights Quarterly* 332, 347; Shekhar Saxena and others, 'Resources for Mental Health: Scarcity, Inequity, and Inefficiency' (2007) 370 (9590) *The Lancet* 878, 878.

states not only to prohibit discrimination but also places a positive obligation on states to ensure equality of opportunity for persons with mental illnesses.[126] This is explicitly captured in *General Comment No. 20*, which requires states to adopt measures to address widespread stigmatization of persons on the basis of their health status, such as mental illness.[127]

The ComESCR stresses that many measures, such as most strategies and programmes designed to eliminate health-related discrimination, can be pursued with minimum resource implications and reiterates that in times of severe resource constraints 'the vulnerable members of society must be protected by the adoption of relatively low-cost targeted programmes'.[128] The ComESCR makes clear that

> [i]nappropriate health resource allocation for example can lead to discrimination that may not be overt. For example, investments should not disproportionately favour expensive curative health services which are often accessible only to a small, privileged fraction of the population, rather than primary and preventive health care benefiting a far larger part of the population.[129]

The principle of 'equity' forms part of the primary health care approach discussed earlier.[130] The concept of health equity has been defined as 'equal access to health care is according to need'[131] and 'equal utilization of health – care according to need'.[132] Access and utilization according to need relates to access to health resources by different groups in society.[133] An essential contribution of equity to the human rights approach is that planning for equity

126 Paul Hunt and Judith Mesquita, 'Mental Disabilities and the Human Right to the Highest Attainable Standard of Health' (2006) 28 *Human Rights Quarterly* 332, 350.

127 ComESCR, *General Comment No. 20, Non-Discrimination in Economic, Social and Cultural Rights*, paragraph 33.

128 ComESCR, *General Comment No. 14, The Right to the Highest Attainable Standard of Health*, paragraph 18.

129 ComESCR, ibid, paragraph 19.

130 Anthony Green, *An Introduction to Health Planning for Developing Health Systems*, 64. Note that the Declaration of Alma-Ata principle 2 notes the gross inequality in the health status of the people, particularly between developed and developing countries, as well as within countries is unacceptable and is, therefore, of common concern to all countries.

131 *Report of the Special Rapporteur on the Right of Everyone to the Enjoyment of the Highest Attainable Standard of Physical and Mental Health*, UN Doc A/HRC/7/11 (2008) paragraph 43; Paul Hunt and Gunilla Backman, 'Health Systems and the Right to the Highest Attainable Standard of Health' (2008) 10 *Health and Human Rights Journal* 81, 83; Green, ibid.

132 Green, ibid 64, argues this interpretation is most in line with the primary health care approach. See also Declaration of Alma-Ata principle 7(6) which also calls for 'priority to those most in need'.

133 Green, ibid 67. Gillian MacNaughton, 'Untangling Equality and Non-discrimination to Promote the Right to Health Care for All' (2009) 11 *Health and Human Rights Journal* 47, 54. See also ComESCR, *General Comment No. 14, The Right to the Highest Attainable Standard of Health*, paragraph 12(b) where equity is mentioned in relation to economic affordability for everyone.

requires the identification of those groups currently disadvantaged in terms of health status, or access to or utilization of services.[134]

General Comment No. 14 also refers to the 'equitable distribution' of health facilities throughout the country.[135] More broadly, one of the core requirements of Article 12 is that there should be an 'equitable distribution of all health facilities, goods and services'.[136] Complementary to that, ComESCR *General Comment No. 20* states that the exercise of rights should not be qualified by a person's place of residence.[137]

Governments must ensure 'even distribution in the availability and quality of primary, secondary, palliative health care facilities' in all localities and regions, including urban and rural areas.[138] Both the ComESCR and the Human Rights Committee view sharp disparities in spending on health care across geographic locations as discrimination.[139]

'Equity' is prominent in relation to the right to health because not all health disparities are unfair, even if they are based on a specific ground such as sex. For example, we expect female newborns to have lower birth weights on average than male newborns.[140] The Article 12 entitlements are therefore to a system of health protection, which provides 'equality of opportunity' for people to enjoy the highest attainable level of health.[141]

The ComESCR has dealt with equality and non-discrimination in health in the UK on various occasions. In relation to the UK's latest country report for example the ComESCR has recommended the UK intensify its efforts to overcome health inequalities and unequal access to health care, in particular for the most disadvantaged and marginalized individuals.[142] The ComESCR

134 Green, ibid 68.

135 ComESCR, *General Comment No. 14, The Right to the Highest Attainable Standard of Health*, paragraph 36. Note also that at paragraph 16 the ComESCR refers to gender equity as well.

136 ComESCR, ibid, paragraph 43 (e) and paragraph 52.

137 ComESCR, *General Comment No. 20, Non-Discrimination in Economic, Social and Cultural Rights*, paragraph 34. See also Gillian MacNaughton, 'Untangling Equality and Non-discrimination to Promote the Right to Health Care for All' (2009) 11 *Health and Human Rights Journal* 47, 53.

138 ComESCR, ibid, paragraph 34. See also MacNaughton, ibid 53.

139 MacNaughton, ibid 56. ComESCR, ibid, paragraph 34. ComESCR, *General Comment No. 13, The Right to Education*, UN Doc E/C.12/1999/10 (1999) paragraph 35. See also Human Rights Committee, *Concluding Observations Suriname*, UN Doc CCPR/CO/80/SUR (2004) paragraph 19; Human Rights Committee, *Concluding Observations Mongolia*, UN Doc CCPR/C/79/Add.120 (2000) paragraph 15.

140 Paula Braveman and Sofia Gruskin, 'Defining Equity in Health' (2003) 57 *Journal of Epidemiology and Community Health* 254, 255.

141 ComESCR, *General Comment No. 14*, paragraph 8.

142 ComESCR, *Concluding Observations of the Committee on Economic Social and Cultural Rights: United Kingdom*, UN Doc E/C.12/GBR/CO/5 (2009) paragraph 32. In the same *Concluding Recommendations* the ComESCR urges the UK to fulfil its commitment to reduce health inequalities by ten per cent by 2010 measured by infant mortality and life expectancy at birth as benchmarks which the State has set for itself. It further recommends that the state gather appropriate disaggregated data on the topic for the next reporting round.

expressed its deep concern regarding the fact that persons with mental disabilities experienced significantly poorer health conditions than those without mental health problems.[143] The ComESCR recommended that the State take immediate steps to address the poor health conditions of persons with mental disabilities as a matter of priority.[144]

In achieving equity in a health system, the first essential step is well-defined, workable criteria of equity and the resultant criteria for monitoring movement towards it. It also requires the identification of those groups currently disadvantaged in terms of health status or access to or utilization of services.[145] In the local context, this disadvantage could be as simple as an issue of location.[146] The role of the planner is not only to identify disadvantaged groups but also to ensure that their voices are heard (see more on participation later).[147]

Geographical equity and the UK

It appears that health spend in Northern Ireland was lower per capita than in Britain (Figure 5.1 above, 2004–2010). This is confirmed in the 2010 McKinsey Report, which indicates that per capita spend in Northern Ireland started to fall behind other parts of the UK in 2009, and that this was exacerbated by the greater need in Northern Ireland.[148] This relates directly to the equity requirement.[149] The ComESCR states that disparities between localities and regions should be eliminated in practice by ensuring, for example, that there is even distribution in the availability and quality of primary, secondary and palliative health care facilities.[150]

The issue of geographical inequity is not limited to overall health expenditure. A similar point may be made by looking more closely at mental health expenditure. One of the indicators proposed by the Special Rapporteur on Health, as well as the Lancet Group spelled out above, relates to the share of mental health funding in relation to the overall health budget.[151]

Despite having a significantly higher level of mental illness as set out above, a recent study estimated that, in 2006/07, mental health received 9.3 per cent

143 ComESCR, ibid, paragraph 32.
144 ComESCR, ibid.
145 Anthony Green, *An Introduction to Health Planning for Developing Health Systems* (2007) 68.
146 Green, ibid.
147 Green, ibid, and Paul Hunt and Gunilla Backman, 'Health Systems and the Right to the Highest Attainable Standard of Health' (2008) 10 *Health and Human Rights Journal* 81, 83.
148 McKinsey Report: *Reshaping the System: Implications for Northern Ireland's Health and Social Care Services of the 2010 Spending Review*, available at www.dhsspsni.gov.uk/index/mckinsey report.htm, 12–14 (accessed 22 May 2013).
149 See section 2.3.2.
150 *General Comment No. 20*, paragraph 34.
151 See Lancet Global Mental Health Group, 'Scale Up Services for Mental Disorders: A Call for Action' (2007) 370 (9594) *Global Mental Health Series* 1241, 1244.

of Northern Ireland's overall health budget compared to 11.1 per cent in Scotland and 11.8 per cent in England.[152] Further, despite the recognized higher need, a study estimated that in 2002/03 per capita expenditure on mental health was 15.6 per cent lower than in England.[153]

In addition to the recognized higher mental health need in Northern Ireland compared with the rest of the UK, it ought to be mentioned that the 2009 UK government report to the ComESCR acknowledges the existing health inequalities in Northern Ireland and identifies people with mental health problems as a vulnerable group who may have problems in accessing healthcare; the report also refers to the rates of suicide among young males in Northern Ireland.[154]

These figures suggest not merely an anomaly, but that the UK's system of funding for health, and specifically mental health, does not respect the principle of geographical equity required by ICESCR.

Equality and mental health in Northern Ireland: Children and adolescent mental health service

The Northern Ireland-based NGO, the Committee for the Administration of Justice, submitted to ComESCR that the incidence of mental health problems is disproportionately high among vulnerable groups of young people including those who have disabilities, live in poverty, are in conflict with the law, are leaving or are in care and who identify as LGBT.[155] The difficulties experienced by children with mental health issues in accessing patient care has also been raised by the Northern Ireland Commissioner for Children and Young People in relation to children suffering from mental health issues such as those with eating disorders and those at risk of self-harm and suicide.[156] In their submission to the ComESCR they pointed out that children in Northern Ireland are sometimes accommodated with adults or sent outside the jurisdiction for treatment because of the lack of available, specialized treatment locally.[157] This would seem to put in question both the availability and appropriateness of the facilities in Northern Ireland.

152 NIAMH, *Mental Health Promotion: Building an Economic Case* (2007) 7.

153 Sainsbury Centre for Mental Health and NIAMH, *Counting the Cost: The Economic and Social Costs of Mental Illness in Northern Ireland* (2004) 9.

154 Paragraph 318 of the UK State Report available at www2.ohchr.org/english/bodies/cescr/cescrs42.htm (accessed 21 September 2010).

155 CAJ, *Submission from the Committee on the Administration of Justice to the UN Committee on Economic Social and Cultural Rights* (2009) available at www2.ohchr.org/english/bodies/cescr/cescrs42.htm (accessed 21 September 2010).

156 Northern Ireland Commissioner for Children and Young People, *Report By NICCY to the UN Committee on Economic, Social and Cultural Rights on the Implementation of ICESCR in Northern Ireland* (2009) available at www2.ohchr.org/english/bodies/cescr/cescrs42.htm (accessed 21 September 2010).

157 Northern Ireland Commissioner for Children and Young People, ibid.

The analysis of children's right to mental health in Northern Ireland is made difficult by the absence of clear budgetary data for allocations to this sector. The Committee on the Rights of the Child, in its general comment regarding the implementation of the Convention on the Rights of the Child, has specifically stated that

> [n]o State can tell whether it is fulfilling children's economic, social and cultural rights 'to the maximum extent of . . . available resources', as it is required to do under Article 4, unless it can identify the proportion of national and other budgets allocated to the social sector and, within that, to children, both directly and indirectly.[158]

Bamford points out that there is no clear budget line for Child and Adolescent Mental Health Services, despite the fact that this is a very vulnerable group. Citing O'Rawe (2003) the Bamford review argued that:

> Budgetary arrangements for CAMH services are not sufficiently clear and increased allocation of resources in proportion to need in order to support CAMH services in NI is urgently required. It is therefore recommended that CAMH services should have their own identifiable budget.[159]

Bamford argued that each CAMH should have six Primary Mental Health (PMH) workers and a minimum of twenty-five whole time equivalents (WTE) per 100,000 population, and a non-teaching service of a minimum twenty WTE.[160]

In Belfast there is one unit that provides adolescent psychiatric inpatient services. However, an investigation into the care and treatment offered to Danny McCartan[161] found that it was 'routine'[162] for no beds to be available in this unit. It further heard evidence that mental health services, particularly CAMH services, were 'under-resourced'[163] and highlighted long waiting lists for referrals to clinical psychiatrists and the unavailability of Child and Adolescent Psychiatrists.[164] Child psychiatrist Dr Peter Gallagher concurred that CAMH

158 Committee on the Rights of the Child, *General Comment No. 5, General Measures of Implementation of the Convention on the Rights of the Child*, UN Doc CRC/GC/2003/5 (2003) paragraph 51.

159 The Bamford Review of Mental Health and Learning Disability (Northern Ireland), *A Vision of a Comprehensive Child and Adolescent Mental Health Service* (2006) 63.

160 The Bamford Review of Mental Health and Learning Disability (Northern Ireland) *A Vision of a Comprehensive Child and Adolescent Mental Health Service* (2006) 67.

161 Danny McCartan committed suicide in April 2005, aged eighteen years, having previously been admitted to an adult ward because no beds were available in the adolescent unit.

162 EHSSB, *Complaint made by Mr and Mrs McCartan Concerning the Mater Hospital Trust and North and West Belfast Trust and South and East Belfast Trust* (2007) 6.

163 Ibid 12.

164 Ibid 13.

services were 'chronically underfunded'[165] and claimed that CAMH represented three to five per cent of mental health expenditure compared to a UK average of ten per cent.[166] This is despite Northern Ireland having a larger proportion of young people (twenty-seven per cent of Northern Ireland's population is aged zero to seventeen years compared to twenty-two per cent of the English population[167]).

The statistics on suicide in Northern Ireland also indicate more grounds for concern about availability of CAMHS. Suicide is a highly important issue for younger people.

Statistics compiled by the Samaritans show that suicide rates in Northern Ireland are above the UK average: in 2010 the suicide rate per 100,000 people was 9.8 in England, 11.7 in Wales, 14.7 in Scotland and 17.4 in Northern Ireland.[168] Furthermore, the suicide rate has increased in Northern Ireland over the period 2001–11.[169]

This also potentially raises an equality issue in that children and young people have particular needs in relation to mental health.[170] In addition to being entitled to the 'general' non-discrimination protections accorded to all right-holders under ICESCR, children as a group are protected against discrimination in terms of the CRC Article 2. The Committee on the Rights of the Child has made clear that prohibited grounds of discrimination under 'other status' in Article 2 CRC also cover health status, including mental health.[171] Indeed, that Committee has made it clear that the child's right to the highest attainable standard of physical and mental health under the CRC requires states to implement measures for the prevention of mental disorders and the promotion of the mental health of adolescents.[172] Further, the ComESCR specifically reconfirms the principle set out in Article 3(1) of the CRC that children and adolescents' best interests shall be a primary consideration in all policies and programmes aimed at guaranteeing their right

165 Tara Mills BBC 'News Anger at Mental Health "Scandal"' 27 February 2006, available at http://news.bbc.co.uk/1/hi/northern_ireland/4756796.stm (accessed 22 May 2013).

166 Mills, ibid.

167 The Bamford Review of Mental Health and Learning Disability (Northern Ireland) *A Vision of a Comprehensive Child and Adolescent Mental Health Service* (2006) 67.

168 Samaritans, *Suicide Statistics Report 2013 Data for 2009–2011* available at www.samaritans.org/sites/default/files/kcfinder/files/research/Samaritans%20Suicide%20Statistics%20Report%202013.pdf (accessed 14 June 2013 22–4).

169 Samaritans, *Suicide Statistics Report 2013 Data for 2009–2011* available at www.samaritans.org/sites/default/files/kcfinder/files/research/Samaritans%20Suicide%20Statistics%20Report%202013.pdf (accessed 14 June 2013).

170 ComESCR, *General Comment No. 14, The Right to the Highest Attainable Standard of Health* at paragraph 23.

171 Committee on the Rights of the Child, *General Comment No. 4, Adolescent Health and Development in the Context of the Convention on the Rights of the Child*, UN Doc CRC/GC/2003/4 (2003), paragraph 6.

172 Ibid, paragraphs 6, 41(a).

to health.[173] The realization of the right to health of adolescents is dependent on the development of what ComESCR calls child- and youth-friendly information and health care, including mental health services.[174] If no special provision is made for children and young people then questions about equality, equity and non-discrimination have to be raised.

The primary point is therefore that appropriately disaggregated budgetary data for youth and adolescent mental health services must be set out if the state is to meet its obligations under ICESCR and the CRC to assess the provision of services for the right to the highest attainable standard of mental health. This duty is highlighted clearly in the Committee on the Rights of the Child's *General Comment on Right of the Child to the Enjoyment of the Highest Attainable Standard of Health*, which requires states (a) to make investment in children visible in the state budget through detailed compilation of resources allocated to them and expended, and (b) to implement rights-based budget monitoring and analysis, as well as child impact assessments on how investments, particularly in the health sector, may serve the best interests of the child.[175]

This section has discussed the interrelated obligations of equality, non-discrimination and equity. It has highlighted the type of issues that need to be considered such as the geographical equity in funding for health and mental health in the UK. The section also emphasizes the need for clear budgetary headings to identify the actual spend on particular vulnerable groups, for example children and adolescents.

Article 2(1) obligations

This section discusses the complex of obligations that are explicit and implicit in Article 2(1) ICESCR. These are the obligations to progressively realize rights, using the maximum of available resources and the implied obligations of non-retrogression and respect for the minimum core of rights.

Progressive realization, non-retrogression and maximum available resources

As with all rights found in ICESCR, the right to physical and mental health is subject to progressive realization and resource constraints.[176] Meier has argued

173 ComESCR, *General Comment No. 14, The Right to the Highest Attainable Standard of Health*, paragraph 22.

174 ComESCR, *General Comment No. 14, The Right to the Highest Attainable Standard of Health*, paragraphs 22 and 23.

175 Committee on the Rights of the Child, *General Comment No. 4, Adolescent health and development in the context of the Convention on the Rights of the Child*, UN Doc. CRC/GC/2003/4 (2003), paragraph 106(c) and (d).

176 Article 2(1) ICESCR.

that the duty to progressively realize the right to health requires states to consider the most 'cost efficient yet effective delivery of life-saving services to the greatest number of people.'[177] However, the duty to move as 'expeditiously and effectively as possible towards the full realization' of the right cannot only refer to life-saving treatment, as the 'full realization of the right to health' refers to a very broad and far-reaching provision and extends far beyond 'life-saving' treatment.

Gostin has argued that the right to mental health is currently still very vague and non-specific and it is thus very difficult to determine what is expected of states in relation to this right.[178] It is also hard to determine an absolute standard of what 'full realization' of mental health may constitute as many factors are outside the control of government.[179]

The ICESCR Reporting Guidelines provide a limited indication of which types of measurements are required in order to assess the degree of realization of the right to the highest attainable standard of mental health, including the extent to which health personnel are trained on health and human rights.[180] The Guidelines also request specific information with regard to measures taken to improve child and maternal health (presumably including mental health),[181] to prevent the abuse of harmful substances as well as treatment and rehabilitation of drugs users and support for their families.[182] The ComESCR also asks about measures taken to ensure adequate treatment and care in psychiatric facilities for mental health patients.[183] Adequate treatment and care in such institutions is essential for the protection not just of the right to health but all of the other human rights that are implicated in such contexts.

The Special Rapporteur further notes that the full realization of the right to mental health will also require the training of an adequate and balanced number of professionals, including psychiatrists, clinical psychologists, psychiatric nurses and social workers, occupational therapists, speech therapists, as well as carers who provide for people with mental health issues in the community in which they live. General Practitioners and other primary care providers should be trained in essential mental health care.[184] A number of

177 Benjamin Meier, 'The Highest Attainable Standard: Advancing a Collective Human Right to Public Health' (2006) 37 *Columbia Human Rights Law Review* 101, 134.

178 Lawrence O. Gostin, 'Beyond Moral Claims: A Human Rights Approach in Mental Health' (2001) 10 *Cambridge Quarterly of Healthcare Ethics* 264, 271.

179 Gostin, ibid 271.

180 ComESCR, *The Guidelines on Treaty-Specific Documents to be Submitted by State Parties under Articles 16 and 17 of the International Covenant on Economic, Social and Cultural Rights*, UN Doc E/C.12/2008/2 (2008) paragraph 56.

181 ComESCR, ibid, paragraph 56(d).

182 ComESCR, ibid, paragraph 57(d).

183 ComESCR, ibid, paragraph 57(g).

184 Paul Hunt, *Report of the Special Rapporteur on the Right of Everyone to the Highest Attainable Standard of Physical and Mental Health*, UN Doc E/CN.4/ 2005/ 51 (2005) 44.

indicators have also been proposed by the Lancet Global Mental Health Group.[185] While their relevance obviously has to be adapted to match local priorities, a selected few are spelled out here for demonstrative purposes. They ask whether there is a specific budget for mental health as the proportion of total health budgets. The indicators question how many trained staff there are and how many mental health professionals are available. Further, they look at the pharmacological treatments available at a primary care level and the proportion of primary health care clinics in which a physician or an equivalent health worker is available.[186] In terms of secondary indicators they look at the balance of expenditure in hospital and community services and the proportion of total mental health expenditure spent on community-based services, including primary and general health care services. In order to measure the least restrictive practices, they ask for the number of involuntary admissions as a proportion of all admissions. Related to that is the indicator looking at whether a human rights institution protecting the interests of people with mental disorders is present. Lastly, they ask for the number of people that have died due to suicide and self-inflicted injury.[187]

Turning to the issue of non-retrogression, let us reiterate that there is a strong presumption that retrogressive measures taken in relation to the right to health are not permissible.[188] Non-retrogression is relevant also in relation to deinstitutionalization – moving from a hospital-based approach to mental health to a more community-based, holistic approach to mental health care. Closing down mental health hospitals in isolation from other initiatives could easily constitute a retrogressive measure if this is not coupled by a complex process of implementing a 'solid network of community alternatives'.[189] 'Closing mental health hospitals without community alternatives' to provide care for the patients is as dangerous according to the WHO 'as creating community alternatives without closing mental hospitals. Both have to occur at the same time.'[190]

Progressive realization is linked to the use of maximum available resources. The obligation to use the maximum of available resources means that departmental allocations in the national budget should not automatically be taken as authoritative. It might be necessary to look beyond the allocations

185 See Lancet Global Mental Health Group, 'Scale Up Services for Mental Disorders: A Call for Action' (2007) 370 (9594) *Global Mental Health Series* 1241, 1242. This research is based on country comparison between estimates for scaling up mental health services. This is done by selecting a core mental health care package which covers three mental health disorders and one risk factor for disease, namely schizophrenia, bipolar affective disorder, and depressive episode as well as hazardous alcohol use.

186 Lancet Global Mental Health Group, ibid 1244.

187 Lancet Global Mental Health Group, ibid.

188 See Chapter 3.

189 WHO, *The World Health Report 2001: New Understanding, New Hope* (2001).

190 Ibid 51.

and take account of all the resources that are available in the country.[191] As discussed in Chapter 2, the duty also implies that where a sum has been allocated it has to be used for its intended purpose. Further, there is a duty to allocate the 'maximum of available resources' necessary to ensure smooth administration of the programme.[192] Progressively, realization includes a duty to expand access and a duty to improve the implementation.[193] Chapman has argued that, as part of the core duty to fulfil health, investments need to prioritize public health measures, primary care, and preventative services and should refrain from investments in expensive tertiary care facilities.[194]

Minimum core obligations

In *General Comment No. 3*, the minimum core of the right to health is loosely referred to as to 'essential primary health care'.[195] The mention of 'essential primary health care' as the minimum core to the right to health is reiterated in *General Comment No. 14*. The minimum core identified in this *General Comment* requires that health facilities, goods and services are accessible on a non-discriminatory basis, especially for vulnerable or marginalized groups; that the distribution of all health facilities, goods and services is equitable; that everyone has access to food, shelter, water and sanitation; access to essential drugs as well as the implementation of a national public health strategy and plan of action. This plan of action is to be developed on the basis of epidemiological evidence, addressing the health concerns of the whole population. It should be devised and reviewed on the basis of a participatory and transparent process. It should include indicators and benchmarks, which allow the progress towards fulfilment to be monitored.[196] As noted above, the WHO urges mental health to be integrated into the primary health care agenda.[197] Primary health care is the basic level of care, which acts as a filter between the general

191 Philip Alston and Gerard Quinn, 'The Nature and Scope of the States Parties' Obligations under the International Covenant on Economic, Social and Cultural Rights' (1987) 9 *Human Rights Quarterly* 156, 178.

192 Geraldine van Bueren, 'Alleviating Poverty through the Constitutional Court' (1999) 15 *South African Journal of Human Rights* 52, 61.

193 Sandra Liebenberg, 'The Right to Social Assistance: the Implications of *Grootboom* for Policy Reform in South Africa' (2001) 17 *South African Journal of Human Rights* 232, 241.

194 Audrey Chapman, 'Core Obligations Related to the Right to Health' in Audrey Chapman and Sage Russell (eds), *Core Obligations: Building a Framework for Economic, Social and Cultural Rights* (Intersentia 2002) 211.

195 ComESCR, *General Comment No. 3, The Nature of States Parties Obligations*, paragraph 10.

196 ComESCR, *General Comment No. 14, The Right to the Highest Attainable Standard of Health*, paragraph 43.

197 WHO, *The World Health Report 2001: New Understanding, New Hope* (2001) 55 and 59. This is one of the key WHO recommendations, along with developing community health services.

population and specialized care.[198] Mental disorders are common and most patients are only seen in primary care but their *mental* disorders are often not detected.[199] WHO argues that training primary and general health care staff in the detection and treatment of common mental and behavioural disorders is an important public health measure.[200]

While *General Comment No. 14* expresses a range of core requirements, some issues identified as the primary health care approach ought to be specifically referred to, not only because of their importance in relation to resource allocation and mental health specifically, but also because there is no direct reference to them in the list of *General Comment No. 14* core obligations.[201] The Declaration of Alma-Ata provides compelling guidance on the core obligations on the right to health.[202] In particular, the obligation to address the main health problems in the community by providing promotive, preventative, curative and rehabilitative services does not enjoy direct reference in *General Comment No. 14*.[203] Further, the requirement for an integrated, functional and mutually supportive referral system leading to the progressive improvement of comprehensive health care for all, had important implications for mental health specifically and thus deserves additional mention as part of the minimum core requirement for the right to the highest attainable standard of health.[204] These can also be referred to as a continuum of care. The other issues covered by PHC approach are to a large degree reflected in the language of *General Comment No. 14*.

In 2008, WHO published a report discussing the integration of mental health services into primary care.[205] In this, the organization noted the failure to integrate mental health services into the primary health care approach.[206] Despite evidence that the treatment of mental health disorders in a primary health care setting (treating the disorder as early as possible; holistically; and

198 WHO, ibid 59.

199 WHO, ibid 59. Note that the WHO also argues that many mental health issues are related to physical complaints which are seen at a primary health care level without the mental health element being picked up on.

200 WHO, ibid 59.

201 Brigit Toebes, 'Towards an Improved Understanding of the International Human Right to Health' (1999) 21 *Human Rights Quarterly* 661, 676 argues that in seeking to define the core content of the right to the highest attainable standard of health one may derive inspiration for the Primary Health Care strategy of the WHO.

202 Paul Hunt and Sheldon Leader, 'Developing and Applying the Right to the Highest Attainable Standard of Health' in John Harrington and Maria Stuttaford (eds), *Global Health and Human Rights* (Routledge 2010) 45.

203 Declaration of Alma-Ata, principle VII, 2.

204 Declaration of Alma-Ata, principle VII, 6.

205 WHO and Wonca (World Organization of Family Doctors), *Integrating Mental Health into Primary Care – A Global Perspective* (2008) available at www.who.int/mental_health/policy/Mental%20health%20+%20primary%20care-%20final%20low-res%20140908.pdf (accessed 28 October 2010).

206 WHO, ibid 9.

close to home; prevention services; as well as adequate referrals) can in many cases lead to improved health outcomes, most countries are still relying on outmoded psychiatric, hospital-based approaches.[207]

WHO recommends the optimal mix of services for mental health commonly represented as a pyramid with primary care services for mental health at the base, followed by psychiatric services in general hospitals as well as community mental health services on the second level and only a small portion at the tip of the pyramid dedicated to long-stay facilities and specialist psychiatric services.[208] WHO defines 'essential services' at the primary care level as including 'early identification of mental disorders, treatment of common mental disorders, management of stable psychiatric patients, referral to other levels where required, attention to the mental health needs of people with physical health problems as well as mental health promotion and prevention.'[209]

This description of the minimum core content of the right to the highest attainable standard of health contains various process requirements as well as a minimum basket of services. The process requirements include a duty to adopt a comprehensive national plan,[210] complete with disaggregated indicators and benchmarks that allow for an assessment of progressive realization.[211] This minimum basket of services does not seem to include any mental health specific aspects. However, upon closer inspection it becomes clear that many of the aspects identified as part of the core obligation are indeed relevant to mental health issues. Considering the lack of explicit consideration of mental health issues with regard to the minimum core of the right, these aspects should be read with the services recommended in relation to the primary health care approach. States thus have to ensure access to, as well as equitable distribution of, mental health facilities, goods and services on a non-discriminatory basis, in particular for vulnerable or marginalized groups. States must ensure that persons with mental illnesses and their representatives are able to participate in the development of a mental health strategy. With regard to the minimum basket of services, maternal, pre-natal and post-natal mental health care is an important issue. Education and access to information regarding substance abuse, for example, is another minimum core adaptation to mental health. Lastly, it is crucial that mental health practitioners are fully aware of the human rights of their patients.

207 WHO, ibid 9.

208 WHO, ibid 16.

209 Importantly the WHO recognizes that continuity of care is a core element of effective primary care (WHO ibid 17).

210 ComESCR, *General Comment No. 14, The Right to the Highest Attainable Standard of Health*, paragraph 43(f) requires states to adopt and implement a national public health strategy and plan of action. See Paul Hunt and Gunilla Backman, 'Health systems and the Right to the Highest Attainable Standard of Health' (2008) 10 *Health and Human Rights Journal* 81, 84.

211 Hunt and Backman, ibid.

Article 2(1) obligations and mental health in Northern Ireland

As mentioned above, the issue of the shift from institutionalization to community care is identified as important both by international observers and by practitioners in Northern Ireland. The figures cited in section 4.5 indicate that there has been a gradual progression towards increased reliance on community-based initiatives, though even the locally indicated split of 40/60 hospital/community-based services is still far from being reached. The Northern Ireland authorities are to be commended for the movement towards the preferred balance between community and hospital care, though it may be legitimate to inquire whether faster progress could be achieved. Secondly, during the transition from hospital-based to community-based care, the overall mental health outcomes have to be closely monitored and mechanisms to encourage user options should be put in place to ensure that the alternative community services are actually effective in addressing the mental health needs of people. The shift towards community-based care must also be coupled with the training and skills development being made available for health care workers.

It was argued above that comprehensive community-based interventions are part of the minimum core approach. Since there is an implicit assumption that all states can provide the minimum core of certain services, a high standard of justification is required for failing to achieve the appropriate level of transition to community-based services. Further, if the cuts and savings would affect the advances made in relation to community-based services the state should have to show that it has done whatever possible, taking into account all the resources that are available. Another issue is that while the shift towards community-based care is welcome, it is important to emphasize that this does not obviate the need for acute, specialized, hospital-based care, in particular for vulnerable persons and those who may have special needs. As noted above, hospitals are part of the community-based service interventions in that they provide crucial and important services that cannot be delivered by anyone else. Hospitals in a community-based setting means that ideally hospitals should also be located in the community to ensure minimal interruption of family life as well as allow for effective outpatient treatment. It is important to note that these two principles are not opposed to each other.

Procedural aspects

The right to the highest attainable standard of health is concerned with both processes and outcomes. The right therefore addresses both how a health system operates and what it achieves.[212] We will now consider selected examples of

212 *Report of the Special Rapporteur on the Right of Everyone to the Enjoyment of the Highest Attainable Standard of Physical and Mental Health*, UN Doc A/HRC/7/11 (2008) paragraph 39.

the procedural aspects relevant to the right to mental health. Are these given effect to in Northern Ireland?

An important aspect of the right to the highest attainable standard of health is the right of the population to participate in all health-related decision-making.[213] Positive measures must be taken to ensure the active and informed participation of disadvantaged individuals, communities and health care workers throughout the planning process for effective provision of health services.[214] Persons with mental health issues may need special assistance to make decisions or communicate preferences.[215] The Participation and Practice of Rights (PPR) project has developed useful indicators that reveal if the right to participation has been honoured: They consider the way meetings work and whose voices are heard; ensuring participants have the resources they need including relevant papers and documents in an accessible format, as well as independent support to service users to assist them in preparing for the meetings. They also consider how participation of service users is encouraged – of particular interest to a consideration of participation in a mental health context is the requirement that service users are given clear and accessible information on resources and staffing to allow them to participate meaningfully.[216] Active and informed participation also incorporates the ability to set the agenda in discussion; policy choices; and implementation as well as monitoring and evaluation.[217] Participation may also include accessible accountability mechanisms.[218] Guidance on participation requirements can also be found in several UK cases and good practice guides.[219]

213 ComESCR, *General Comment No. 14, The Right to the Highest Attainable Standard of Health*, paragraph 11. From a primary health care perspective 'participation' can have a variety of meanings. See Anthony Green, *An Introduction to Health Planning for Developing Health Systems*, 69–71: community participation can refer to the individuals responsibility for health, the individual or community involvement in self-help and financing schemes; and the individual or community involvement in decisions about health care. See also Helen Potts, *Participation and the Right to the Highest Attainable Standard of Health* (Human Rights Centre, University of Essex 2009) 9.

214 *Report of the Special Rapporteur on the Right of Everyone to the Enjoyment of the Highest Attainable Standard of Physical and Mental Health*, UN Doc A/HRC/7/11 (2008) paragraph 93.

215 Paul Hunt and Judith Mesquita, 'Mental Disabilities and the Human Right to the Highest Attainable Standard of Health' (2006) 28 *Human Rights Quarterly*, 332, 351. This article talks about the rights of people with mental disabilities and not illnesses, but some of the issues are transferable.

216 PPR, 'Participation and mental health: Monitoring your engagement with Government' available at www.pprproject.org/sites/default/files/documents/mh%20participation%20 pamphlet.pdf (accessed 26 August 2010).

217 Helen Potts, *Participation and the Right to the Highest Attainable Standard of Health* (Human Rights Centre, University of Essex 2009) 18.

218 Potts, ibid 14–15.

219 UK Government, *Code of Practice on Consultation* (Department for Business, Enterprise and Regulatory Reform, London 2008).

The ComESCR states that a national health plan must be based on the principles of accountability and transparency. Good governance according to the ComESCR is essential to the effective implementation of all human rights, including the realization of the right to health.[220] Accountability ensures that reasonable balances between competing demands are struck and have been arrived at by way of fair processes.[221] Accountability includes the monitoring of conduct, performance and outcomes. An equally essential feature of an effective health system is transparency, which forms part of the core content of the right to the highest attainable standard of health.[222] Monitoring and accountability is essential to ascertain if progressive realization is taking place.[223] Adequately funded national human rights institutions are a crucial part of this requirement as they are likely to be more accessible to vulnerable groups, such as persons dealing with mental health issues.[224]

Northern Ireland has a regime for monitoring of mental health services. Previously carried out by the Mental Health Commission under the Mental Health (Northern Ireland) Order 1986, this function has now been transferred to the Regulation and Quality Improvement Authority (RQIA) under the Health and Social Care (Reform) Act (Northern Ireland) 2009, which authority has a Mental Health and Disability team. The functions transferred to the RQIA include those to inquire into any deficiency in treatment, improper detention or other inadequacy in the care of mental health patients; and to visit and interview patients detained under mental health provisions.[225]

When it comes to the general organization of mental health services, one commentator has noted that, despite an increased formal concern with participation, the mental health systems in Northern Ireland seem resistant to such processes in practice.[226] A human rights analysis of the Northern Ireland budgetary process 2010–11 regarding the health budget must support this concern. The consultation process surrounding the Budget during December 2010 to February 2011 was flawed in several respects. The consultation period

220 ComESCR, *General Comment No. 14, The Right to the Highest Attainable Standard of Health*, paragraph 55.

221 *Report of the Special Rapporteur on the Right of Everyone to the Enjoyment of the Highest Attainable Standard of Physical and Mental Health*, UN Doc A/HRC/7/11 (2008) paragraph 64.

222 Hunt, ibid, paragraph 40.

223 Paul Hunt and Sheldon Leader, 'Developing and Applying the Right to the Highest Attainable Standard of Health' in John Harrington and Maria Stuttaford (eds), *Global Health and Human Rights* (Routledge 2010) 38.

224 ComESCR, *General Comment No. 14, The Right to the Highest Attainable Standard of Health*, paragraph 59; Hunt and Leader, ibid 39. See also Paul Hunt, *Report submitted by the Special Rapporteur on the Right of Everyone to the Highest Attainable Standard of Physical and Mental Health, Mission to Romania*, UN Doc E/CN.4/ 2005/51/Add.4. (2005) paragraph 68.

225 Mental Health (Northern Ireland) Order 1986, Article 86.

226 Deirdre Heenan, 'Mental Health Policy in Northern Ireland: The Nature and of Extent of User Involvement' (2009) 8 *Social Policy and Society* 451, 459.

was very short given the late appearance of the DHSSPS Consultation Paper, allowing for less than five weeks of consultation. The consultation process did not provide very many details on proposals for addressing the budgetary situation. Despite the possibility to send in responses to the consultation, it was not clear from the DHSSPS consultation paper what proposals were open to amendment as a result of any consultation. While the DHSSPS consultation paper recognized that the budgetary proposals might impact negatively on vulnerable groups ('equality groups'), and undertook to ensure there was a neutral impact on such groups, there was no detailed equality assessment published during the consultation period indicating what the impacts might be or how they might be alleviated. Overall, one has to agree with the assessment of one Assembly Committee that the absence of details: 'makes it almost impossible for any meaningful public consultation to be undertaken or any detailed scrutiny by the committees.'[227]

Conclusion

This chapter has sought to identify the key ICESCR obligations that are relevant to any analysis of funding for mental health services as an aspect of the realization of the right to health. It has also presented the context for the funding of mental health services in Northern Ireland. As part of its presentation of the relevant ICESCR obligations, it has highlighted how funding for mental health services in Northern Ireland might fall short of international human rights standards.

The chapter highlights equality-based obligations in relation to mental health. This notes that health funding throughout the UK appears to be inequitable. The chapter summarizes evidence, which establishes that there is higher need in Northern Ireland for mental health services, but this region receives less funding overall. Addressing regional inequity is an issue that deserves a high place on the agenda as ICESCR requires geographical equity. The data shows that the Health and Social Care Budgets is incongruent with estimates of incidences of mental illness. The chapter then looks at child and youth mental health care services as this was identified as an important issue during the last reporting round to the ComESCR. Unfortunately, there is no clear budget for child and youth mental health services making an exact analysis impossible. This fact might constitute a potential discrimination against children and young people, especially given the special mental health needs of this group. It highlights the need for production of data that is useful in order to measure outcomes in human rights terms, and not merely as conventionally categorized.

227 Finance and Personnel Committee, *Report on the Executive's Draft Budget 2011–2015*, paragraph 384, views of Committee for Employment and Learning.

The chapter presented the Article 2(1) obligations of progressive realization, maximum available resources, non-retrogression and the minimum core. The case study assesses community-based care services as another area where further inquiry could be useful. The data shows that there has been a gradual progression towards community-based services. Unfortunately, the progression towards community-based care is still behind the recommended split between community financing and psychiatric hospitals.

Finally, there are important procedural obligations. As argued previously, it is not clear that the funding available for mental health will enable the Article 12 rights to be progressively realized, and may leave open the possibility of actual retrogression. If a state wishes to justify possibly retrogressive measures then it is essential that it considers all alternatives; this requires a transparent and participatory process. There was not an adequately participatory debate and discussion of all alternatives during the finalization of the Health Budget in 2010–11.

In summary, this chapter has highlighted the parameters of a human rights budget analysis approach to mental health care. The geographical inequity within the UK will be a matter of concern to international monitoring bodies like ComESCR. It will be necessary to have data that indicates how well resourced are the provisions made for vulnerable groups such as children and young adults. It will be necessary to monitor how the right to health is being progressively realized; this will include considering the impact of reductions in expenditure and whether these are accompanied by compensatory measures. Finally, procedural obligations require adequate consultation of those affected by the delivery of mental health services. A human rights approach to mental health needs to address these principles – of equality (and equity), progressive realization, maximum use of available resources, protection of minimum core rights, and procedures (including participatory ones) – if the right to mental health is to be realized.

6 Social housing

Introduction

Adequate housing is a human right, essential to human dignity, security and well-being. Disturbingly, there is strong evidence to suggest that many in Northern Ireland do not enjoy this right. Over the first decade of this century, a time of optimism and prosperity for many, waiting lists for social housing increased, as did levels of homelessness. House prices soared and then crashed as recession struck. In this context, the funding of social housing becomes crucial in realizing the right to adequate housing. This chapter examines the funding of social housing in Northern Ireland from a human rights perspective.

In demonstrating how the human rights-based budget analysis framework can be applied in practice, this chapter assesses selected elements of the social housing budget against the budget-specific obligations stemming from the International Covenant on Economic, Social and Cultural Rights (ICESCR).

The chapter opens with an overview of the applicable human rights principles, with a focus on those associated with the right to adequate housing. A brief outline of the historical context to social housing is followed by a review of a number of indicators used to monitor and assess the progressive realization of the right to adequate housing. The indicators selected are particularly relevant to social housing. The chapter then looks at selected budget issues that relate to social housing including the levels of investment, the model of mixed funding for social housing, and the use of the private rented sector. The chapter examines these issues from a human rights perspective focusing on Article 2 ICESCR obligations of progressive realization and maximum available resources, as well as the procedural obligations imposed by that instrument.

The right to adequate housing

The right to adequate housing is a component of the right to an adequate standard of living in Article 11 ICESCR. The meaning of the right to adequate housing can be largely determined from the ComESCR *General Comment No. 4*[1] on the right to adequate housing and *General Comment No. 7* on evictions.[2]

In *General Comment No. 4*, the ComESCR interprets the right to adequate housing to refer to the right of all persons, regardless of their income or economic resources, to 'live somewhere in security, peace and dignity'.[3]

According to the ComESCR the right to 'adequate' housing includes more than just a roof over one's head. Aspects of 'adequacy' include:

- Legal security of tenure.
- Availability of services, material, facilities and infrastructure.
- Affordability, in that housing costs should be in general commensurate with income levels.
- Habitability.
- Accessibility for all disadvantaged groups.
- Location that allows access to employment opportunities and other services and facilities.
- Cultural adequacy.[4]

Article 2(1) obligations

Article 2(1) requires states to progressively move forwards in the realization of the full right to adequate housing for everyone using the maximum of their available resources.[5] The most appropriate means of achieving the full realization will vary significantly from one state party to another.[6] Measures employed by states may reflect whatever public/private mix is most suitable for the local context.[7] Overall, the ComESCR has explicitly stated that, 'the obligation is to demonstrate that, in aggregate, the measures being taken are sufficient to realize the right for every individual in the shortest possible time in accordance with the maximum of available resources'.[8]

According to the ComESCR, such measures could include the provision of housing subsidies and ensuring that levels of housing finance adequately reflect housing needs.[9] The Special Rapporteur on the Right to Adequate Housing

1 ComESCR, *General Comment No. 4, The Right to Adequate Housing*, UN Doc E/1992 /23 annex III at 114 (1991) paragraph 8.
2 ComESCR, *General Comment No. 7, Forced Evictions and the Right to Adequate Housing*, UN Doc E/1998/22, annex IV at 113 (1997).
3 ComESCR, *General Comment No. 4, The Right to Adequate Housing.*
4 Ibid, paragraph 8.
5 A detailed interpretation of this section can be found in Chapter 3.
6 ComESCR, *General Comment No. 4, The Right to Adequate Housing*, paragraph 12.
7 Ibid, paragraph 14.
8 Ibid, paragraph 14.
9 Ibid, paragraph 8(c).

(hereafter the Special Rapporteur) recommends that alternatives to private mortgage and ownership-based housing systems ought to be developed to assist those that have not been well served by such existing mechanisms.[10] She has argued that interventions in the market such as equitable land-use policies, public financing and housing provision, appropriate rent regulation and reinforcement of legal securities of tenure should be explored.[11]

The Article 2(1) requirement that a state use the maximum of its available resources means that a state must use the maximum amount of resources that can be expended for a particular purpose without sacrificing other, essential services.[12] In relation to housing, the 'particular purpose' is the full realization of the right to adequate housing for everyone. Implicit in this duty is a process requirement, that states may be requested to show that adequate consideration has been given to all the possible resources available to satisfy each of the ICESCR's requirements, even if the effort to give effect to full realization is not immediately possible. The state must take into consideration the full scope of resources available at a national level in relation to the entire range of obligations under the ICESCR; if the state does not, then there is a failure to adhere to a principled policymaking process.[13]

The obligation to progressively advance the right to adequate housing logically entails a duty to avoid retrogression or a step back in the enjoyment of that right. For example, the ComESCR points out that, especially during economic contraction, states are obliged to guard against a general decline in living and housing standards.[14] In many contexts, this necessarily entails states not reducing expenditure on housing. On the contrary, public funding for, and the construction of, public housing will need to increase in order to mitigate the impact of the crisis on the most vulnerable.[15] States have the immediate duty to refrain from taking retrogressive measures. States therefore ought to refrain from taking any deliberate steps backwards in the realization of ESR,

10 Raquel Rolnik, *Report of the Special Rapporteur on Adequate Housing as a Component of the Right to an Adequate Standard of Living, and the Right to Non-discrimination in this Context: Promotion and Protection of All Human Rights, Civil, Political, Economic, Social and Cultural Rights, including the Right to Development*, UN Doc A/HRC/10/7 (2009) paragraph 83.

11 Ibid, paragraph 87. See more recently Raquel Rolnik, *Report of the Special Rapporteur on Adequate Housing as a Component of the Right to an Adequate Standard of Living*, A/67/286 (2012).

12 Philip Alston and Gerard Quinn, 'The Nature and Scope of the States Parties' Obligations under the International Covenant on Economic, Social and Cultural Rights' (1987) 9 *Human Rights Quarterly* 156, 178.

13 Ibid 181.

14 ComESCR, *General Comment No. 4, The Right to Adequate Housing*, paragraph 11.

15 Raquel Rolnik, *Report of the Special Rapporteur on adequate housing as a component of the right to an adequate standard of living, and the right to non-discrimination in this context: Promotion and Protection of All Human Rights, Civil, Political, Economic, Social and Cultural Rights, including the Right to Development*, UN Doc A/HRC/10/7 (2009) paragraph 83.

such as the reduction of public funding on housing in the face of increasing need or the withdrawal or limitation of existing ESR programmes. Evictions, repossessions of houses and a decrease in persons enjoying the right to housing can constitute retrogressive measures if caused by deliberate action or inaction of the state.

Immediate obligations

As discussed in Chapter 4, the right to non-discrimination is not subject to progressive realization.[16] Thus, states must ensure full and sustainable access to housing and housing-related resources to all disadvantaged groups.[17] The right to non-discrimination and equality covers both formal and substantive equality.[18] Non-discrimination may, therefore, sometimes require states to take positive measures or affirmative action in order to ensure to vulnerable and disadvantaged groups equal enjoyment of the right to adequate housing.[19] The aim of these measures is to improve the situation of the targeted group so as to place them in equal situations with other, more privileged groups.[20]

The state also has an immediate duty to ensure that it gives effect to the minimum core obligations imposed by the right to adequate housing. As highlighted in Chapter 3, while the ComESCR has not spelled out in detail what the minimum core of the right to housing is (the terminology of 'minimum core' is not used in either *General Comment No. 4* or *No. 7*) the ComESCR has stated that if a significant number of individuals are deprived of basic shelter the state is *prima facie* violating its obligations.[21] One can thus assume that 'basic shelter' constitutes the minimum core of the right to adequate housing.

Certain procedural requirements must also be put in place immediately because they enable progressive realization of the right to adequate housing. States are required to adopt a national housing strategy that 'identifies the resources available to meet [the] goals and the most cost-effective way of using them and sets out the responsibilities and time-frame for implementation'.[22] This strategy should reflect extensive, genuine consultation with and

16 ComESCR, *General Comment No. 3, The Nature of States Parties Obligations*, UN Doc E/1991/23 annex III (1990) paragraph 1.

17 ComESCR, *General Comment No. 4, The Right to Adequate Housing*, paragraph 8(e).

18 ComESCR, *General Comment No. 20 Non-Discrimination in Economic, Social and Cultural Rights*, UN Doc E/C.12/GC/20 (2009) paragraph 8.

19 Ibid, paragraph 9.

20 María Magdalena Sepúlveda Carmona, *The Nature of the Obligations under the International Covenant on Economic, Social and Cultural Rights* (Intersentia 2003) 401.

21 ComESCR, *General Comment No. 3, The Nature of States Parties Obligations*, UN Doc E/1991/23 annex III at 86 (1990), paragraph 10.

22 ComESCR, *General Comment No. 7, Forced Evictions, and the Right to Adequate Housing*, paragraph 12.

participation by all of those affected, including the homeless, the inadequately housed and their representatives. In addition, the state must ensure that there is coordination between Ministries and regional and local authorities in order to reconcile related policies relevant to the right to adequate housing, in particular and the adequate standard of living in general.[23] The state must monitor the extent of non-realization of ESR and devise strategies and programmes for their promotion.[24] This duty is not eliminated by resource constraints[25] and is of immediate effect. Finally, the state has to collect disaggregated data that enables it to ascertain the full extent of homelessness and inadequate housing within its jurisdiction.[26]

Tripartite typology

The obligations imposed by the right to adequate housing can also be classified using the 'tripartite typology' approach of respect, protect and fulfil. At the most basic level, the obligation to respect obliges states not to interfere with existing access to housing (for example, through the state carrying out evictions and repossessions). It also incorporates positive obligations when necessary to maintain existing access. The Special Rapporteur has noted that the current economic climate threatens the realization of housing rights, especially if bank losses are covered by public funds at the expense of state programmes for housing and other social areas.[27] If the enjoyment of the ESR is diminished because the state has 'bailed out' financial institutions, the obligation to respect ESR is likely to have been breached.[28]

The obligation to protect requires states to guard against interference with the enjoyment of the right to adequate housing by third parties. This is particularly relevant where housing is being provided or facilitated by the private sector. In the Northern Ireland context, the conduct of non-state actors such as banks, lending agencies and private landlords has had an important impact on enjoyment of the right to adequate housing.

As stated in Chapter 4, the obligation to fulfil has been divided into the obligations to facilitate, promote and provide. The state must facilitate people's ability to secure their own housing, that is to say the state must engage in

23 ComESCR, *General Comment No. 4, The Right to Adequate Housing*, paragraph 12.

24 ComESCR, *General Comment No. 3, The Nature of States Parties Obligations*, paragraph 13.

25 Ibid, paragraph 11.

26 ComESCR, *General Comment No. 4, The Right to Adequate Housing*, paragraph 13.

27 Raquel Rolnik, *Report of the Special Rapporteur on Adequate Housing as a Component of the Right to an Adequate Standard of Living, and the Right to Non-discrimination in this Context: Promotion and Protection of All Human Rights, Civil, Political, Economic, Social and Cultural Rights, including the Right to Development*, UN Doc A/HRC/10/7 (2009) paragraph 16.

28 Ibid, paragraphs 15–16. Even though the obligation to respect is not mentioned specifically in relation to bank bailouts, the Special Rapporteur notes that the rescue of the banking sector must be accountable and must not have negative impacts on human rights.

activities to ensure that people have access to resources to ensure the full enjoyment of their rights. The state must promote access to adequate housing by, among other things, adhering to various procedural and administrative requirements relevant to housing rights. Finally, the state must provide that right directly where persons or groups are unable to enjoy the right, for reasons beyond their control.[29]

The ComESCR on the right to adequate housing in Northern Ireland

ComESCR has considered the steps taken by the UK to give effect to the right to adequate housing on various occasions. In 1994, the ComESCR recognized that imposed budgetary constraints caused economic and social exclusion.[30] The national housing policy was found to be inadequate in addressing the problems faced by the most vulnerable groups of society, which the ComESCR identified as private tenants who were single parents or in general had low incomes.[31] The ComESCR urged the UK to improve the monitoring of the problem of inadequate housing and to develop more focused and active measures to improve the situation.[32] Housing was again a subject of concern for the ComESCR in 1997.[33] In 2002, the ComESCR expressed its concern about the considerable levels of poverty in Northern Ireland[34] and the persistence of homelessness throughout the UK as a whole; it especially highlighted poor-quality housing and fuel poverty.[35]

The latest (fifth) UK periodic report did not contain much information on the Northern Ireland housing situation. No delegate from Northern Ireland was present when the UK presented its report to the ComESCR or attended the question-and-answer session with the ComESCR.[36] The lack of a Northern

29 The language of 'respect, protect and fulfil' was developed after the adoption of *General Comment No. 4* on housing. The understanding of these terms is taken from later *General Comments*. ComESCR, *General Comment No. 12, The Right to Adequate Food*, UN Doc E/C.12/1999/5 (1999a) paragraph 15.

30 ComESCR, *Conclusions and Recommendations of the Committee on Economic, Social and Cultural Rights, United Kingdom of Great Britain and Northern Ireland*, UN Doc E/C.12/1994/19 (1994) part 1, paragraph B.

31 Ibid, part 1, paragraph C.

32 Ibid, part 1, paragraph D.

33 ComESCR, *Conclusions and Recommendations of the Committee on Economic, Social and Cultural Rights, United Kingdom of Great Britain and Northern Ireland*, UN Doc E/C.12/1 Add.19 (1997) paragraph 17.

34 ComESCR, *Concluding Observations of the Committee on Economic, Social and Cultural Rights: United Kingdom of Great Britain and Northern Ireland*, UN Doc E/C.12/1/Add.79 (2002) paragraph 18.

35 Ibid, paragraph 20.

36 ComESCR, *Concluding Observations of the Committee on Economic, Social and Cultural Rights, United Kingdom*, UN Doc E/C.12/GBR/CO/5 (2009) paragraph 2.

Ireland representative meant that the ComESCR's questions with regards to housing in the region, and in Belfast in particular, were left unanswered.[37] During its discussion of the report with the UK delegation, ComESCR members addressed the chronic shortage of social housing among disadvantaged groups in Northern Ireland, in particular Catholics in north Belfast.[38] In response, the delegation stated that the UK government was aware of the problem and that it intended to invest over £8 billion for the provision of new social houses.[39] Since reference to both Scotland and Northern Ireland is made throughout the report it can be assumed that this allocation does not refer to Northern Ireland specifically.

Consequently, the ComESCR's 2009 *Concluding Observations* express concern about the chronic shortage of housing, in particular social housing, for the most disadvantaged and marginalized individuals and groups in Northern Ireland, in spite of the financial resources provided and other measures taken in this regard.[40] The ComESCR recommended that the UK review its existing policies and develop effective strategies – including a gender impact assessment – to increase the levels of affordable housing, including social housing.[41] Overall, the ComESCR specifically pointed to the persistent levels of deprivation and inequality in relation to the right to an adequate standard of living (Article 11) throughout Northern Ireland, despite the adoption of Equality Impact Assessments.[42] In particular, in the context of urban regeneration programmes, the ComESCR highlighted that a human rights framework ought to be adopted, ensuring the participation of the affected populations to promote adequate housing programmes for the poor.[43] Crucially, the ComESCR noted the lack of a national strategy to implement the Covenant in all the territories in the state party, including Northern Ireland.[44]

This section has explained the budget-related ICESCR obligations regarding the right to adequate housing. It has shown what areas the ComESCR is concerned about in the realization of this right in the UK and specifically in Northern Ireland. The next section moves from the global to the local and examines the historical context to social housing policy and expenditure in Northern Ireland.

37 Treaty Body Monitor, Committee on Economic, Social and Cultural Rights, 42nd session, United Kingdom of Britain and Northern Ireland 4–5th report 12–13th of May 2009, Human Rights Monitor Series (2009) available at www.ishr.ch (accessed 25 August 2009).

38 Treaty Body Monitor, Committee on Economic, Social and Cultural Rights, 42nd session, United Kingdom of Britain and Northern Ireland 4–5th report 12–13th of May 2009, Human Rights Monitor Series (2009) 4.

39 Ibid.

40 ComESCR, *Concluding Observations of the Committee on Economic, Social and Cultural Rights, United Kingdom*, UN Doc E/C.12/GBR/CO/5 (2009) paragraph 29.

41 Ibid, paragraph 29.

42 Ibid, paragraph 31.

43 Ibid, paragraph 31.

44 Ibid, paragraph 12.

The historical context to social housing in Northern Ireland

This section reviews key developments in housing policy and expenditure in Northern Ireland. It begins with the creation of the Northern Ireland Housing Executive (NIHE) in the context of the civil rights campaign of the 1960s, before examining the shift in housing policy inaugurated in 1979. It then highlights the introduction of devolution following the 1998 Belfast/Good Friday Agreement and Northern Ireland Act 1998 and concludes with a review of the recent global economic crisis.

Prior to 1971, responsibility for the provision and management of social housing was a matter for a variety of local government bodies. Following the civil rights movement's highlighting of sectarian and political discrimination in the building and allocation of public housing,[45] the Northern Ireland Housing Executive (NI) Act 1971 established the NIHE.[46] Between 1971 and 1973, the NIHE inherited the stock and functions of the former Housing Trust, sixty-one Local Authorities and three Commissions.[47]

Throughout the 1970s, the NIHE undertook a large-scale programme of new social build. Between 1971 and 1979 a total of 57,223 homes were constructed (an average of 6,358 per year).[48]

In 1976, in the context of a deteriorating economic environment (including a growing budget deficit), the UK government approached the International Monetary Fund (IMF) for a loan. The loan conditions stipulated a significant cut in public expenditure, prompting disinvestment in public housing. Consequently, between 1976–7 and 1977–8 government expenditure on housing in Northern Ireland fell by fifteen per cent in real terms.[49]

The election of Margaret Thatcher as Prime Minister in 1979 ushered in a dramatic change in social and economic policy. The Conservative government departed from the social democratic consensus, which had previously obtained and which had accorded an important role to social housing (defined as housing provided by the state on a non-profit basis)[50] as part of the welfare state. The 'neoliberal'[51] ideology that underpinned the government's agenda advocated the extension of markets, an expanded role for the private sector in the provision of public services and the withdrawal of welfare services. In the sphere of housing this provoked a shift from support for social housing to

45 Cameron Report, *Disturbances in Northern Ireland: Report of the Commission appointed by the Governor of Northern Ireland* (HMSO, Belfast 1969) Cmnd. 532.

46 In 2013, the DSD announced plans to abolish the Housing Executive.

47 Housing Rights Service, *Housing Rights Manual* (2008) page 3:1.

48 Personal communication with the DSD dated 10/06/09, unpublished, on file with authors.

49 Frank Gaffikin and Mike Morrissey, *Northern Ireland: The Thatcher Years* (Zed Books 1990) 157.

50 Cited in Stephen Harriott, Lesley Matthews and Grainger Paul, *Introducing Social Housing* (Chartered Institute of Housing 2004) 5.

51 Neoliberalism advocates the extension of market relations as providing the basis for human freedom and prosperity. Key texts include Milton Friedman, *Capitalism and Freedom* (Chicago UP 1962) and Friedrich von Hayek, *The Constitution of Liberty* (Routledge 1960). For a survey see David Harvey, *A Brief History of Neoliberalism* (Oxford UP 2005).

home ownership.[52] From a rights perspective, this could be understood as a shift in the role of the state from provider to facilitator.[53] The ComESCR specifically recognizes that states may not be able to satisfy the need for housing by providing publicly built accommodation, and may have to facilitate the enjoyment of the right through 'enabling strategies'.[54] Therefore, the use of government resources to support home ownership can be commendable if it forms part of an overall scheme towards the full realization of everyone's right to housing in line with the ICESCR obligations.[55] A number of financial developments helped to engineer this transfer, including a fall in new build expenditure.[56] Between 1983–4 and 1988–9 expenditure on new build halved in real terms in Northern Ireland (Figure 6.1).

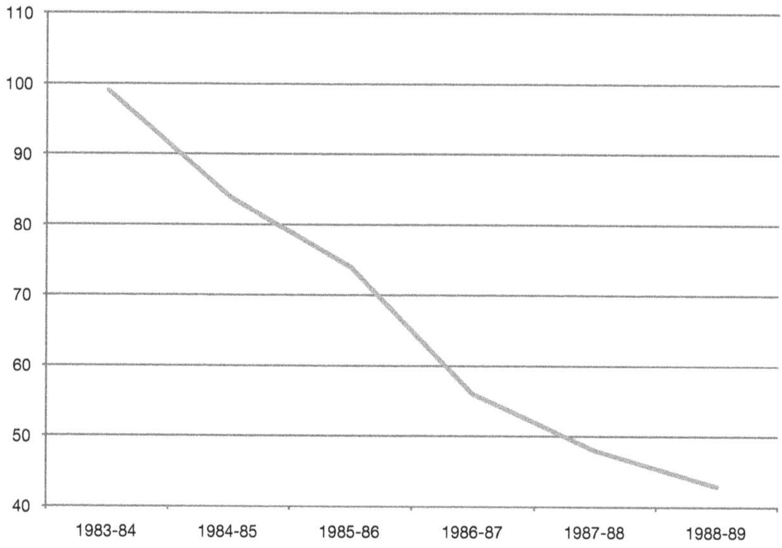

Figure 6.1 Public expenditure on new build (£m) 1983–4 to 1988–9.[57]

Source: DFP (1989) NI Commentary on Public Expenditure Plans 1989–90 to 1991–2.[58]

52 According to Mullins and Murie this shift was also motivated by electoral considerations, specifically the belief that property owners were more likely to adopt Conservative outlooks and voting patterns: David Mullins and Alan Murie, *Housing Policy in the UK* (Palgrave 2006) 64.

53 Raquel Rolnik, *Report of the Special Rapporteur on Adequate Housing as a Component of the Right to an Adequate Standard of Living, and the Right to Non-discrimination in this Context: Promotion and Protection of All Human Rights, Civil, Political, Economic, Social and Cultural Rights, Including the Right to Development*, UN Doc A/HRC/10/7 (2009) paragraph 27.

54 ComESCR, *General Comment No. 4, The Right to Adequate Housing*, paragraph 14.

55 Ibid, paragraph 8(a), adequacy of housing includes legal security of tenure which can take a variety of forms, including owner-occupation.

56 Other such initiatives included mortgage interest tax relief and abolition of capital gains tax. See Frank Gaffikin and Mike Morrissey, *Northern Ireland: The Thatcher Years* (Zed Books 1990) 155.

57 1983–4 values.

58 The figure for 1988–9 was an estimate.

The House Sales Scheme, introduced in Northern Ireland in 1979, was also important in orienting housing towards home ownership. Under this scheme, social housing tenants could purchase their home at a discount on the market price.[59] More than 100,000 properties in Northern Ireland were sold under this scheme between 1979 and 2003.[60] This enabled many low-income households to access home ownership and presented the UK government with a significant source of capital receipts.[61] Thus, disinvestment in new social stock occurred at the same time as significant resources were being generated via the sale of existing social housing units.

States have an obligation to give due priority to social groups living in unfavourable conditions and, where necessary, to provide housing to those who cannot do so through the market.[62] However, low levels of funding soon had a dramatic impact on the NIHE's ability to maintain its new build programme.[63] Figure 6.2 shows the decrease in new build between 1983 and 1998.

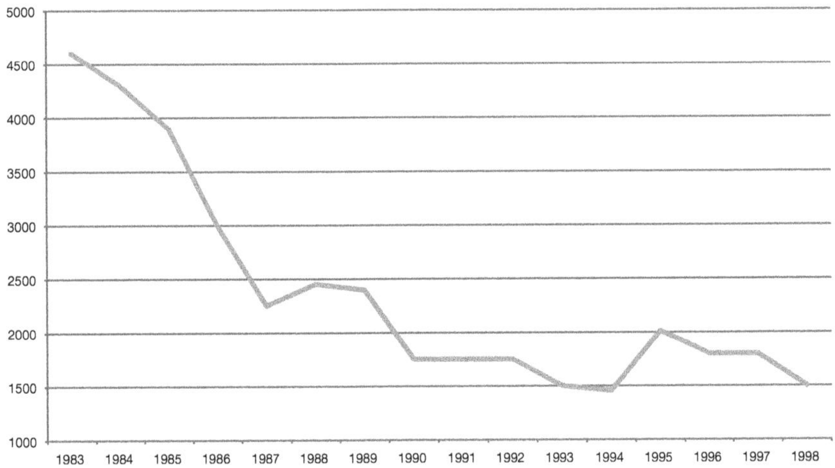

Figure 6.2 New social build 1983–98.

Source: NI Housing Statistics 1999–2000.

59 The size of the discount has changed a number of times during the operation of the policy, and at its height stood at sixty per cent of market value. The discount is currently capped at £24,000. This represents fourteen per cent of the average property price or 19.5 per cent of the average terraced house price in Northern Ireland.

60 NIHE, *The House Sales Scheme and the Housing Market* (2004) 8.

61 David Mullins and Alan Murie, *Housing Policy in the UK* (Palgrave 2006) 39.

62 ComESCR, *General Comment No. 14, The Right to the Highest Attainable Standard of Health*, paragraph 11.

63 For example, in 1990 the NIHE announced that as a result of government budget cuts, it could provide 1,000 rather than the planned 1,300 new homes for the year. Cited in Frank Gaffikin and Mike Morrissey, *Northern Ireland: The Thatcher Years* (Zed Books 1990) 160.

Indeed with house sales exceeding new build, the overall size of the social sector declined by 17.3 per cent between 1987 and 1998 (Figure 6.3). Over the same period the number of households that owned their own homes increased by 34.5 per cent.[64]

In this context, the NIHE began to explore alternative sources of funding. Central government borrowing rules prevented the NIHE from augmenting its allocation from central government with borrowing from private financial institutions.[65] A solution appeared to be provided by the 1992 Housing (NI) Order, which permitted housing associations that had previously been restricted to borrowing from government to obtain loans from private sources. Housing associations had previously complemented the large-scale NIHE developments with small-scale specialized developments. As housing associations were designated as private bodies, their borrowing was not counted as part of public sector borrowing. Therefore, in order to circumvent central government restrictions on borrowing, a 1996 government review of housing policy recommended that responsibility for building and managing *all* new social housing be transferred to housing associations.[66] In 1998, housing associations assumed building and landlord responsibilities for new stock. Housing associations fund new build with a mixture of government grants (the Housing Association Grant), borrowing and their own reserves.

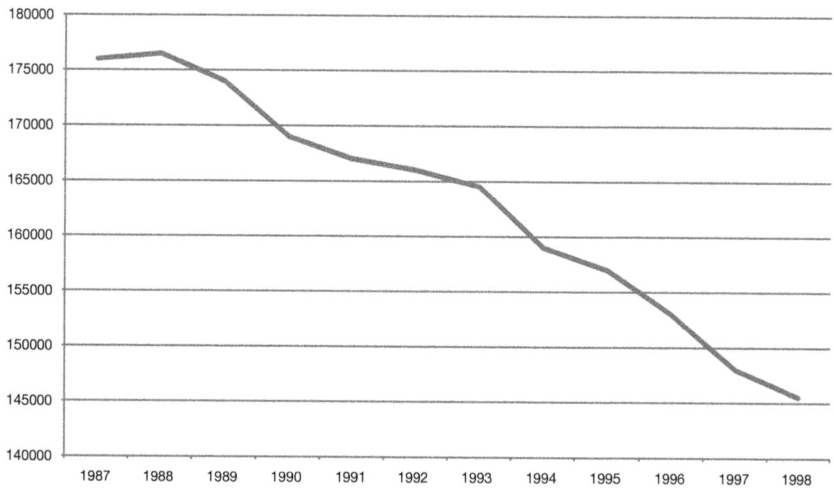

Figure 6.3 Social housing stock 1987–98.

Source: NI Housing Statistics 1999–2000.

64 DSD, *Northern Ireland Housing Statistics 1999–2000* (2000) 16.

65 House of Commons Northern Ireland Affairs Select Committee, *Social Housing Provision in Northern Ireland: Sixth Report of Session 2003–04* (HC 2003–2004 493) Memorandum submitted by CIH.

66 Department of the Environment, *Building for Success* (1996) Northern Ireland Economic Development Office, Belfast.

Devolution

The Northern Ireland Assembly (NIA) was established a result of the 1998 Belfast/Good Friday Agreement. The Assembly, established by the Northern Ireland Act 1998, assumed its full functions in December 1999.[67] Responsibility for housing policy, for example, was transferred to the NIA. However, the NIA operated intermittently and was suspended over the entire period from October 2002 to May 2007. Given this, it is perhaps unsurprising that a review of Northern Ireland housing policy between 1998 and 2007, found 'little evidence that devolution has made much difference'.[68]

Upon the restoration of devolution, Margaret Ritchie (SDLP) was appointed Minister for Social Development. In February 2008, Minister Ritchie launched a new agenda for housing, stating that 'there can be no more fundamental right than having a roof over your head and that is why . . . I have made the alleviation of our housing crisis my foremost priority'.[69]

While the Department for Social Development (DSD) has primary responsibility for social housing, it is important to remember that other agencies are involved. First, some areas of decision-making fall outside the legislative competence of the NIA. Taxation, financial services and investment business, as well as certain aspects of social security, are issues outside the responsibility of the devolved authorities, even though they have important impacts on the resources that are available for the realization of the right. Second, the right to adequate housing is directly related to a range of human rights. These include the right to the highest attainable standard of health and mental health (ICESCR, Article 12), the right to education (ICESCR, Article 13), the right to work (ICESCR, Article 6), and the right to equality (International Covenant on Civil and Political Rights, Articles 2 and 26). As a result, the enjoyment of the right to adequate housing impacts on the enjoyment of these other rights and vice versa. Therefore, giving full effect to the right to adequate housing cannot be achieved by one department alone.

Economic crisis

The NIA assumed its functions on the cusp of the global economic crisis that developed in the latter part of 2007. A range of practices in areas such as lending, investment, insurance and risk analysis, facilitated by a lack of effective government regulation, contributed to the crisis.[70] Ironically, housing

67 As amended. See Chapter 1 for more on the institutional context.

68 Chris Paris, 'Changing Housing System in Northern Ireland 1998–2007' (2008) 7 *Ethnopolitics* 119, 120.

69 DSD, A *New Agenda for Housing – Statement by Margaret Ritchie MLA, Minister for Social Development* (26/02/08). Available at www.dsdni.gov.uk/index/publications/ministers_speeches/offps-new-agenda-housing.htm (accessed 21 June 2010).

70 For a more comprehensive review of the origins of the financial crash see Vincent Cable, *The Storm: the World Economic Crisis and What It Means* (Rev. ed. Atlantic 2010).

also played a central role in the crisis, most clearly manifested in the 'sub-prime' mortgage crisis in the US.[71]

As a result of the crisis, the UK economy went into recession and the property market in Northern Ireland collapsed, with average house prices falling from £250,586 in quarter three of 2007 to £156,857 in quarter one of 2009 (a decrease of 37.4 per cent).[72] The crash left many households in negative equity (i.e., the market value of their home was less than the purchase price they paid for it). In addition, as people struggled to meet their mortgage costs, actions for repossession in Northern Ireland increased by 62.2 per cent from 2,401 in 2007/08 to 3,894 in 2008/09.[73]

Many of the macro policy instruments required to address the economic crisis reside with the UK government rather than devolved institutions.[74] For example, the ability of the Northern Ireland devolved institutions to regulate banking practices is limited.[75] The UK government injected substantial finance[76] into the banking system, and the Bank of England cut interest rates, in an effort to provide that system with the necessary liquidity to kick-start lending. The combination of huge public borrowing to rescue the financial system, and falling government revenue due to recession, had a significant impact upon the public finances.

In sum, the 1970s saw the NIHE pursue a committed programme of building new housing. However, the economic crisis of the 1970s and the Conservative government policies after 1979 created a different context for social housing, in which home ownership was encouraged. During the 1990s, more responsibility was placed on housing associations, because of their ability to access private sector borrowing. Devolution raised the possibility of Northern Ireland politicians developing their own policies. However, devolution operated intermittently until 2007 and its return coincided with the emergence of a global economic crisis.

Social housing from a human rights perspective

The provision of social housing is a crucial aspect of the right to adequate housing, particularly for members of vulnerable groups. This section explains why social housing has emerged as an important human rights issue in

71 On the development of the sub-prime market see Raquel Rolnik, *Report of the Special Rapporteur on Adequate Housing as a Component of the Right to an Adequate Standard of Living*, A/67/286 (United Nations, 2012) paragraphs 23–8.

72 UUJ, *Northern Ireland Quarterly House Prices Index* (2009).

73 DSD, *Northern Ireland Housing Statistics 2008–09* (2009) 68.

74 V. Hewitt, *Mitigating the Recession: Options for the Northern Ireland Executive*, Research Paper No. 37 (Economic Research Institute of Northern Ireland 2009) 5.

75 Ibid 3.

76 Some £140bn by September 2009. See BBC News, *Public Sector Borrowing Soaring* (19 September 2009). Available at http://news.bbc.co.uk/1/hi/business/8262434.stm (accessed 21 November 2009).

Northern Ireland. It considers the extent of progressive realization of different aspects of the right to adequate housing, to which social housing makes a key contribution. The section shows that several key indicators suggest that, for most of the first decade of this century, the right to adequate housing was not progressively achieved; rather, these indicators suggest that the housing situation worsened. This section also looks at the affordability of the private sector and its ability to provide suitable alternatives to social housing in this context.

Two key indicators used to measure the realization of the right to adequate housing are waiting lists for social housing and rates of homelessness. For example, the reporting guidelines issued by the ComESCR require states to indicate whether a national survey on homelessness and inadequate housing has been undertaken and to publish the findings. Further, with regard to the realization of the right to adequate housing, the ComESCR inquires about the impact of social housing measures, such as the provision of low-cost social housing units. The ComESCR also asks for information regarding the waiting lists for such housing and the average length of waiting time.[77]

The UN *Report on Indicators for Promoting and Monitoring the Implementation of Human Rights* also provides a good indication of how the realization of the right to adequate housing can be measured. Recommended indicators include the share of public expenditure on social housing; the share of public expenditure spent on basic amenities (sanitation, water, electricity, etc.) and the share of the population receiving housing benefits or subsidies. Housing affordability is measured by looking at the proportion of households receiving housing assistance, including those that live in subsidized rented housing and home ownership. Comparison between the proportion of households spending more than a certain percentage of their monthly income on housing or rent in the bottom three and top three income deciles also provides an indication of affordability.[78] As these are all aspects of the right to adequate housing, the obligation to progressively realize the right requires a progressive improvement on all these fronts.

The first indicator examined is the waiting list for social housing. The Common Selection Scheme, introduced in November 2000, records the number of applicants for social housing accommodation. A points system is used to assess the housing needs of all applicants and, in general, each available dwelling is offered to the household with the highest number of points.[79]

77 ComESCR, *The Guidelines on Treaty-Specific Documents to be Submitted by State Parties under Articles 16 and 17 of the International Covenant on Economic, Social and Cultural Rights*, UN Doc E/C.12/2008/2 (2008) article 50.

78 United Nations, *Report on Indicators for Promoting and Monitoring the Implementation of Human Rights*, UN Doc HRI/MC/2008/3 (2008) 29. See now Office of the High Commissioner for Human Rights, *Human Rights Indicators: A Guide to Measurement and Implementation* (2012) HR/PUB/12/5.

79 The Housing Selection Scheme is available at www.nihe.gov.uk/housing_selection_scheme.pdf (accessed 26 August 2013).

Applicants with thirty or more points are regarded as being most in need of social housing and are designated as being in 'housing stress'. The waiting list provides perhaps the most direct indicator of social housing need. Figure 6.4 shows there was strong growth in both the overall waiting list for social housing and those on the waiting list categorized as being in housing stress. Between 2000–01 and 2008–09, the waiting list increased by 76.5 per cent, from 22,054 to 38,923 households. Over this same period the number of households in housing stress increased from 10,639 to 20,481 (a rise of 92.5 per cent). Having increased each successive year since 2000–01, both the waiting list and housing stress declined between 2007–08 and 2008–09 by 1.9 per cent and 4.1 per cent respectively.

The second key indicator is the measure of 'homelessness'. In Northern Ireland the term 'homeless' means that a person does not have accommodation, in the sense that there is no accommodation in which the person has an entitlement to reside, or that there is no accommodation where it would be reasonable to expect the person to reside.[80]

Figure 6.5 shows that the period between 1998–99 and 2008–09 witnessed a 56.5 per cent rise in the number of households presenting themselves to the NIHE as homeless (from 11,552 to 18,076). The number of households presenting as homeless, however, decreased in the last two financial years.

These figures show an increase in the numbers on the waiting list for social housing, in housing stress and presenting as homeless for most of the period

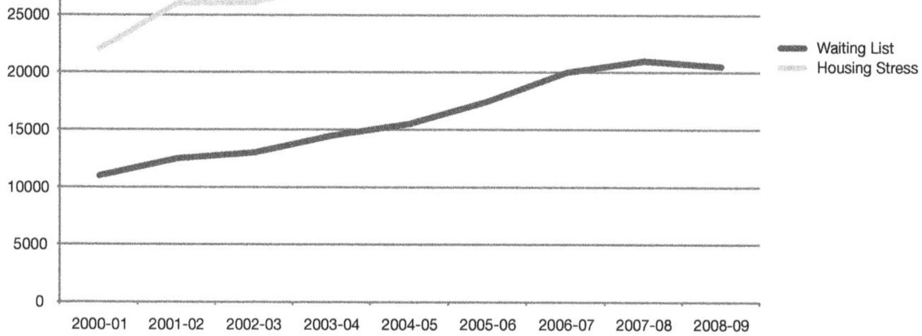

Figure 6.4 Social housing waiting list and housing stress 2000–01 to 2008–09.
Source: NI Housing Statistics 2003–04 and 2008–09.

80 Defined under Article 3 of the Housing (Northern Ireland) Order 1988.

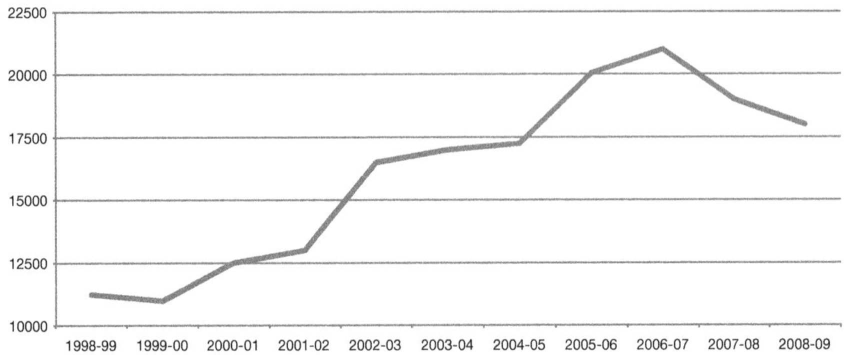

Figure 6.5 Households presenting as homeless 1998–99 to 2008–09.
Source: NI Housing Statistics 2003–04 and 2008–09.

since 2000 (except for decreases in the last one to two years of the research). This follows a period where expenditure on new build decreased (1983–9, Figure 6.1), new social build decreased (1983–98, Figure 6.2) and the social housing stock decreased (1987–98, Figure 6.3). The state's decision to reduce funding for social housing could be justifiable under the ICESCR if that decision delivered progressive realization of the right to adequate housing as expeditiously as possible in the context of the maximum of available resources.

However, the increase in the number of households on the common waiting list for social housing, in housing stress and presenting as homeless, evidences a failure to progressively realize the right to housing.[81] Indeed, these factors suggest that during most of the first decade of this century there was retrogression in the enjoyment of the right to adequate housing.

The above indicators of need are widely accepted as being directly related to the provision of social housing.[82] It is also important to acknowledge that the social housing sector is part of an interconnected housing system that also comprises home ownership and private renting. These sectors are interdependent in that changes in the demand and supply in one sector can impact on the others. Thus, for example, the Special Rapporteur has established 'a clear link between the rise in housing prices – and resulting affordability problems

81 The ComESCR specifically asks reporting states about the numbers of people on waiting lists for obtaining accommodation, the average length of waiting time and the measures taken to *decrease* such lists. ComESCR, *The Guidelines on Treaty-Specific Documents to be Submitted by State Parties under Articles 16 and 17 of the International Covenant on Economic, Social and Cultural Rights*, UN Doc E/C.12/2008/2 (2008) paragraph 3(b)(vi).

82 NIHE and NIFHA, *Response to the Recommendations of the Review into Affordable Housing Interim Report* (2007) 10.

– and the demand for public and affordable housing'.[83] If households are unable to access home ownership, they will turn to private renting or social housing in order to meet their needs and vice versa.[84] In this context, the declining capacity of the social sector to accommodate households is likely to represent one of multiple factors that contributed to demand for home ownership.[85] The first decade of the century witnessed remarkable growth in house prices in Northern Ireland, as shown in Figure 6.6, which provides the average real price of housing in Northern Ireland. Figure 6.7 shows that house price inflation was far in excess of the Consumer Price Index (CPI).[86]

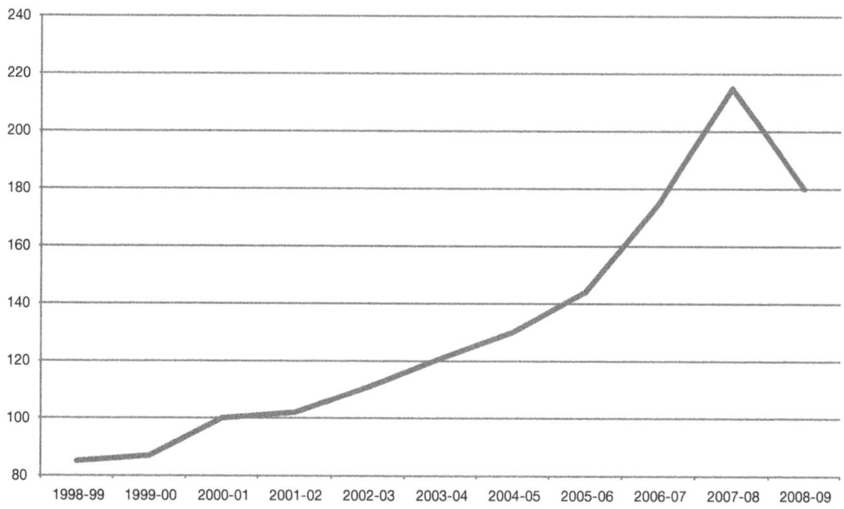

Figure 6.6 Average real house prices (in thousands) in Northern Ireland 1998–9 to 2008–09 (2008–09 values).

Source: NI Housing Statistics 2001–02, 2004–05 and 2008–09

83 Raquel Rolnik, *Report of the Special Rapporteur on Adequate Housing as a Component of the Right to an Adequate Standard of Living, and the Right to Non-discrimination in this Context: Promotion and Protection of All Human Rights, Civil, Political, Economic, Social and Cultural Rights, including the Right to Development*, UN Doc A/HRC/10/7 (2009) paragraph 34.

84 Differences in 'supply, by the very fact that it tends to eliminate some or all of the other possible ways of satisfying housing need (for example, the renting of single-family houses), contributes to imposing a particular way of satisfying this need'. Pierre Bourdieu, *The Social Structures of the Economy* (Polity 2005) 22.

85 Other factors include demographic trends such as population growth and family breakdown, changing lending practices that offer mortgages at a higher loan-to-value ratio (the value of the mortgage as a percentage of the cost of the house), low interest rates, high levels of employment and speculation. For a comprehensive discussion of the drivers of the housing market see NIHE, *The NI Housing Market: Drivers and Policies* (2007).

86 CPI is a key measure of inflation in the economy. It measures the average change in prices of a range of household goods and services.

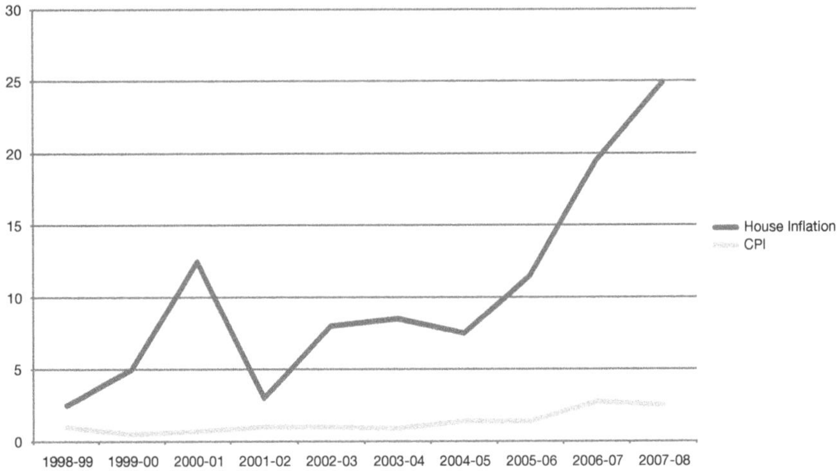

Figure 6.7 House price inflation and consumer price index (CPI) 1998–9 to 2007–08. Source: ONS.

In the absence of an equivalent rise in real incomes, home ownership became increasingly unaffordable. This was evident in the fall in the proportion of first-time buyers accessing mortgages from sixty per cent to thirty-six per cent between 2000 and 2005.[87] Further, the income multiple[88] for first-time buyers increased from 2.36 to 2.85 over this five-year period.[89] In September 2006, the DSD commissioned John Semple to carry out a review of housing affordability. The *Review into Affordable Housing* (2007) defined housing costs as 'affordable' if they did not exceed thirty-five per cent of household income.[90] In order to provide an indication of the level of affordability in Northern Ireland, Semple considered how many properties in each District Council would be considered affordable for a household on a median income. According to this measure, Semple found that in eighteen of the twenty-six council areas, less than ten per cent of homes were 'affordable'.[91]

This situation raises issues in relation to the ComESCR statement that the right to adequate housing should be ensured to all persons irrespective of income or access to economic resources.[92] Affordability as an aspect of the right to adequate housing means that personal or household financial costs associated with housing should be at such levels that the satisfaction of other basic needs

87 Council of Mortgage Lenders, *Housing Finance* (2006) 8.
88 The cost of the house divided by the household income.
89 Council of Mortgage Lenders, *Housing Finance* (2006) 8.
90 John Semple, *Review into Affordable Housing: Final Report* (2007) 11. Available at www.dsdni.gov.uk/affordable_housing_final.pdf (accessed 26 August 2013).
91 Ibid 56.
92 ComESCR, *General Comment No. 4, The Right to Adequate Housing*, paragraph 7.

is not threatened or compromised.[93] The ComESCR requires states to indicate in their reports the number of persons whose housing expenses are above the government set limit of affordability, which in terms of the Semple report is thirty-five per cent of income.[94] From this it follows that, in 2006, housing in the private sector was not 'adequate' in that it was unaffordable for a large group of people.

As stated previously, having peaked at £250,586 in the third quarter of 2007, average house values subsequently collapsed.[95] While this may have increased the affordability of housing, restrictions on lending[96] meant that accessing mortgages became more difficult.[97] Indeed, despite the fall in prices, the number of house sales fell from 6,136 in 2006–07 to 2,878 in 2007–08 and 2,141 in 2008–09.[98]

To conclude, this section has examined some key indicators that can be used to assess whether the right to adequate housing is being progressively realized. During most of the first decade of the century, the number of persons on the waiting list for social housing, in housing stress and presenting as homeless increased (though the figures show an improvement towards the end of the period). Problems with the affordability of housing in the private sector made this an unsuitable alternative for many vulnerable households. Overall, for much of the decade, these factors indicate a failure to progressively realize the right to adequate housing.

Analysis of selected aspects of the social housing budget

The previous section suggests that progressive realization is not occurring in areas in which social housing makes a significant contribution to the enjoyment of the right to adequate housing. These indicators of need particularly affect vulnerable members of society. In that context, this chapter now turns to analyze some elements of the social housing budget using the human rights framework outlined in Section 2. It begins by providing an overview of the Northern Ireland housing budget. The subsequent three sub-sections focus on three financial aspects of social housing: the model of mixed funding for social housing, investment in social housing, and the use of the private rented sector to accommodate low-income households.

93 Ibid, paragraph 8(c).

94 ComESCR, *The Guidelines on Treaty-Specific Documents to be Submitted by State Parties under Articles 16 and 17 of the International Covenant on Economic, Social and Cultural Rights*, UN Doc E/C.12/2008/2 (2008) paragraph 3(v).

95 Source: UUJ, (2009) Northern Ireland Quarterly House Price Index.

96 V. Hewitt, *Mitigating the Recession: Options for the Northern Ireland Executive*, Research Paper No. 37, Economic Research Institute of Northern Ireland (2009) 3.

97 'Lending criteria have tightened across the UK in response to funding constraints and the worsening economic outlook'. Council of Mortgage Lenders, *Northern Ireland Factsheet: Housing and Mortgage Market Update* (2009) 2.

98 DSD, *Northern Ireland Housing Statistics 2008–09* (2009) 69.

The housing budget: An overview

The budget for 2003–04 to 2007–08

One source of information on the Northern Ireland budget is provided by the UK Treasury's Public Expenditure Statistical Analysis (PESA) data. PESA categorizes public expenditure by function, with housing expenditure collated under 'Housing and Community Amenities'. Table 6.1 shows that over the five-year period from 2003–04 to 2007–08, total expenditure on services increased each year while expenditure on Housing and Community Amenities increased in every year but one (2006–07). The percentages provided in Table 6.1 identify expenditure on Housing and Community Amenities as a proportion of total expenditure. It is reassuring to see that this figure also increased each year with the exception of 2006–07. Table 6.1 shows that per head of the Northern Ireland population, total expenditure on services increased each year, while Housing and Community Amenities expenditure increased in each year with the exception of 2006–07.

Figure 6.8 breaks total expenditure on Housing and Community Amenities into its sub-functions. Again, it is encouraging that expenditure on Housing Development increased in each year, with the exception of 2006–07.

The Budget for 2008–09 to 2010–11

Following the restoration of devolution in May 2007, the Northern Ireland Executive largely inherited its budget for 2007/08 from the direct rule administration. However, it was operational in time to shape the 2008–11 budget. The Northern Ireland Executive's Programme for Government (PFG)

Table 6.1 Identifiable expenditure on services in Northern Ireland in real terms.[99]

	2003–204	*2004–05*	*2005–06*	*2006–07*	*2007–08*
NI Total (£m)	14,848	15,380	15,871	16,053	16,863
Housing and Community Amenities (£m)	710 (4.8%)	866 (5.6%)	956 (6.0%)	889 (5.5%)	1,130 (6.7%)
PER CAPITA					
NI Total (£)	8,721	8,993	9,204	9,217	9,577
Housing and Community Amenities (£)	417	506	554	510	642

Source: PESA 2009 Tables 9.3, 9.4, 9.15.

99 2007–08 values.

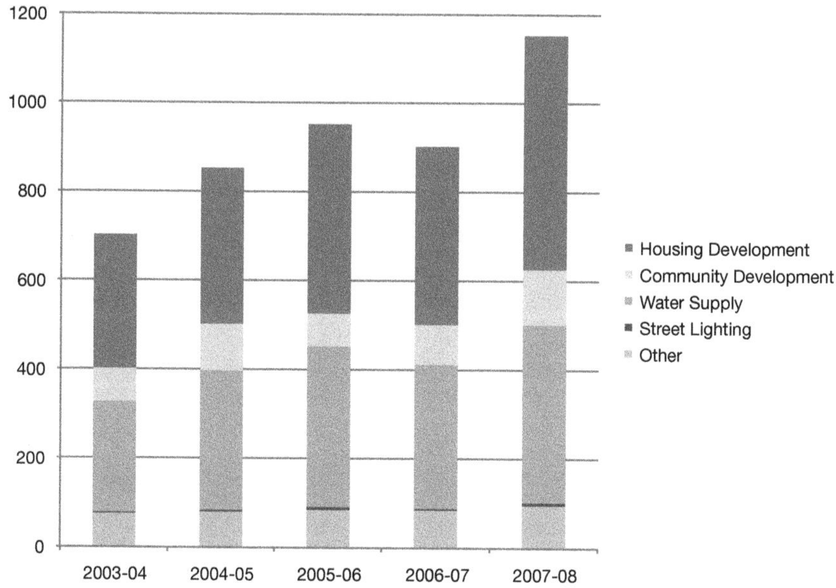

Figure 6.8 Housing and Community Amenities expenditure by sub-component (£m).[100]
Source: PESA 2009 Table 10.4.

2008–11 included social housing as a component of one of its twenty-three Public Service Agreements.[101]

Table 6.2 demonstrates how the budget attached to this PFG allocated current and capital (net of receipts) resources to the DSD, and how the DSD planned to divide its budget between its three main areas of responsibility (social security and child support, housing, and urban regeneration and community development). Percentages are provided for the DSD budget as a proportion of the total budget and for housing as a proportion of the DSD budget. It shows that, as a proportion of the Northern Ireland Executive's total budget, the DSD was much more significant in terms of capital expenditure (17.6 per cent net and 24.9 per cent gross) than current expenditure (6.1 per cent). Housing was the single most important area of current expenditure for the DSD (41.9 per cent) and constituted a majority (58.1 per cent) of its capital account.

To conclude, the figures presented in this section indicate that, during the period 2003–08 (with the exception of one year), funding for housing and community amenities increased. During the same period, however, housing

100 2007–08 values.

101 Public Service Agreements set out the NI Executive's objectives and associated actions and targets.

Table 6.2 Northern Ireland budget 2008–11 (£m).

	2008/09	*2009/10*	*2010/11*	*Total*	
CURRENT EXPENDITURE					
NI Total	8,308.8	8,596.9	8,972.4	25,878.1	
DSD	530.3 (6.4%)	523.4 (6.1%)	523.1 (5.8%)	1,576.8 (6.1%)	
Social Security and Child Support	243.5	242.5	244.2	730.2	
Housing	222.2 (41.9%)	219.5 (41.9%)	218.7 (41.8%)	660.4 (41.9%)	
Urban Regeneration and Community Development		63.6	522.7	60.1	646.4
CAPITAL EXPENDITURE (NET OF RECEIPTS)					
NI Total	1,318.5	1,393.1	1,412.9	4,124.5	
DSD	223.7 (17.0%)	220.3 (15.8%)	283.4 (20.1%)	727.4 (17.6%)	
Social Security and Child Support	65.4	2.9	2.9	71.2	
Housing	90.6 (40.5%)	153.8 (69.8%)	178.0 (62.8%)	422.4 (58.1%)	
Urban Regeneration and Community Development		67.4	63.0	101.3	231.7
CAPITAL EXPENDITURE (GROSS)					
NI Total	1,804.5	1,659.6	2,025.3	5,489.40	
DSD	407.8 (22.6%)	388.5 (23.4%)	571.7 (28.2%)	1,368.00 (24.9%)	

Source: *Northern Ireland Executive. Budget 2008–11*, pages 58, 112, 113 and 146.

waiting lists as well as households presenting to be in housing stress increased, indicating a worsening housing situation. There is evidence of a disjunction between the progress of realization of the right to adequate housing in Northern Ireland and the resources directed towards this end. For this reason, the next three sections will look in more depth at the model of mixed funding for social housing, investment in social housing, and the role of the private rented sector in accommodating low-income households.

The model of mixed funding for social housing

As explained in 'The Historical Context to Social Housing', housing associations have been given important responsibilities for the provision of social housing. This section explains how housing associations finance social housing. It then considers this funding model from a human rights perspective. The analysis raises doubts about whether this model represents the most effective use of the available resources in giving effect to all aspects of the right to adequate housing. The section then outlines concerns about levels of affordability in housing-association-provided housing. Finally, issues relating to transparency and accountability are identified.

Housing Association finance

Since 1998 housing associations have financed their responsibilities for social housing from three main sources:

- Housing Association Grant (HAG) from the DSD;
- Borrowing;
- Reserves (including revenue from rent and receipts from house sales).

The Housing Association Grant typically constitutes approximately two-thirds of the funding for social housing with the remaining third covered by a mixture of private finance and its own financial reserves.[102] This model effectively means that social housing is financed through Public-Private Partnership (PPP). However, PPP models can take various forms. Two features of the use of housing associations are of particular note. First, the private partners in this case (housing associations) do not operate on a profit-making basis.[103] Instead, housing association surpluses are reinvested in housing. Second, in this instance, a PPP was not adopted on the commonly asserted basis that the private sector (housing associations) could provide services more efficiently and effectively than the public sector (NIHE).[104] As Paris stated, the Housing Executive 'demonstrated over many years its ability to produce good quality new social housing'.[105] The single rationale was that housing associations could raise additional finance while central government rules barred the NIHE from doing so.[106]

102 V. Hewitt, *Mitigating the Recession: Options for the Northern Ireland Executive,* Research Paper No. 37, Economic Research Institute of Northern Ireland (2009) 3.

103 See Housing Northern Ireland Order 1992 Article 3(b) – definition of a 'housing association': body of trustees or company which does not trade for profit or whose constitution or rules prohibit the issue of capital with interest or dividend exceeding such rate as may be prescribed by the Department of Finance and Personnel, whether with or without differentiation between share and loan capital.

104 For example, Wilson refers to 'the repeated- though not evidence-based – assertion [. . .] that the private sector has "skills" which make it *inherently* more efficient than the public sector'. Robin Wilson, 'Private Partners and the Public Good' (2002) 53 *Northern Ireland Legal Quarterly* 454, 457.

105 House of Commons Northern Ireland Affairs Select Committee, *Social Housing Provision in Northern Ireland: Sixth Report of Session* (HC 2003–04 493) Q317.

106 Ibid, memorandum submitted by CIH.

In transferring its responsibilities to third parties, such as housing associations (and there is a question mark as to whether housing associations are, in fact, non-state third parties[107]) states are required to protect against interference with the enjoyment of the right to housing by third parties. States have to ensure that existing access is maintained and that the obligation to fulfil is not hampered or negatively affected by the transfer or delegation of the service. Even if the state has delegated a function or service to a private body, the state retains its duties under international human rights law.

Maximum available resources

In this context, it is important to consider the ESR implications of borrowing through housing associations rather than the NIHE. The former DSD Minister Ritchie articulated the main benefit in the following manner:

> Housing associations, unlike the Housing Executive, can attract private finance without it scoring as public expenditure. Therefore housing associations can deliver more social housing for a given amount of public funding. Since the introduction of private finance, housing associations have raised some £340 million in private funding, which means that they have provided the equivalent of about 5,000 new homes at no cost to the Exchequer.[108]

At face value, by generating resources additional to government allocation, this business model seems entirely consistent with the duty to employ the MAR. However, it is important to challenge the notion, commonly expressed in relation to PPP, that the borrowing of the private partners imposes 'no cost to the Exchequer.'[109] For it is typically government that guarantees, if not provides, the revenue streams with which the debt is repaid. Thus, in the case of housing associations, debt is repaid using rental income[110] and capital receipts from the sale of housing units – revenue foregone by the NIHE in the transfer

107 In England, Housing Associations have been declared to be examples of a 'hybrid public authority' for the purposes of the Human Rights Act; they are also amendable to judicial review. See *R. (Weaver) v London and Quadrant Housing Trust* [2009] EWCA Civ 587, [2010] 1 WLR 363. There does not seem to be any reason why this would not apply to housing associations in Northern Ireland. From a human rights perspective, the main point is that the state remains ultimately responsible regardless of whether housing associations are considered private, public or hybrid bodies.

108 NI Assembly Debate, *Official Report* (Hansard), 2 July 2007. Available at http://archive.niassembly.gov.uk/record/reports2007/070702.htm (accessed 10 May 2013).

109 This sentiment is described as the 'something for nothing' fallacy in Robin Wilson, 'Private Partners and the Public Good' (2002) 53 *Northern Ireland Legal Quarterly* 454, 457.

110 In 2008–09 total rental income collected by housing associations was £117.2m. DSD, *Northern Ireland Housing Statistics 2008–09* (2009) 64.

of responsibility for new build to housing associations. Therefore, the main financial benefit of the use of housing associations is that it defers a proportion of the capital expenditure for new build, and allows it to be repaid over a longer period. Of course, this benefit could also have been realized if the NIHE had been permitted to supplement its grant with borrowing. The *financial* benefits of using housing associations as a proxy for borrowing, as opposed to equipping the NIHE to borrow, are therefore questionable in the long term. Indeed, as we shall see below, the use of housing associations has introduced both financial and non-monetary costs. The primary value of PPP may therefore derive from the fact that, as an exercise in 'creative accounting'[111] the borrowing of private bodies is not counted as public sector debt. By keeping such debt off-budget,[112] governments could comply with EU restrictions on capital borrowing at the same time as enjoying the political benefits[113] of high levels of investment and the appearance of fiscal prudence.[114]

In addition, the use of PPP often carries costs. In relation to the financing of social housing in Northern Ireland, one potential issue relates to the terms upon which housing associations can access borrowing. It is generally the case that public sector bodies will be able to borrow on more favourable terms than non-public sector organizations.[115] This is aggravated by the small size of many housing associations.[116]

Furthermore, with housing associations negotiating multiple loans, as opposed to a single body such as the NIHE, additional transaction costs are likely to be incurred. If housing associations are unable to borrow on as favourable a basis as the NIHE, it raises a concern in relation to the MAR. The NIFHA has acknowledged that 'private borrowing is expensive and limited'.[117] That said, in the benign economic environment that prevailed before the recent economic crisis, these weaknesses were unlikely to have been fully exposed. A 2009 House of Commons Committee report on *Housing and the*

111 Bernardino Benito, Vincente Montesinos and Francica Bastida, 'An Example of Public Sector Creative Accounting in Public Sector: The Private Financing of Infrastructures in Spain" (2008) 19 *Critical Perspectives on Accounting* 963, 965.

112 That is, not counted in the budget.

113 Michael Spackman, 'Public-Private Partnerships: Lessons from the British Approach' (2002) 26 *Economic Systems* 283, 288.

114 'PFI contracts allow incumbents to invest in new infrastructures, which have a positive impact on voters' opinion about them, while deferring the payments of the infrastructure'. Bernardino Benito, Vicente Montesinos and Francisco Bastida, 'An Example of Creative Accounting in Public Sector: The Private Financing of Infrastructures in Spain' (2008) 19 *Critical Perspectives on Accounting* 963–86, 966.

115 Michael Spackman, 'Public-Private Partnerships: Lessons from the British Approach' (2002) *Economic Systems* 283, 295.

116 House of Commons Northern Ireland Affairs Select Committee, *Social Housing Provision in Northern Ireland: Sixth Report of Session 2003–04* (HC 2003–2004 493) Q11.

117 NIFHA, *Evidence to the Commission on the Future for Housing in Northern Ireland* (2009) 3.

Credit Crunch noted that, prior to the economic downturn, housing associations in England were 'recognized as a good Triple A investment' and were 'able to secure loans at very competitive rates'.[118] However, in the difficult financial environment that has followed the global economic crisis, this may no longer obtain. The aforementioned House of Commons Committee found evidence that since the credit crunch, lending institutions have become more stringent in regard to both the amount and terms of borrowing to associations,[119] and are even 'seeking to toughen up the terms of existing loans to housing associations'.[120]

There is also a potential loss of economies of scale in moving from a single body to a multiple provider system. The NIHE had anticipated that housing associations would merge in order to reclaim economies of scale,[121] but this has not materialized to date. The House of Commons Committee report on *Housing and the Credit Crunch* (2009) noted that lending institutions may actually create a barrier to such restructuring.[122]

As the obligation of MAR refers to all resources (including those of a human, organizational or technical nature), and not just financial resources, a further issue is the potential loss of the NIHE's expertise in bringing forward large-scale developments. This concern was raised during an investigation by the Northern Ireland Affairs Select Committee into *Social Housing Provision in Northern Ireland* (2004). In his testimony to the Committee, John Perry, a Policy Advisor with the Chartered Institute of Housing, stated that 'one of the difficulties with the [housing] associations is that only a handful really have the capacity to undertake new development'.[123] The Committee also received a testimony from Professor Paddy Gray who, in response to the question 'what would you see as the major reason why the housing association movement in Northern Ireland has not been able to hit the targets that have been set?' declared that 'possibly the [housing] association movement is still relatively small and does not have the expertise of delivering a new build programme that the Housing Executive has'.[124]

If this loss of expertise has impacted on the delivery of new build it would represent a failure to maximize resources that consequently impinges on the progressive realization of the right to housing. However, when the interim report of the *Review into Affordable Housing* voiced 'doubts about the capacity

118 House of Commons Communities and Local Government Committee, *Housing and the Credit Crunch: Third Report of Session 2008–09* (HC 2008–2009 101) 27.

119 Ibid 27.

120 Ibid 28.

121 NIHE, *Building on Success: Northern Ireland Housing Executive Response* (1996) 39.

122 Ibid 28.

123 House of Commons Northern Ireland Affairs Select Committee, *Social Housing Provision in Northern Ireland. Sixth Report of Session 2003–04* (HC 2003–2004 493) Q9.

124 Ibid Q318.

of housing associations to deliver an enhanced social [housing] programme'[125] the NIHE and the NIFHA rejected this.[126]

Affordability

Another issue relevant to the use of PPP is that additional costs are often incurred by the public in the form of user fees. Figure 6.9 compares real average weekly rent levels within the NIHE and housing associations. However, caution should be exercised in directly comparing the NIHE and housing association rents as they do not account for factors such as differences in house size, age of dwellings, and standard of design area.

Nevertheless comparing average weekly rent levels does provide an indication of different levels of affordability. Figure 6.9 shows that between 2000–01 and 2008–09 average rents increased much more dramatically in relation to housing association tenancies (41.6 per cent) than was the case

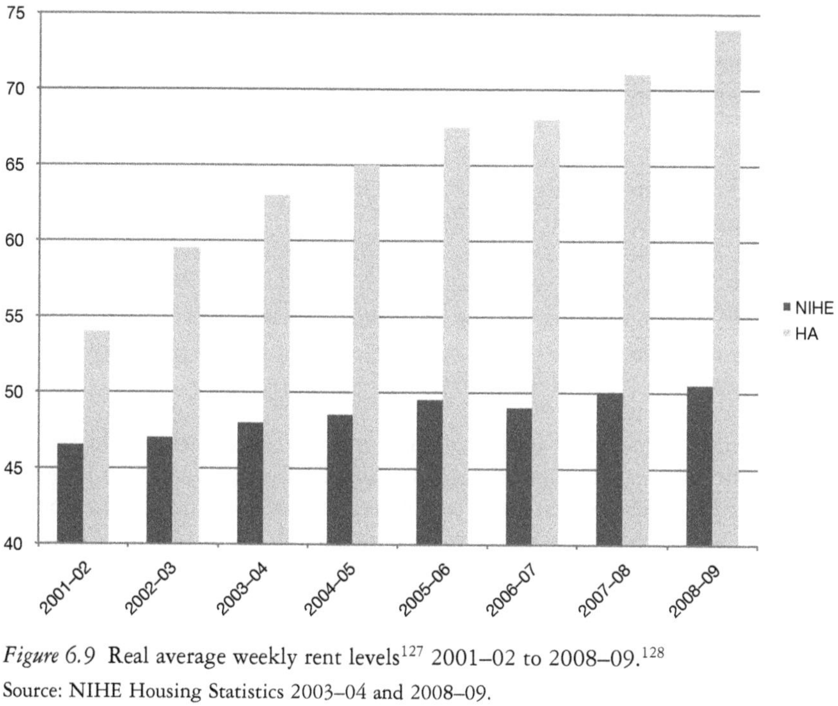

Figure 6.9 Real average weekly rent levels[127] 2001–02 to 2008–09.[128]

Source: NIHE Housing Statistics 2003–04 and 2008–09.

125 John Semple, *Review into Affordable Housing: Interim Report* (2006) 29.

126 NIHE and NIFHA, *Response to the Recommendations of the Review into Affordable Housing Interim Report* (2007) 10.

127 Inclusive of rates and service charges.

128 2008–09 values.

with regard to NIHE tenancies (10.3 per cent). Consequently, the difference in real average rent levels between the NIHE and housing associations increased from £4.81 per week in 2000–01 to £22.63 per week in 2008–09.

According to the ComESCR, housing-related costs should be affordable and commensurate with income levels[129] and tenants must be protected against unreasonable rent levels.[130] In this context, the ability of housing associations relative to the NIHE to provide affordable rent levels is a matter of concern, given that both NIHE and housing associations are typically providing accommodation to lower-income groups.[131]

Transparency and accountability

Having taken over significant public functions, it is a crucial aspect of the right to adequate housing that the practices and performance of housing associations are transparent and subject to the scrutiny and oversight of the state. With this in mind, it is of concern that housing associations, unlike the NIHE, are not listed under 'public bodies' in Schedule 1 of the Freedom of Information Act 2000. This was highlighted in the course of the research for this chapter; following a DSD press release publicizing a loan obtained by housing associations, the authors submitted the following questions to the DSD:[132]

- How is the interest rate calculated (including any floors and ceilings)?
- What is the repayment schedule?
- What other costs are associated with the borrowing (e.g., arrangement fees)?
- What security was provided by Housing Associations?
- What precisely is the borrowing to be used to deliver (e.g., how many housing units will the loan finance)?

The response of the DSD indicated that the only information held by the department was that 'the investment will help deliver a total of 26 schemes across Northern Ireland' that are to be delivered by five housing associations.[133] While not subject to FOI legislation, housing associations may well be covered

129 ComESCR, *General Comment No. 4, The Right to Adequate Housing*, paragraph 8(c).

130 Ibid, paragraph 8(c).

131 In 2007 the average gross weekly household income for a household in social housing was £260 compared to £579 for those who owned their home outright and £739 who owned their home with a mortgage. DSD, *Northern Ireland Housing Statistics 2008–09* (2009) 76.

132 Northern Ireland Executive, *Record £30 million European Housing Investment Welcomed – Ritchie* (09/12/09). Available at www.northernireland.gov.uk/news/news-dsd/news-dsd-0312009-record-european-housing.htm (accessed 21 June 2010).

133 Specifically, Fold (3 schemes), Helm (3), North and West (2), Oaklee (4), and Trinity (14).

by other legislation requiring transparency in at least some situations; e.g., they may be covered by the Environmental Information Regulations (EIR).[134] The DSD stated that these regulations cover a similar release for much material covered by FOI and could therefore in effect deliver the same results.[135]

Given that housing associations receive the majority of their funding from the public purse and exist to provide a public service, a greater degree of governmental scrutiny of the financial transactions carried out by housing associations is to be expected. The fact that the DSD does not have details of this loan suggests that such accountability is not in place and that the DSD is lacking in oversight over these bodies.

The issue of accountability was also highlighted in the course of a Northern Ireland Public Accounts Committee investigation into the DSD's regulation of housing association rent arrears management. It noted a failure by the DSD's regulatory framework to detect 'significant deficiencies in the quality and completeness of the annual data collected from [Housing] Associations'[136] and reported an acknowledgement by the DSD Accounting Officer that:

> in the past, the Department has not afforded a top priority to regulating Housing Associations, partly because they represented a small proportion of the housing stock and partly because they are not public bodies. He pointed to recent expansions in staff numbers and regulatory activity in the Department as evidence that things have moved on.[137]

A multi-provider system may also lead to confusion around roles, provoke difficulties in co-ordination and facilitate greater scope for variation in standards on service provision,[138] impacting on the equal enjoyment of the right to housing.

In conclusion, this section has explained how housing associations finance social housing. The chapter has raised a number of key concerns about this model. Specifically there are questions as to whether this use of resources ensures

134 Relevant decisions of the Information Commissioner Office are Belfast Improved Housing Association Decision Notice FER 0152607 and Wesley Housing Association Decision Notice FER 149772 taken from www.ico.org.uk/upload/documents/decisionnotices/2008/fer_0152607.pdf (accessed 20 May 2013).

135 Personal communication dated 14 May 2010 with DSD, on file with the authors.

136 Public Accounts Committee, *Report on the Management of Social Housing Rent Collection and Arrears* (2009) paragraph 37 available at http://archive.niassembly.gov.uk/public/2007mandate/reports/2009/Report_16_09_10R.htm (accessed 20 May 2013).

137 Ibid, paragraph 37.

138 Eoin Rooney, *Failing to Deliver* (St Patrick's and St Joseph's Housing Committee, Belfast 2007); NIFHA, *Evidence to the Commission on the Future for Housing in Northern Ireland* (2009) 1; Commission on the Future for Housing in Northern Ireland, *A Key Issues Paper from the Independent Commission* (2009) 28.

the most effective and expeditious progression towards the full right to adequate housing; questions of the affordability of rent in housing association tenancies, and finally questions about transparency and accountability. The next section examines the levels of finance that this model has levered into new social housing build.

Investment in social housing

This section examines issues relating to investment in social housing. The first part looks at the statistics concerning overall levels of investment and compares them with NIHE projections of the level of new build required in Northern Ireland. It then discusses land costs, which represents a major proportion of expenditure on new social housing. Finally, this section examines the issue of the reliance on capital receipts to fund social housing new build.

Total expenditure on new build

Figure 6.10 shows the level of expenditure on new build between 1998–9 and 2008–09. In the graph:

- 'Public' expenditure refers to HAG as well as NIHE expenditure, which sharply receded after 1998.

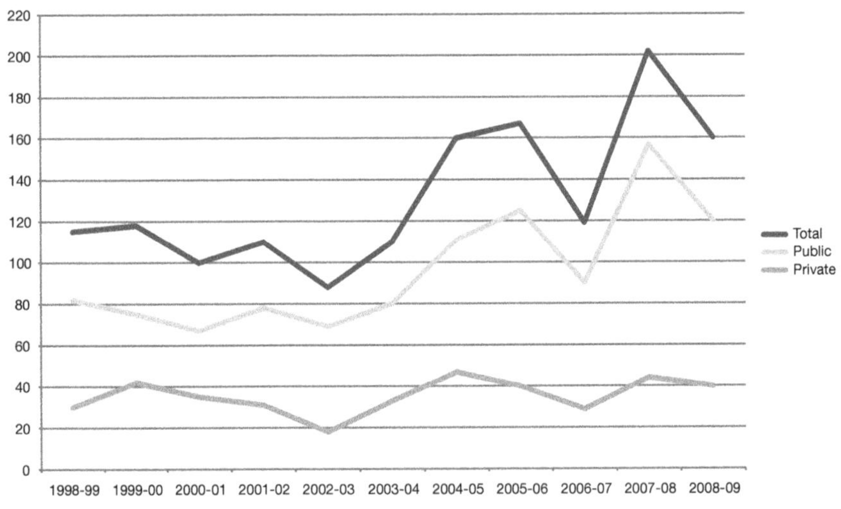

Figure 6.10 Investment in new social build (£m) 1998–9 to 2008–09.[139]

Source: NI Housing Statistics 2001–02, 2004–05 and 2008–09.

139 2008–09 values.

- 'Private' expenditure refers to the investment of housing associations (through borrowing and reserves).
- 'Total' expenditure represents the sum total of public and private expenditure.

Given the increase in need highlighted in the section 'Social Housing from a Human Rights Perspective' above, a corresponding increase in investment might be expected in order to ensure progressive realization of the right to housing. However, Figure 6.10 reveals that there has not been a consistent linear increase in total investment. That said, the highest levels of both public and private expenditure are in the second half of this eleven-year period, with a peak of £201.3m of total expenditure on new build in 2007–08.

A key issue is the extent to which such financial investment is translated into housing units. In the context of rising need, an increasing level of completions might be expected in order to prevent retrogression. However Figure 6.11, which displays the level of new build for the period from 1998–9 to 2008–09, shows that this did not occur. Indeed with house sales continuing to exceed new build,[140] the total stock of social housing continued to decline, although there has been a slight improvement since 2006–07 (Figure 6.12) due to the collapse in house sales.

The NIHE acknowledges that '[s]ince 2001 the Social Housing Development Programme has failed to keep pace with the steadily rising need for

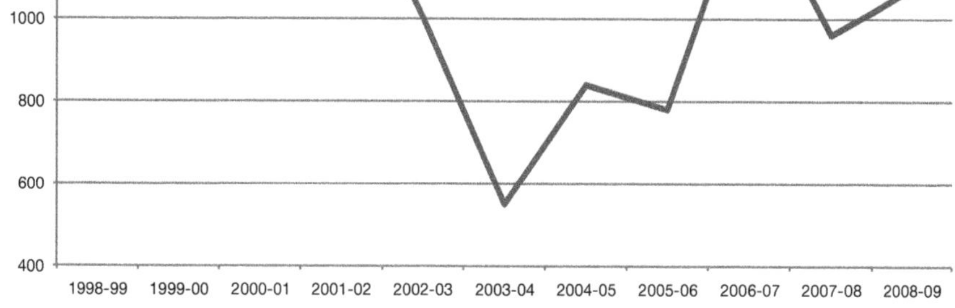

Figure 6.11 New social build 1998–9 to 2008–09.

Source: DSD. NI Housing Statistics 2000–01, 2004–05 and 2008–09.

140 Previous to 2001–02 stock data was collected on an annual year basis and is not comparable with post 2001–02 financial year figures.

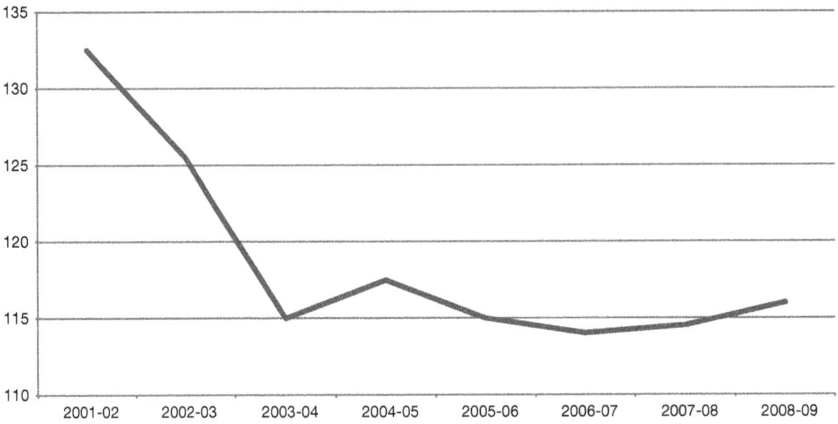

Figure 6.12 Social housing stock (000's) 2003–04 to 2008–09.
Source: NI Housing Statistics 2003–04 and 2008–09.

social housing'.[141] Since 2001, the NIHE has largely based its own estimate of the need for new build on the Net Stock Model and Cambridge Model.[142] In 2001, these respective models indicated a need for an average of 1,400 and 1,500 new homes per year over the period 2001–11. A 2004 review of the Net Stock and Cambridge models indicated a need for 1,600 and 1,700 new builds respectively. However, as the models did not account for the failure to hit new build targets in previous years, the NIHE estimated that 2,000 new dwellings were required between 2004 and 2011. Further updates of the Net Stock Model occurred in 2006 and 2008. On the basis of the most recent estimate in 2009, and taking into account an accumulated backlog of 4,465 new builds between 2001 and 2008, the NIHE estimates that 'at least 3,000 new social dwellings should be constructed each year'.[143] There is not necessarily a direct relationship between more investment and new build as a variety of factors will determine the amount of dwellings produced for a given level of expenditure. However, it seems that a substantial increase in funding is essential, if not in itself sufficient, to deliver the level of new build that is both deemed necessary by the NIHE and required if the right to adequate housing is to be progressively realized.

141 NIHE, *Northern Ireland Housing Market: Review and Perspectives 2009–2012* (2009) 18.
142 These models base their projections on a range of demographic and housing data. For more information see NIHE, ibid 44.
143 Ibid 45.

Expenditure on land

One reason why more expenditure on new build will not necessarily result in more housing is that the costs of development may increase. One such cost is the purchase of land. Land costs have been linked to the rise in housing prices by the Special Rapporteur.[144] This international trend appears to be reflected in Northern Ireland. In the period following the establishment of devolution, the market value of land increased at a remarkable rate. Table 6.3 shows the land values for Northern Ireland using a simple average of land costs in each District Council. In 2006, the market value for 'small sites' was 3.7 times that of 2000. For 'bulk land', the 2006 value was 3.1 times the 2000 price.[145]

This rise in land costs has impacted upon housing expenditure for social housing, as the NIHE purchases land at market value. The NIHE stated that in 2007 'the escalation in land values means that 50% of the cost of a new build property is now attributable to the price of land, with £100,000 typically being the land cost for a new semi-detached house'.[146] The NIHE has also commented that despite demand from elderly people for bungalows, these 'are not being built due to high land values'.[147] High land costs may also encourage the development of high-rise accommodation. While permitting more homes to be built on a given area of land, high-rise flats may be less conducive to health[148] and family life[149] than houses.

According to the Semple *Review into Affordable Housing* the 'very rapid rise in land costs [was] fuelled by land banking and speculation'.[150] Land banking

Table 6.3 Northern Ireland nominal residential building land costs (£'000 per Ha).[151]

	2000	*2001*	*2002*	*2003*	*2004*	*2005*	*2006*
Small Sites	397	449	519	666	862	1,315	1,878
Annual Increase	–	13.1%	15.6%	28.3%	29.4%	52.6%	42.8%
Bulk Land	406	457	515	608	810	1,191	1,666
Annual Increase	–	12.6%	12.7%	18.1%	33.2%	47.0%	39.9%

Source: Review into Affordable Housing, Interim Report Annex 2.

144 Ibid, paragraph 46.

145 The 2006 values are the most recent values available. The Semple report did not provide a definition of 'small sites' or 'bulk land'.

146 NIHE, *The NI Housing Market: Drivers and Policies* (2007) 16.

147 Ibid 45.

148 Tim Blackman, Eileen Evason, Martin Melaugh and Roberta Woods, 'Housing and Health: A Case Study of Two Areas in West Belfast' (1989) 18 *Journal of Social Policy*, 1.

149 This is, however, a contentious and complex matter. See J.S. Fuerst and Roy Petty, 'High-rise Housing for Low-Income Families' (1991) 103 *Public Interest*, 108.

150 John Semple, *Review into Affordable Housing: Interim Report* (2006) 10.

151 The figure for Northern Ireland is a simple average of the average land costs in each District Council.

involves purchasing land and leaving it dormant, in the expectation (or knowledge) that the area will, at a later point in time, be 'zoned' for development, multiplying its market value. Discussing this practice in the Republic of Ireland, Drudy and Punch describe it as representing 'unearned' financial gain as it yields substantial profits without adding social value.[152] Indeed it may represent a social cost if it involves taxpayers paying more to secure land for social housing.[153]

Land is a crucial resource in the progressive realization of the right to adequate housing. If land is not productively used to contribute to that progressive achievement it may represent a failure on the part of the state to use maximum available resources. By taking up an excessive proportion of the housing budget, high land costs leave less funding available for other components of building social housing (for example, construction costs). In turn, this hampers the progressive realization of the right to adequate housing. As has already been highlighted, the ComESCR states in its *General Comment No. 4* that policies and legislation should 'not be designed to benefit already advantaged social groups at the expense of others'.[154] Excessive land costs unduly benefit a privileged group of landowners at the expense of both homebuyers (who have land costs passed on to them in the form of higher house prices, consequently impacting on their right to affordable housing) and taxpayers (who pay more for land for social housing). While the recent economic collapse might suggest that land prices will reduce to a more affordable level, landowners may be reluctant to sell in such an economic climate. Indeed, due to the reliance of the new build programme on capital receipts, the funding difficulties may, if anything, be further exacerbated by the collapse in property values. This is discussed in more detail in the sub-section below.

Reliance on capital receipts

The new build programme relies in part on receipts from the NIHE land and house sales. Consequently, the collapse in property values has had a direct impact on the resourcing of social housing. Figure 6.13 shows the fall in NIHE capital receipts from land and house sales.

The DSD estimated that this created a shortfall of £85m in the social housing programme for 2009/10. According to former DSD Minister Ritchie this was

152 P.J. Drudy and Michael Punch, *Out of Reach: Inequalities in the Irish Housing System* (TASC 2005) 16.

153 The profits to be made from zoning decisions are potentially corrupting of political and administrative systems. For example, in the Republic of Ireland corruption in relation to planning permission and re-zoning has been under investigation by the Mahon Tribunal since 1997 and its revelations contributed to the resignation of the Irish Taoiseach in 2008.

154 ComESCR, *General Comment No. 4, The Right to Adequate Housing*, paragraph 9.

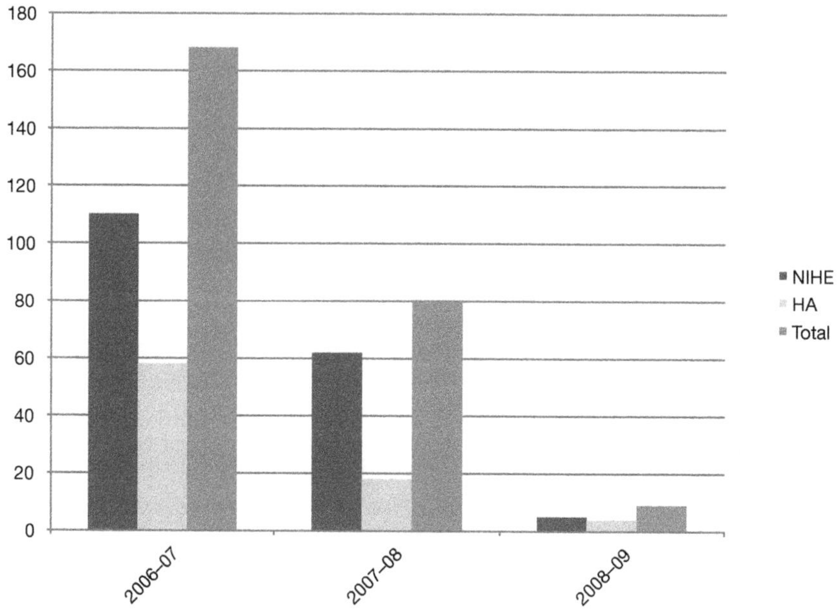

Figure 6.13 NIHE capital receipts (£m) 2006–07 to 2008–09.[155]
Source: NI Housing Statistics 2008–09.

reduced to £35m 'through in-year monitoring rounds and diversions of DSD resources from other budget lines'.[156] However, the Minister added that a shortfall of £100m was anticipated for each of the next two financial years, which 'is equivalent to the loss of 1,000 new build houses per annum'.[157] The reliance of the social housing budget on land and house sales means that the new build programme is continually at risk.

While it appears that the new build programme is expected to bear the brunt of the cost of any shortfall in projected receipts from house and land sales, any surpluses from house and land sales are not automatically invested in new stock. Indeed, a Northern Ireland Affairs Select Committee heard evidence that the budget for new social build was cut at the same time as a substantial surplus from social house sales was generated. When the Minister of State in the Northern Ireland Office (John Spellar) informed the Committee

155 2008–09 values.
156 NI Assembly, *Debate. Official Report* (Hansard) 2 February 2009. Available at http://archive.niassembly.gov.uk/record/reports2008/090202.htm (accessed 15 September 2009).
157 Ibid.

that the DSD had reduced its new build target to 1,300 as the Department 'only have funding for 1,300',[158] the Committee concluded that it was:

> wrong that the target has been arbitrarily reduced from 1,750 to 1,300 houses in the current year because funding has only been made available for the smaller number. This is particularly unfortunate when, despite strong evidence of escalating housing stress and homelessness, around £37 million annually from record levels of sales of existing Housing Executive stock is returned to the Treasury, when that could be used for the benefit of the homeless.[159]

The inflated nature of the land market was highlighted by the 'correction' that followed the economic collapse of 2007. This provided a politically opportune time to address land banking and excessive land prices, which had hampered the social housing programme. There are a number of ways in which land costs could be maintained at a level that would be fair and reasonable to all parties. The NIHE and the NIFHA 'agree that appropriate measures should be put in place to discourage developers from "sitting on" land that is appropriate or zoned for housing provision while its value inflates'[160] and suggested a range of measures that might assist in delivering land at a reasonable price, including making greater use of the NIHE's existing vesting powers.[161] Even before the current economic crisis, the Semple review also made various proposals on this issue. It called on the Planning Service to 'take advantage of any opportunity that arise to dezone housing land which is being withheld for speculative reasons'[162] and requested that the DSD 'monitor the effectiveness of the Northern Ireland Housing Executive's existing powers and consider strengthening them, if necessary'.[163] More broadly, Semple recommended that the Department for Regional Development and the Department of the Environment devise a new system for planning by 2009.

The Executive had an opportunity to address the issue of speculation in the course of a DFP review of the domestic rating system, commissioned in 2007. The review considered a tax on derelict land:

> The rationale behind this proposal was that it would act as a disincentive to excess land banking, whereby developers and others hold on to land with the aim of making capital gains. The intention was that this

158 House of Commons Northern Ireland Affairs Select Committee, *Social Housing Provision in Northern Ireland: Sixth Report of Session 2003–04* (HC 2003–2004 493) 17.

159 Ibid.

160 NIHE and NIFHA, *Response to the Recommendations of the Review into Affordable Housing Interim Report* (2007) 15.

161 Ibid 5.

162 John Semple, *Review into Affordable Housing: Final Report* (2007) 4.

163 Ibid.

would free up further sites for development, assist with the issue of housing affordability, as well as bringing broader economic development and regeneration benefits.[164]

However, in October 2008 the former DFP Minister, Nigel Dodds, announced that the tax would not be introduced, on the following basis:

> the market conditions which led to the development of this proposal have reversed since the time of the rating review in 2007. The supply of development land has increased and prices have dropped dramatically, with increasing pressures on the development sector and in particular the viability of house building . . . It would not be right to proceed further with the proposal during the life of this current Assembly, a move which I hope will be welcomed by the development sector, which has enough to contend with at the moment, without the prospect of a new tax on land holdings.[165]

The ComESCR has noted that the Covenant obligations 'are perhaps even more pertinent during times of economic contraction'.[166] However, the above rationale suggests that the interests of landowners, who benefited considerably from the bubble in land and property values during the 'boom years', at the expense of the general public, are also to be prioritized in the midst of a property crash. The DFP's rejection of a derelict land tax is arguably a lost opportunity to bring land into productive use at a price that provides the taxpayer with value for money, as it fails to challenge the attractiveness to landowners of retaining derelict land. This raises issues in relation to the obligation to fulfil the right to adequate housing if the practice of land banking impedes the state's ability to directly provide adequate housing to those who need, and are entitled to it. A tax on derelict land is only one option available to government and if other means prove more effective then it may be unnecessary. The key point is that the rationale proffered by the DFP does not appear to be consistent with the state's obligations under ICESCR.

Diverting resources away from ESR realization, rather than reinvesting them, raises serious issues with regard to the duty to use the MAR. The DSD has argued for 'a decoupling of the housing budget from asset sales'.[167] In the context of declining resources, the state has a duty to give priority to the protection of the poor. Given the importance of social housing to the most

164 DFP, *Review of Domestic Rating: A Consultation Report* (2009) 50.

165 Northern Ireland Executive, *Dodds Announces Decision Not to Introduce Derelict Land Tax* (23 October 2008). Available at www.northernireland.gov.uk/news-dfp-231008-derelict-land-tax (accessed 14 November 2009).

166 ComESCR, *General Comment No. 4, The Right to Adequate Housing*, paragraph 11.

167 H. Cousins, *Housing is a Bright Star in the Executive Firmament. Irish News* (2 January 2010).

deprived sections of the population, the state would be expected to seek to protect the social housing budget and to make any necessary cuts in areas that do not impact to the same extent on the most deprived. This raises issues around equality as the ComESCR has specifically stated that the most vulnerable need to receive a certain degree of priority protection in the housing sphere.[168] Therefore, a human rights perspective would lend support to the position of the DSD that new housing should not be reliant on receipts from the sale of land and dwellings.

To sum up, this section has highlighted some of the issues affecting investment in social housing. While there was an overall increase in investment, there had not been a steady progression. Crucially, the investment still failed to provide adequate levels of new build. One reason for this is that a high proportion of the budget for new build was being expended on excessive land costs. Investment was also put at risk by the reliance on capital receipts from sales. In a turbulent economic climate this attracts obvious risks. Given the lack of social housing, many low-income households have had to rely on the private rented sector for accommodation. The implications of this use of the private sector for the right to adequate housing are considered in the next section.

Use of the private rented sector

With home ownership increasingly unaffordable and access to social housing increasingly limited, a greater number of households looked to the Private Rented Sector (PRS) for accommodation.[169] This section considers the role of the PRS in addressing housing need and identifies concerns about this approach. Specifically, the provision for transparency, participation and consultation in the PRS is weak when compared to social housing. There are problems of affordability of PRS housing. Finally, the use of the PRS to house tenants in receipt of housing benefit may not constitute the most effective use of available resources in progressively realising the right to adequate housing.

The role of the private rented sector

In 2001/02, the private rented sector constituted 7.0 per cent of occupied housing stock (Figure 6.14). By 2008/09, its share had risen to 13.1 per cent.[170]

168 ComESCR, *General Comment No. 4, The Right to Adequate Housing*, paragraph 8(e).

169 A tenant survey identified 'difficulties in accessing social housing as the main reason for choosing to live in private rented accommodation'. NIHE, *The Private Rented Sector in Northern Ireland* (2007) 33.

170 DSD, *Northern Ireland Housing Statistics 2008–09* (2009) 24.

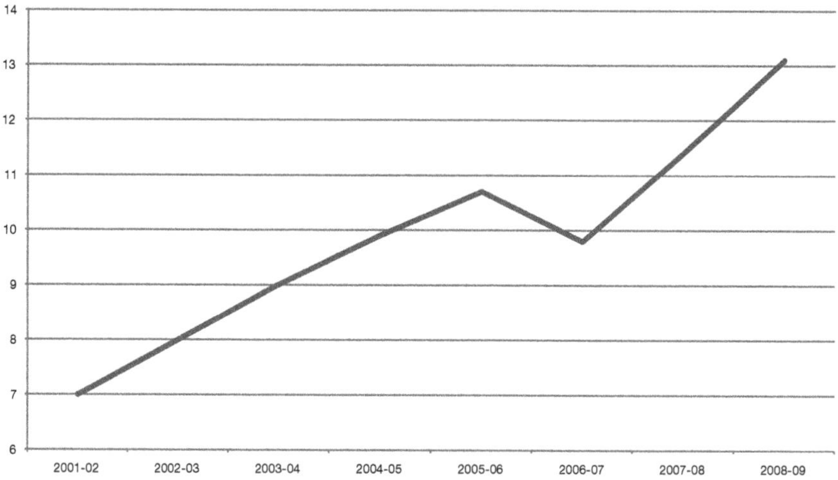

Figure 6.14 Private rented sector as percentage of occupied housing stock, 2001–02 to 2008–09.

Source: DSD. NI Housing Statistics 2004–05 and 2008–09.

Of particular interest to this research, which is focused on expenditure related to social housing, is the fact that with low-income households increasingly unable to access social housing, the private rented sector has been increasingly 'housing the type of tenants traditionally associated with social housing.'[171] As many low-income tenants have their rent subsidized by housing benefit, this in effect means that the government is subsidizing the private rented sector.

Indeed, such is the level of public subsidy, it could be argued that the private rented sector has largely become an extension of social housing provision: in 2004/05, 38,300 private rented sector tenants were in receipt of housing benefit. In some areas, this constituted as much as ninety per cent of private renting tenants.[172]

The practice of subsidizing the private rented sector to accommodate low-income households has multiple ESR-related consequences. It arguably constitutes a creative attempt to facilitate access to housing in the context of the state's failure to allocate sufficient resources to new build. However, the suitability of the private rented sector to accommodate low-income households, relative to social housing, is a concern.

171 NIHE, *The Private Rented Sector in Northern Ireland* (2007) 8.
172 Ibid 31.

Transparency, participation and consultation

Transparency is one issue. While the rights of NIHE tenants are clearly set out in the NIHE Tenants' Handbook, the private rented sector is weakly regulated. For example, private landlords are currently not required to register with the state, albeit proposals to increase protection of private sector tenants are currently under debate.[173] Legislation provides better protection for NIHE and housing association tenants than for tenants in the private sector; this is especially true as regards participation and information rights. The Housing (Northern Ireland) Order 1983 and the Housing Northern Ireland Order 2003 grant the right to consultation and access to information for housing associations and NIHE tenants.[174] There are some gaps in this protection in relation to the scope of issues subject to consultation and limitations in terms of introductory tenants.[175] The point is, however, that such protection is completely absent from the private rented sector. In addition, tenant associations in the social housing sector provide tenants with an opportunity to organize, raise concerns collectively and participate in decision-making. Such mechanisms contribute to the right to freedom of association and the right to participate in public decision-making.[176] They are not available in the private rented sector.

The duty to ensure that those who are affected by the decisions taken have an opportunity to participate in the decision-making is an integral aspect of the rights under ICESCR and is of immediate effect.[177] The right to participate

173 Registration of Private Landlords was included in the *Private Rented Sector Strategy* (March 2010). See also Northern Ireland Executive, *Landlords to be regulated for the first time, announces Ritchie* (24 March 10) available at www.northernireland.gov.uk/news/news-dsd/news-dsd-240310-landlords-to-be.htm (accessed 11 June 2010). The relevant legislation has more recently been introduced with the Landlord Registration Scheme Regulations (Northern Ireland) 2012.

174 Article 38 and 39 of the 1983 of the Housing (NI) Order grants right to information to secure tenants in both NIHE and registered housing association tenancies. Article 40 of the same Order grants the right to consultation with respect to certain issues excluding changes to rent, service charges of facilities. Introductory tenant's rights are spelled out in the Housing (NI) Order 2003. Article 18 sets out the rights to information and Article 19 sets out rights of consultation with respect to introductory tenants. No similar protection is available for tenants in the private rented sector.

175 Since 5 April 2004, all new Housing Executive tenancies are introductory tenancies. A registered housing association may elect to introduce an introductory tenancy scheme. See Article 6 of the Housing (Northern Ireland) Order 2003.

176 ComESCR, *General Comment No. 4, The Right to Adequate Housing*, paragraph 9 states that the full enjoyment of other rights – such as the right to freedom of expression, the right to freedom of association (such as for tenants and other community-based groups), the right to freedom of residence and the right to participate in public decision-making – is indispensable if the right to adequate housing is to be realized and maintained by all groups in society.

177 *Report of the High Commissioner for Human Rights on Implementation of Economic, Social and Cultural Rights*, UN Doc E/2009/90 (2009) paragraph 33.

is specifically mentioned by the High Commissioner for Human Rights, who stated that the institutional framework for implementing ESR should include mechanisms that ensure the participation of relevant stakeholders, provide for transparency and access to information, establish accountability mechanisms, respect due process in decision-making, and provide remedies in case of violations.[178] Failure to include mechanisms to satisfy these procedural requirements may also amount to violations of international obligations.[179] The ComESCR has reiterated that the human rights framework includes the right of those affected by key decisions to participate in the decision-making processes. It adds that policies or programmes formulated without the active and informed participation of those affected are least likely to be effective.[180] The private rented sector provides accommodation for tenants who may not be able to access social housing. The ComESCR has specifically said that the state must use any mix of public and private initiatives that are appropriate in the national context.[181] This ought not to distract from the fact that, regardless of how the national housing strategy is delivered, in terms of ICESCR the state remains ultimately responsible for ensuring that the full range of international human rights, including those of participation and consultation, are adhered to.

Affordability

The affordability of rent levels is also a concern. Research has found that tenants renting privately have reported difficulties 'in paying the shortfall between housing benefit and the rent charged',[182] which on average amounted to £28 per week.[183] Difficulty in paying PRS rent has contributed to the rise in homelessness in Northern Ireland.[184] More generally, the subsidization of the PRS via housing benefit makes the buy-to-let market a more attractive investment. The rise of buy-to-let has in turn contributed to excessive house price inflation – directly impacting on the affordability of housing.

178 Ibid.

179 Ibid.

180 ComESCR, *Substantive Issues Arising in the Implementation of the International Covenant on Economic, Social and Cultural Rights; Poverty and the International Covenant on Economic, Social and Cultural Rights*, UN Doc E/C.12/2001/10 (2001) paragraph 12. Specifically in relation to the state's duty to devise a strategy or a plan of action for realization of the right to adequate housing, the ComESCR has stated that such a plan or strategy should reflect extensive genuine consultation with, and participation by, all of those affected, including the homeless, the inadequately housed and their representatives. ComESCR, *General Comment No. 4, The Right to Adequate Housing*, paragraph 12.

181 ComESCR, *General Comment No. 4, The Right to Adequate Housing*, paragraph 14.

182 NIHE, *The Private Rented Sector in Northern Ireland* (NIHE 2007) 6.

183 Ibid 36.

184 Ibid.

The problem of affordability for social housing tenants is mentioned in the DSD's *Building Solid Foundations Strategy for the Private Rented Sector*. The Department's response is said to centre upon arrangements that safeguard rent deposits and provide a means to allow disputes between landlords and tenants to be dealt with quickly and efficiently.[185] Arguably, the affordability problem extends far beyond the issue of rent deposits and it appears that the larger concerns are not addressed in this strategy.

Maximum available resources

The issue of subsidizing the PRS raises interesting questions in relation to the state's use of resources. The PRS has become an important form of accommodation for low-income households as a result of the inadequacy of the social housing stock. Therefore, housing benefit paid into the private rented sector represents a 'hidden cost' of the low levels of funding for new build; in 2010–11 for example, this cost was likely to have been approximately £270 million.[186] Another hidden cost is that housing benefit paid into the public sector is re-invested in social housing, while that paid into the PRS is not. If housing benefit is to be used in a way that maximizes the available resources for the progressive realization of the right to adequate housing, it is therefore preferable for it to be paid to social rather than private landlords. The financial balance sheet is further complicated by the fact that the use of the private rented sector avoids the capital costs associated with building new homes but also misses out on the economic benefits of social build.[187]

In conclusion, this section has discussed the role of the PRS in addressing social housing need. It has identified problems with the role of the PRS in this area. There are issues about the level of transparency, consultation and participation, while rents in the PRS are less affordable than in the social housing sector. In addition, the use of the PRS to house tenants who require social housing and are in receipt of housing benefit possibly represents a failure to use maximum available resources for the progressive realization of the right to adequate housing as rents are not reinvested in social housing.

Conclusion

This chapter has examined a number of issues relevant to the resourcing of social housing in Northern Ireland from a human rights-based perspective.

185 DSD, *Building Solid Foundations – A Strategy for the Private Rented Sector* (2009) 11.

186 Eoin Rooney and Mira Dutschke, 'The Right to Adequate Housing: A Case Study of the Social Housing Budget in Northern Ireland' in Aoife Nolan, Rory O'Connell and Colin Harvey (eds), *Human Rights and Public Finance* (Hart 2013).

187 Mike Smyth and Mark Bailey, *Addressing the Economic Downturn: The Case for Increased Investment in Social Housing* (School of Economics, University of Ulster 2009) page numbers not included.

The pre-devolution decisions of central government to put more emphasis on home ownership have created an extremely challenging financial environment for the public bodies directly responsible for the provision of social housing in Northern Ireland. In the context of severe budgetary and borrowing constraints, local housing bodies have explored creative ways of using existing resources and generating additional finance. One DSD official has described the task as trying to work 'something of an economic miracle'.[188] Initiatives such as the transfer to housing associations that could borrow off-budget and greater use of the PRS have helped to circumvent some of the difficulties – but not without costs. Crucially, the state's use of resources appears to have been insufficient to progressively realize the right to adequate housing over time during the timeframe of this research.

In terms of ICESCR, the UK is bound to ensure that everyone enjoys the right to an adequate standard of living. The state is obliged to take steps to the maximum of its available resources with a view to progressively achieving the right to adequate housing. In abstract terms, this means that the state must use all the resources it can, without neglecting any other vital obligations, to gradually and continually improve all aspects of the right to adequate housing. Various duties stemming from this obligation are to be adhered to immediately. For example, the state must not tolerate retrogression in the realization of rights. A basic minimum core entitlement, as well as a duty to ensure equality, are both of immediate effect. Even though resources might be inadequate to realize all aspects of the right immediately, this does not relieve the state from the immediate duty to plan for full realization as well as for the future acquisition of resources necessary for implementation. The state therefore has to develop a national housing strategy in which these plans are spelled out. In terms of process, the state also has to ensure that those likely to be affected by decision-making in the housing sphere have the ability to participate meaningfully in those decisions.

What then is required in order for the state to better fulfil its ESR obligations? A variety of possible solutions are feasible in terms of ensuring state compliance with its international obligations in relation to the right to adequate housing. It is, therefore, not appropriate to be overly prescriptive about what policies should be adopted. However, a number of points arise from the above analysis.

The use of housing associations as a mechanism for raising finance off-balance, while politically convenient, is highly questionable from a human rights perspective. While it appears to offer a cost-free mode of providing housing, in practice it only does so by foregoing revenue that would otherwise accrue to the public purse. If borrowing is required, it may be more efficient to provide the appropriate public body with a borrowing capacity.

188 H. Cousins, *Housing is a bright star in the executive firmament. Irish News* (2 January 2010).

It is necessary for proper transparency and accountability processes to be in place, even in a multi-agency system that relies on hybrid bodies to deliver important services. Indeed, arguably, it is more important to pay attention to transparency and accountability questions in such a context, as otherwise the complexities created by a multi-agency system might undermine these values.

Public authorities should allocate financial resources to address perceived need, based on adequate planning. It is problematic if resources are dependent on the unpredictable raising of revenue. In particular, a system of funding for ESR based on the contingencies of the land market, as practised in Northern Ireland, should be avoided. Such a system means that an economic crisis reduces the resources available for the provision of ESR in the very situation they are arguably most needed.

The need for careful planning does not just relate to the direct provision of ESR resources like social housing. State agencies need to manage the wider resources in society to make sure that vital resources such as land remain affordable. A failure to address these wider issues does not just make the state provision of ESR resources problematic; it also makes it difficult for individual persons and families to realize their rights through their own efforts; and fundamentally may cause longer-term economic problems.

The state needs to consider the relationship between public and private provision of housing, and reconsider policies that rely on short-term use of the private sector. A short-term approach that relies on the private sector may overlook issues about the adequacy of rights fulfilment in the private sector, as well as channelling resources in such a way as to benefit the already advantaged (private landlords) rather than investing in public services for the benefit of the less well-off.

More broadly, however, change in how housing is perceived is necessary to ensure that social housing is adequately valued in the long term. If financial support for social housing has been lacking in the context of a neoliberal ideology that emphasizes market solutions, the engendering of a discourse which views housing as a right, essential to human dignity, security and well-being, may promote a firmer footing for social housing.

7 Conclusion

Local meets global

In this final chapter our aim is to summarize the principal conclusions of our work, and to indicate possible ways forward for the effective application, implementation and enforcement of economic and social rights. Although our title for this chapter is 'local meets global' the book as a whole demonstrates the complex interactions that currently exist between a globalized discourse and practice of rights and local realities of budget processes, outcomes and the intricacies of public finance. In significant senses we show how embedded each is in the other, and just how dynamic the interactions are. For the purpose of clarity, and to aid future attempts to advance the human rights agendas outlined here, we separate out the various normative orders to understand better all the practical implications. Our attempt to promote explanatory precision, however, does not seek to underplay overlapping and intertwined agendas. We are aware of the interconnected nature of local activism and global human rights discourse and practice.

The global rights regime

The book is in two parts, a global perspective and the use of localized case studies. In Part 1, we outline the context and examine in detail available guidance material. Through this forensic exploration of existing resources we identify contemporary difficulties and challenges. The framework for our work, and critical engagement, is international human rights law, in particular ICESCR. Our decision to locate the analysis within the fabric of global human rights is a deliberate one. We believe, and demonstrate, that localized study of economic and social rights in action must be based on an understanding of the international discourse of human rights, and the wider institutional context for its development. That is why we devote so much time in this book to outlining the international normative order and surrounding environment.

Effective mobilization around rights today is frequently guided by intricate interactions between international standards, differing normative orders, national and sub-national contexts, localized politics of law, and – in scholarly terms – the reality of disciplinary boundaries. Although we might wish economics and human rights law 'to talk to each other coherently', there are genuine dilemmas to address in any such exchange. We do not avoid facing them in this work. Human rights lawyers in particular must always remain mindful of how to bring interpretative clarity to the meaning of norms to any discussion of economic and social rights. They must do so in ways that do not end in a dilution of the standards that are there. One of the issues highlighted in this book is how precisely to use an international human rights framework within the micro-dynamics of particular practical contexts. In undertaking this task we found the global perspective consistently invaluable; it is difficult to clarify the local human rights dynamics without a firm basis in existing international norms, and to understand how these shape national debates. In doing so, and in holding to this perspective, we demonstrate the sophistication of modern approaches employed by advocates and activists to advance the cause of human rights. These approaches are based on international law, including broadly worded treaty provisions but also detailed legal analysis in a range of official documents and academic commentaries. This point must be underlined. Too much commentary on economic and social rights in the public sphere continues to function with a degraded and impoverished version of human rights. There remains much basic misunderstanding of what the standards are. The result is that due regard is not paid to the nuanced nature of international human rights law.

This is in no way to be uncritical defenders of the present legal framework. As our work shows, there is still some way to travel before sufficient consensus exists globally on definitional clarity. There is scope for further development of international and regional standards. We also remain conscious of the limitations of mechanistic discourses of law and economics that would seek to reduce or even eradicate the complexity and diversity of human experience and potentially undercut the humane, moral values of human rights and human dignity. We are aware of the contested nature of legal norms, and the politics of law that flows through international and transnational conversations about rights. We know that restrictive arguments premised upon particular conceptions of utility only can retain a suffocating hold on the languages of law and economics.

Why did we select ICESCR? As we highlighted in Chapter 1, the formal reason is that the UK has signed and ratified this international instrument and is thus bound in international law – a legal obligation exists. In our view, it is important to insist on the legally binding character of these international obligations. What are the international legal obligations that flow from this covenant and what do they mean for the area under examination? How are these of relevance to budget decisions?

We are concerned that the view advanced by the UK Government and others on economic and social rights, often triggered by discussions of incorporation, promotes widespread misunderstanding of the law and its implications. There is a recurrent tendency on the part of state actors and political partisans to stress the programmatic nature of these human rights to the detriment of a proper grasp of the legal obligations that exist now. As we discuss in Chapter 1, the default position of international human rights law is that all human rights – civil, cultural, economic, social and political – are universal, indivisible, interdependent and interrelated. The international human rights law corpus rejects the view that economic and social rights are goals without any real normative obligation. Despite this, governments like the United Kingdom's still assert a position that challenges the normativity of economic and social rights. This is precisely why the normativity of economic and social rights still needs to be defended. The suggestion that these are somehow not proper law has still not been eradicated from public discourse, and we believe it remains vital to stress the legal nature of the obligation.

There is another dimension to this that is sometimes neglected. The failure to give national life to economic and social rights in the UK denies constitutional actors the ability to shape the global human rights conversation around these rights and related issues such as poverty and development. The UK Government's endemic, historic unwillingness to 'bring economic and social rights home' by means of domestic incorporation of explicit standards, denies national constitutional actors an influential voice. What do we mean by this? We do not mean that UK-based civil society organizations, NHRIs and others fail to make full and effective use of the international standards in their advocacy work. On the contrary, these organizations make considerable use of these standards in a range of settings. The difficulty is that significant national constitutional actors – from legislatures to judiciaries within the UK – are excluded from giving effective shape to the global rights debate as a consequence of the failure to incorporate the standards. The exclusion of economic and social rights from the domestic legal order, and from a range of constitutional configurations, denies participants the opportunity to give meaning in law to these rights and concepts. In bringing economic and social rights into the conversation about budgets and public finances, we are explicitly resisting this exclusionary state agenda. While discussion of the Human Rights Act 1998 in the UK continues to rage one thing seems apparent: national judges are making full and effective use of the rights under the European Convention on Human Rights in ways that are influencing European debates. There is good sense in giving national constitutional actors such a guiding role, and there is evidence from around the UK that economic and social rights are beginning to emerge in discussions about future constitutional change and reform.[1] We would strongly encourage this trend and hope that our book is a small contribution to it.

1 See, for instance, the inclusion of economic and social rights in Northern Ireland Human Rights Commission advice on a Bill of Rights for Northern Ireland, *A Bill of Rights for Northern Ireland* (NIHRC 2008); similarly the second most popular suggestion for additional rights in any UK Bill of Rights was economic and social rights: Commission on a Bill of Rights, *Final Report: A UK Bill of Rights? The Choice Before Us* (Commission on a Bill of Rights, UK 2012) paragraph 53.

Our argument in this work thus rests on the centrality of the global human rights regime, and the job of bringing that into domestic arenas. Economic and social rights are a secure part of the international normative order. If the nature and scope of particular obligations varies one thing is no longer in doubt: they are *law*. One concern we iterate and reiterate, is that this fact must be better understood in the circumstances of national and sub-national legal analysis.

What general conclusions do we reach? We identify the requirement for more comprehensive definitions of ESR principles. As we show, these are currently applied inconsistently, and there is a need for clarification. We ask the question: can a consistent approach be adopted given the variation and diversity identified and the widely differing contexts? Is consistency possible in terms of the formulation and application of indicators of compliance? We believe that in this book we make a start, along with many others, in answering these questions. By explaining in considerable detail the human rights framework, starting with Article 2(1) ICESCR, we spell out all the main budget-related obligations. We proceed to introduce the established tripartite typology that is now widely accepted and endorsed internationally, as well as focussing on the implementation of 'immediate obligations' under the international ESR framework. We are aware here of the risks involved, and we acknowledge the many barriers that remain. Some of the problems include a lack of clarity on matters like the degree of progress required by progressive realization; the specific content of a state's 'maximum available resources'; on the relationship between equity and non-discrimination (equality); and on the definition of the minimum core and other immediate obligations. We believe, nevertheless, that conceptual and practical clarity on the meaning of these international standards and their implications is possible, and that Chapters 3 and 4 have contributed to this project.

Budgets, public finance and human rights

Our intention with this work is to enter the world of budgets and public finance with a view to exploring the consequences of bringing rights-based approaches to the table. We do not do so lightly, and we nowhere underestimate the potential for misunderstanding, resistance and unintended consequences. Central to our work is the desire to draw in relevant expertise into these reflections, with the resulting acceptance that lawyers and the legal mind can only take us part of the way. As we highlight in Chapter 1, the Universal Declaration of Human Rights speaks of the obligations on every individual and every organ of society to promote and protect human rights, not just lawyers or judges. Without wishing to diminish the standing of human rights lawyers and advocates, one of the continuing dilemmas is how to ensure rights are taken seriously at times when the entire discourse is under sustained assault, as it currently is in the UK. We hope that we demonstrate here how this might be achieved.

Budget processes are not uniform. Part of the argument in our work is the need to appreciate the sheer multiplicity of approaches that exist internationally; thus one major blockage to reform will remain the practical implementation of global standards in varying contexts. We do not believe it is a challenge that is insurmountable and clear themes do emerge. These include transparency and participation. For example, the importance of access to relevant useful information is vital to ESR-based budget analysis efforts and advocacy. Chapter 6 identifies problems with accessing information in a multi-agency system where non-state bodies may not be straightforwardly subject to freedom of information laws. Chapter 5 highlights that information possessed by public authorities may not actually be in a format that enables us to assess whether human rights obligations are being met; the problem is not just that government does not release information, but that it does not possess it in a relevant form itself.

As Chapter 1 highlights, modern budgeting approaches are frequently highly centralized and technocratic, allowing for little genuine participation and debate; Chapter 5 provides the example of the Draft Budget 2011–15 for health in Northern Ireland, where the consultation period was five weeks and departmental proposals were often lacking in detailed information. These sorts of practices seriously hamper the possibility for citizens and civil society to participate. This can even be true of existing constitutional actors who should, in theory, already have an established role. Even existing legislatures can struggle to assume an effective and influential role in shaping the budget process and its outcome.

Again, our aim is not to dismiss the formidable impediments and genuine dilemmas in play. We do, however, conclude that rights-based approaches have a place in promoting more participatory principle-based approaches to budgets, and in shaping the discussions of the use of public finances and resources in the wider public interest. It is important to emphasize that this is not just a matter of process (though process is fundamental, and an aspect of the human rights obligations discussed in this work) but also about the substantive terms of the debate. International human rights law provides guidance and standards on how such decisions should be made. We show how those wishing to advance this work might proceed.

There is a democratization challenge that remains during budget processes but also in the practical assessment of budget outcomes. While some societies have the capacity to generate impressive levels of independent assessment of budget outcomes, this is not a universal picture. The issue of capacity is significant. A rights-based approach is strongly suggestive of the need to allocate resources for proper and systematic analysis of governmental budgets with reference to ESRs. How, for example, is rights-based proofing resourced? Should such work be done entirely independently of the state? If so, how is the capacity to undertake this work supported? Who will assume 'ownership' of such assessment and how will this impact on the sometimes elitist nature of budget formulation, implementation and, indeed, assessment? Dialogue and debate can be encouraged by subjecting the budget process and its outcomes to rigorous assessment using human rights standards in ways that capture concisely the nature of the relevant obligations. The question of how this work is facilitated remains a pressing one.

Human rights in action: Case studies from Northern Ireland

In this work, we include detailed consideration of case studies from Northern Ireland. We believe that Northern Ireland offers an intriguing sub-national context for investigation and analysis. It exists in a devolved regional setting within the UK, on the island of Ireland, and rests within the broader EU context. Although it is framed and embedded within a 'liberal democratic' environment of constitutionalism, it is also a transitional society emerging steadily from a violent and protracted conflict, one with novel features and where the advancement of economic and social rights is frequently viewed as a core element in sustainable and principled peace building and reconciliation. This allows our research to speak credibly to a broad international debate, and adds a significant dimension to our work; others may find this of value when considering how conflict impacts on the implementation of economic and social rights in situations of profound ethno-national division. We thus demonstrate how a rights-based approach to budget analysis might be used in societies emerging from conflict within a constitutional architecture that is well established.

Our approach is not confined to reflecting on Northern Ireland in general or generic terms. We delve into the micro-dynamics of rights application in the specific contexts of mental health and social housing. The right to the highest attainable standard of mental health is used as a contextualized case study, with the present position in Northern Ireland subjected to careful scrutiny. By doing this we hope to show why our approach can be of such value in highlighting problems and probing ways to secure rights-based approaches. Here we identify several recommendations for progress based on our framework and local advances.

The right to adequate housing is also used to examine the reality of economic and social rights realisation in this society in transition. The area has particular resonance, in a place where the allocation of social housing initially fuelled conflict, and remains an area of controversy and debate. The historical background thus assumes particular importance, and it displays considerable localized complexity, difficulty and challenge. This book advances several conclusions that would assist in aligning social housing provision, and the approach to the whole area, with the right to adequate housing. Again, we identify what the problems are. Thus, for instance, we question the current balance between 'the public and private' in housing policy; this is an issue that will resonate with others considering the right to adequate housing elsewhere. In Chapter 6 we demonstrate how a reliance on private actors to secure the right to adequate housing may not provide the cost-free solution that is sometimes imagined; we also question the reliance on a heavily subsidized private rented sector and highlight issues in relation to transparency and participation in a hybrid multi-agency system. These, we believe, will strike a chord with others working on the right to adequate housing. As well as identifying problems, we also seek to outline what is required to secure rights-compliant improvements.

Ways forward

This book originated in a research project inspired by our shared desire to demonstrate what the global human rights regime might mean at a local level. In this work, the local and global meet precisely because we demonstrate that there is interaction already, and we show the benefits of a rights-based approach in bringing clarity to these conversations. A challenge for the human rights movement at any level will remain the realization of norms in practice, and ensuring they have meaningful life in situations where they matter most to individuals and communities who need them. Human rights are for everyone; yet there are many socio-economically marginalized, vulnerable and alienated communities whose plight demands that these norms are embodied in the world they face daily. Human rights lawyers and advocates must promote nuanced and mature approaches that acknowledge and address structural inequality and persistent socio-economic marginalization – locally and globally.

This is not a straightforward task of implementation, precisely because one of the difficulties we face is contestation around the meaning of norms. That is why the work of legal clarification we have undertaken here is of such significance. We need to understand the normative content of economic and social rights as a starting point. It remains surprising how often this point is lost. Rights do need to be 'brought home' in the sense that rights discourse and advocacy must speak to people where they are, and not solely in a narrowly legalistic way. We stress throughout the centrality of knowing the international *legal* basis for the discussions, but we also underline in this book the urgency of carrying these norms into the public sphere in meaningful and effective ways. In undertaking this task we have consistently engaged with the practical economics of budgets and sought to grasp and explain the intricacies of public finances. We do not underestimate the challenges in bringing distinctive disciplinary perspectives together. Modern societies are now dominated by discursive formations that struggle to speak in a coherent way across disciplines and where shared languages are hard to unearth and advance. We believe that in this book we show how this might function.

The world remains an unequal and unjust place, where the idealized normative standards of human rights, and the lofty rhetorical pleas on behalf of our shared humanity, can appear as a cruel joke or irrelevancy to too many people. The imperative thus remains to explore how these norms can be given life for societies, communities and individuals whose right to a dignified existence is at stake. In assisting in this broader task, our aim in this book is to indicate the depth, range and sophistication of modern international law approaches to human rights. We do so not to glorify in any complacent way our own specialism, but to resist some of the reductionist narratives around human rights-based legal methods. We simply do not see ourselves in the caricatures of human rights and human rights law. We believe our project and its outcomes prove that defensible ways forward are possible. If we have a hope it is that the work will assist those struggling to realize these normative ideals in practice. If we have produced useful tools, and provided a secure evidential base, to assist those who mobilize thoughtfully and skilfully within human rights movements, then we will be content.

Bibliography

Secondary literature (books, book sections, journal articles, working papers)

Alston P. and Quinn G., 'The Nature and Scope of the States Parties' Obligations under the International Covenant on Economic, Social and Cultural Rights' (1987) 9 *Human Rights Quarterly* 156.

Anderson B., 'The Value of a Nonpartisan, Independent, Objective Analytic Unit to the Legislative Role in Budget Preparation' in Pelizzo R., Stapenhurst R. and Olson D. (eds) *The Role of Parliaments in the Budget Process* (World Bank Institute, Washington, DC 2008).

Barraclough K. and Dorotinsky B., 'The Role of the Legislature in the Budget Drafting Process: A Comparative Review' in Pelizzo R., Stapenhurst R. and Olson D. (eds) *The Role of Parliaments in the Budget Process (World Bank Institute*, Washington, DC 2008).

Bates E., 'The United Kingdom and the International Covenant on Economic, Social and Cultural Rights' in M. Baderin and R. McCorquodale (eds) *Economic, Social and Cultural Rights in Action* (Oxford UP 2007).

Benito B., Montesinos V. and Bastida F., 'An Example of Creative Accounting in Public Sector: The Private Financing of Infrastructures in Spain' (2008) 19 *Critical Perspectives on Accounting* 963.

Besselink L.F.M. and Reestman J.H., 'The Fiscal Compact and the European Constitutions: "Europe Speaking German"' (2012) 8 *European Constitutional Law Review*, 1.

Bew P., Gibbon P. and Patterson H., *Northern Ireland 1921–2001: Political Forces and Social Classes* (Rev. and updated Serif 2002).

Bhagwati P.N., 'Judicial Activism and Public Interest Litigation' (1985) 23 *Columbia Journal of Transnational Law* 561.

Bilchitz D., 'Towards a Reasonable Approach to the Minimum Core: Laying the Foundations for Future Socio-Economic Rights Jurisprudence' (2003) 19 *South African Journal on Human Rights* 1.

Blackman T., Evason E., Melaugh M. and Woods R. 'Housing and Health: A Case Study of Two Areas in West Belfast' (1989) 18 *Journal of Social Policy* 1.

Blake C., 'Normative Instruments in International Human Rights Law: Locating the General Comment' in *Centre for Human Rights and Global Justice*, Working Papers No. 17 (2008) New York University, School of Law.

Blyberg A., 'Government Budgets and Rights Implementation: Experience from Around the World' in J. Heymann J. and A. Cassola (eds), *Making Equal Rights Real* (Cambridge UP 2012).

Bogdanor V., *The New British Constitution* (Hart 2009).

Boyle K., Hadden T. and Hillyard P., *Law and State: The Case of Northern Ireland* (Robertson 1975).

Bourdieu P., *The Social Structures of the Economy* (Polity 2005).

Bowyer Bell J., *The Irish Troubles: A Generation of Political Violence, 1967–1992* (St Martin's Press 1993).

Braveman P. and Gruskin S., 'Defining Equity in Health' (2003) 57 *Journal of Epidemiology and Community Health* 254.

Buckland P., *A History of Northern Ireland* (Gill & Macmillan 1981).

Buergenthal T., *International Human Rights in a Nutshell* (West Publishing Co 1995).

Buergenthal T., 'International Human Rights in an Historical Perspective' in Janusz Symonides (ed) *Human Rights: Concepts and Standards* (Ashgate 2000).

Burchardt T. and Holder H., 'Inequality and the Devolved Administrations: Scotland, Wales and Northern Ireland' in J. Hills, T. Sefton and K. Stewart (eds) *Towards a More Equal Society? Poverty Inequality and Policy since 1997* (Policy Press 2009).

Cable V., *The Storm: The World Economic Crisis and What it Means* (Rev. ed Atlantic 2010).

Campbell C., Ní Aoláin F. and Harvey C., 'The Frontiers of Legal Analysis: Reframing the Transition in Northern Ireland' (2003) 66 *Modern Law Review* 317.

Carozza P., 'From Conquest to Constitutions: Retrieving a Latin American Tradition of the Idea of Human Rights' (2003) 25 *Human Rights Quarterly* 281.

Chapman A.R. and Russell S., 'Introduction' in A. Chapman and S. Russell (eds) *Core Obligations: Building a Framework for Economic, Social and Cultural Rights* (Instersentia 2002).

Chapman A.R., 'Core Obligations Related to the Right to Health' in A. Chapman and S. Russell (eds) *Core Obligations: Building a Framework for Economic, Social and Cultural Rights* (Instersentia 2002).

Chapman A.R., 'Violations Approach for Monitoring the International Covenant on Economic, Social and Cultural Rights' (1996) 18 *Human Rights Quarterly* 23.

Chapman A.R., 'The Status of Efforts to Monitor Economic, Social and Cultural Rights' in S. Hertel and L. Minkler (eds), *Economic Rights: Conceptual, Measurement and Policy Issues* (Cambridge UP 2007).

Chayes A., 'The Role of the Judge in Public Law Litigation' (1976) 89 *Harvard Law Review* 1281.

Chirwa D.M., 'Privatisation of Water in Southern Africa: A Human Rights Perspective' (2004) 4 *African Human Rights Journal* 218.

Coogan T.P., *The Troubles: Ireland's Ordeal, 1966–1996 and the Search for Peace* (Arrow 1996).

Coogan T.P., *The IRA* (Palgrave for St Martin's Press 2002).

Costa F.D., 'Poverty and Human Rights: From Rhetoric to Legal Obligations – A Critical Account of Conceptual Framework' (2008) 9 *SUR International Journal on Human Rights* 81.

Cox M., Guelke A. and Stephen F., *A Farewell to Arms? Beyond the Good Friday Agreement* (Manchester UP 2006).

Cottrell J., 'Ensuring Equal Rights in Constitutions: Public Participation in Drafting Economic Social and Cultural Rights' in Jody Heymann and Adele Cassola (eds) *Making Equal Rights Real* (Cambridge UP 2012).

Courtis C., 'Argentina: Some Promising Signs' in M. Langford (ed), *Social Rights Jurisprudence: Emerging Trends in International and Comparative Law* (Cambridge UP 2008).

Craven M., *The International Covenant on Economic, Social and Cultural Rights – A Perspective on its Development* (Oxford UP 1995).

Dankwa V., Flinterman C. and Leckie S., 'Commentary on the Maastricht Guidelines on Violations of Economic, Social and Cultural Rights' (1998) 20 *Human Rights Quarterly* 705.

Darby J., 'The Historical Background' in Darby J (ed) *Northern Ireland: The Background to the Conflict* (Syracuse UP 1983).

Darrow M., *Between Light and Shadow: The World Bank, the International Monetary Fund and International Human Rights Law* (Hart 2003).

Dawson J.P., *The Oracles of the Law* (University of Michigan Press 1968).

De Vos P., 'Pious Wishes or Directly Enforceable Human Rights? Social and Economic Rights in South Africa's 1996 Constitution' (1997) 1 *South African Journal of Human Rights* 67.

Dickson B., 'The Protection of Human Rights – Lessons from Northern Ireland' (2000) *European Human Rights Law Review* 213.

Dixon P., *Northern Ireland: The Politics of War and Peace* (Palgrave 2001).

Eide A., 'Economic and Social Rights' in J. Symonides (ed), *Human Rights: Concepts and Standards* (UNESCO 2000).

Eide A., 'Realization of Social and Economic Rights and the Minimum Threshold Approach' (1989) 10 *Human Rights Law Journal* 35.

Elson D., Balakrishnan R. and Heintz J., 'Public Finance, Maximum Available Resources and Human Rights' in Aoife Nolan, Rory O'Connell and Colin Harvey (eds) *Human Rights and Public Finance* (Hart 2013).

English R., *Armed Struggle: The History of the IRA* (Oxford UP 2003).

Evans C. and Evans S., 'Evaluating the Human Rights Performance of Legislatures' (2006) 6 *Human Rights Law Review*, 545.

Fay M.T., Morrissey M. and Smyth M., *Northern Ireland's Troubles: The Human Costs* (Pluto Press in association with The Cost of the Troubles Study 1999).

Felner E., 'A New Frontier in Economic and Social Rights Advocacy? Turning Quantitative Data into a Tool for Human Rights Accountability' (2008) 9 *SUR International Journal on Human Rights* 109.

Forestiere C. and Pelizzo R., 'Does the Parliament Make a Difference? The Role of the Italian Parliament in Financial Policy' in R. Pelizzo, R. Stapenhurst and D. Olson (eds) *The Role of Parliaments in the Budget Process* (World Bank Institute, Washington, DC 2005).

Fredman S., *Human Rights Transformed – Positive Rights and Positive Duties* (Oxford UP 2008).

Friedman M., *Capitalism and Freedom* (Chicago UP 1962).

Fuerst J.S. and Petty R., 'High-rise Housing for Low-Income Families' (1991) 103 *Public Interest* 108.

Gaffikin F. and Morrissey M., *Northern Ireland: The Thatcher Years* (Zed Books 1990).

Godechot J., *France and the Atlantic Revolution of the Eighteenth Century, 1770–1799* (Free Press 1965).

Goldsmith J., 'The Paradigm Shift: Transforming from an Acute to Chronic Care Model' (1990) *Decisions in Imaging Economics* 13.

Gostin L.O., 'Beyond Moral Claims: A Human Rights Approach in Mental Health' (2001) 10 *Cambridge Quarterly of Healthcare Ethics* 264.

Gostin L.O., 'The Human Rights of Persons with Mental Disabilities: A Global Perspective on the Application of Human Rights Principles to Mental Health' (2004) 63 *Maryland Law Review* 20.

Green A., *An Introduction to Health Planning for Developing Health Systems* (Oxford UP 2007).

Green M., 'What We Talk About When We Talk About Indicators: Current Approaches to Human Rights Measurement' (2001) 23 *Human Rights Quarterly* 1062.

Hadfield B., 'Devolution: A National Conversation?' in Jeffrey Jowell and Dawn Oliver (eds) *The Changing Constitution* (7th edition, Oxford UP 2011).

Hannum H., 'The Rights of Persons belonging to Minorities' in Janusz Symonides (ed) *Human Rights: Concepts and Standards* (Ashgate 2000).

Harriott S. and Matthews L., *Introducing Social Housing 2004* (Chartered Institute of Housing 2004).

Harvey D., *A Brief History of Neoliberalism* (Oxford UP 2005).

Hayek F., *The Constitution of Liberty* (Routledge 1960).

Haysom N., 'Constitutionalism, Majoritarian Democracy and Socio-Economic Rights' (1992) 8 *South African Journal of Human Rights* 451.

Heenan D., 'Mental Health Policy in Northern Ireland: The Nature and Extent of User Involvement' (2009) 8 *Social Policy and Society* 451.

Hennessey T., *A History of Northern Ireland, 1920–1996* (Macmillan 1997).

Hirschl R., *Towards Juristocracy: The Origins and Consequences of the New Constitutionalism* (Harvard UP 2004).

Hoffman P.T. and Norberg K., *Fiscal Crises, Liberty, and Representative Government, 1450–1789* (Stanford UP 1994).

Hunt M., 'Enhancing Parliament's Role in Relation to Economic and Social Rights' (2010) *European Human Rights Law Review* 242.

Hunt P. and Backman G., 'Health Systems and the Right to the Highest Attainable Standard of Health' (2008) 10 *Health and Human Rights Journal*, 81.

Hunt P. and Leader S., 'Developing and Applying the Right to the Highest Attainable Standard of Health' in J. Harrington and M. Stuttaford (eds) *Global Health and Human Rights* (Routledge 2010).

Hunt P. and Mesquita J., 'Mental Disabilities and the Human Right to the Highest Attainable Standard of Health' (2006) 28 *Human Rights Quarterly* 332.

Ishay M., *The History of Human Rights: From Ancient Times to the Globalization Era* (University of California Press 2004).

Jackson A., *Ireland, 1798–1998: Politics and War (A History of the Modern British Isles)* (Blackwell 1999).

Kang S.L., 'The Unsettled Relationship of Economic and Social Rights and the West: A Response to Whelan and Donnelly' (2009) 31 *Human Rights Quarterly* 1006.

Khagram S., de Renzio P. and Fung A., 'Overview and Synthesis: The Political Economy of Fiscal Transparency, Participation, and Accountability Around the World' in Khagram S., Fung A. and de Renzio P. (eds) *Open Budgets: The Political Economy of Transparency, Participation, and Accountability* (Brookings Institution Press 2013).

King A.S., *The British Constitution* (Oxford UP 2007).

King J.A., 'United Kingdom: Asserting Social Rights in a Multi-layered System' in M. Langford (ed) *Social Rights Jurisprudence: Emerging Trends in Comparative and International Law* (Cambridge UP 2009).

Kirkup A. and Evans T., 'The Myth of Western Opposition to Economic, Social, and Cultural Rights?: A Reply to Whelan and Donnelly' (2009) 31 *Human Rights Quarterly* 221.

Klein A., 'Judging as Nudging: New Governance Approaches for the Enforcement of Constitutional Social and Economic Rights' (2008) 39 *Columbia Human Rights Law Review* 351.

Koch I.E., 'Dichotomies, Trichotomies or Waves of Duties?' (2005) 5 *Human Rights Law Review* 81.

Koch I.E., 'The Justiciability of Indivisible Rights' (2003) 72 *Nordic Journal of International Law* 3.

Koven S., *Ideological Budgeting: The Influence of Political Philosophy on Public Policy* (Praeger 1988).

Lancet Global Mental Health Group 'Scale up Services for Mental Disorders: A Call for Action' (2007) 370 (6) *Lancet Global Mental Health Series* 1241.

Langford M. and Nolan A., *Litigating Economic, Social and Cultural Rights: A Legal Practitioner's Guide* (COHRE Centre for Housing Rights and Evictions 2006).

Langford M., Khalfan A., Fairstein, C. and Jones H., *Legal Resources for the Right to Water: International and National Standards* (COHRE Centre for Housing Rights and Evictions 2003).

Langford M. (ed), *Social Rights Jurisprudence: Emerging Trends in International and Comparative Law* (Cambridge UP 2009).

Lauren P.G., *The Evolution of International Human Rights: Visions Seen* (3rd edition, University of Pennsylvania Press 2011).

Liebenberg S., 'Socio-Economic Rights' in M. Chaskalson, J. Kentridge, J. Klaaren, G. Marcus, D. Spitz and S. Woolman (eds), *Constitutional Law of South Africa* (Juta 1996).

Liebenberg S., 'Taking Stock: Jurisprudence on Children's Socio-economic Rights' (2004) 5 *ESR Review* 2.

Liebenberg S., 'The International Covenant on Economic, Social and Cultural Rights and its Implementation for South Africa' (1995) 11 *South African Journal on Human Rights* 359.

Liebenberg, S. 'The Right to Social Assistance: The Implications of Grootboom for Policy Reform in South Africa' (2001) 17 *South African Journal of Human Rights* 232.

Lienert I., *Who Controls the Budget: The Legislature or the Executive?* (International Monetary Fund Working Paper 05/115 2005).

Livingstone S. and Murray R., 'The Effectiveness of National Human Rights Institutions' in Simon Halliday and Patrick Schmidt (eds) *Human Rights Brought Home* (Hart 2004).

Lynch M., 'Political Adjudication or Statutory Interpretation – Robinson v Secretary of State for Northern Ireland' (2002) 53 *Northern Ireland Legal Quarterly* 327.

Marx K., 'On the Jewish Question' in Loyd Easton and Kurt Guddat (ed) *Writings of the Young Marx on Philosophy and Society* (Doubleday Books 1967, 1843).

MacNaughton G., 'Untangling Equality and Non-discrimination to Promote the Right to Health Care for All' (2009) 11 *Health and Human Rights Journal* 47.

McBeth A., 'A Right by Any Other Name: The Evasive Engagement of International Financial Institutions with Human Rights' (2009) *George Washington International Law Review* 40.

McBeth A., *International Economic Actors and Human Rights* (Routledge 2010).

McCrudden C., 'Mainstreaming Equality in the Governance of Northern Ireland' (1999) 22 *Fordham International Law Journal* 1696.

McCrudden C., 'Northern Ireland, The Belfast Agreement, and the British Constitution' in Jeffrey Jowell and Dawn Oliver (eds) *The Changing Constitution* (Oxford UP 2007).

McGarry J. and O'Leary B., *Explaining Northern Ireland: Broken Images* (Blackwell 1995).

McKittrick D., *Lost Lives: The Stories of the Men, Women and Children who Died as a Result of the Northern Ireland Troubles* (Mainstream 2001).

McKittrick D. and McVea D., *Making Sense of the Troubles: A History of the Northern Ireland Conflict* (Revised edition, Viking 2012).

McKeever G. and Ní Aoláin F., 'Thinking Globally, Acting Locally: Enforcing Socio-Economic Rights in Northern Ireland' (2004) *European Human Rights Law Review* 158.

Meier B., 'The World Health Organization, the Evolution of Human Rights, and the Failure to Achieve Health for All' in J. Harrington and M. Stuttaford (eds) *Global Health and Human Rights Legal and Philosophical Perspectives* (Routledge 2010).

Meier B., 'The Highest Attainable Standard: Advancing a Collective Human Right to Public Health' (2006) 37 *Columbia Human Rights Law Review* 101.

Moloney E., *A Secret History of the IRA* (Penguin 2003).

Morison J. and Livingstone S., *Reshaping Public Power* (Sweet & Maxwell 1995).

Morsink J., *The Universal Declaration of Human Rights: Origins, Drafting and Intent* (University of Pennsylvania Press 2000).

Mullins D. and Murie A., *A Housing Policy in the UK* (Palgrave 2006).

Ní Aoláin F., *The Politics of Force* (Blackstaff Press 2000).

Nolan A. and Dutschke M., 'Article 2(1) ICESCR and States Parties' Obligations: Wither the Budget' [2010] *European Human Rights Law Review* 280.

Nolan A., 'A Report of Discussions and Outcomes at the Economic, Social and Cultural Rights Litigation Strategy Workshop' in M. Langford and B. Thiele (eds) *Road to a Remedy: Current Issues in Litigation of Economic, Social and Cultural Rights* (University of New South Wales Press 2005).

Nolan A., 'Rising to the Challenge of Child Poverty: the Role of the Courts' in G. van Bueren (ed) *Fulfilling the Law's Duty to the Poor* (OUP/UNESCO 2010).

Nolan A., 'Addressing Economic and Social Rights Violations by Non-State Actors Through the Role of the State: A Comparison of Regional Approaches to the "Obligation to Protect"' (2009) 9 *Human Rights Law Review* 225.

Nolan A., Porter B. and Langford M., 'The Justiciability of Social and Economic Rights: An Udpated Appraisal' (2007) 15 *Centre for Human Rights and Global Justice Working Paper*.

Nolan A. (ed), *Economic and Social Rights after the Global Financial Crisis* (Cambridge UP 2014).

Normand R. and Zaidi S., *Human Rights at the UN: The Political History of Universal Justice* (Indiana UP 2008).

O'Connell R., 'Recovering the History of Human Rights: Public Finances and Human Rights' in Aoife Nolan, Rory O'Connell and Colin Harvey (eds) *Human Rights and Public Finance* (Hart 2013).

Palley C., 'The Evolution, Disintegration and Possible Reconstruction of the Northern Ireland Constitution' (1972) 1 *Anglo-American Law Review* 368.

Palmer E., *Judicial Review, Socio-Economic Rights and the Human Rights Act* (Hart Publishing 2009).

Paust J., 'The Other Side of Right: Private Duties Under Human Rights Law' (1992) 5 *Harvard Human Rights Journal* 51.

Paris C., 'The Changing Housing System in Northern Ireland 1998–2007' (2008) 7 *Ethnopolitics* 119.

Pegram T., 'Diffusion Across Political Systems: The Global Spread of National Human Rights Institutions' (2010) 32 *Human Rights Quarterly* 729.

Petrie M. and Shields J., 'Producing a Citizens' Guide to the Budget: Why, What and How?' (2010) OECD *Journal on Budgeting* 2.

Prior P.M., 'Mental Health Policy in Northern Ireland' in J. Campbell and R. Manktelow, *Mental Health Social Work in Ireland: Comparative Issues in Policy and Practice* (Ashgate 1998).

Prior P.M., 'Removing Children from Care of Adults with Diagnosed Mental Illnesses – A Clash of Human Rights' (2003) 6 *European Journal of Social Work* 179.

Prior P.M., *Mental Health and Politics in Northern Ireland* (Avebury 1993).

Ramkumar V. and Shapiro I., *Guide to Transparency in Government Budget Reports: Why are Budget Reports Important, and What Should They Include?* (International Budget Partnership, 2010).

Robertson R., 'Measuring State Compliance with the Obligation to Devote the "Maximum of Available Resources" to Realizing Economic, Social and Cultural Rights' (1994) 16 *Human Rights Quarterly* 693.

Rooney E. and Harvey C., 'Better on the Margins? A Critique of Mainstreaming Economic and Social Rights' in Aoife Nolan, Rory O'Connell and Colin Harvey (eds) *Human Rights and Public Finance* (Hart 2013).

Rooney E. and Dutschke M., 'The Right to Adequate Housing: A Case Study of the Social Housing Budget in Northern Ireland' in Aoife Nolan, Rory O'Connell and Colin Harvey (eds), *Human Rights and Public Finance* (Hart 2013).

Saiz, I. 'Resourcing Rights: Combating Tax Injustice from a Human Rights Perspective' in Aoife Nolan, Rory O'Connell and Colin Harvey (eds) *Human Rights and Public Finance* (Hart 2013)

Saiz I., 'Rights in Recession? Challenges for Economic and Social Rights Enforcement in Times of Crisis' (2009) 1 *Journal of Human Rights in Practice* 277.

Savela E., 'Homelessness and the Affordable Shortage: What Is to be Done?' (1990–1) 9 *Law and Inequality* 279.

Saxena S., Thornicroft G., Knapp M. and Whiteford H., 'Resources for Mental Health: Scarcity, Inequity, and Inefficiency' (2007) 370 (9590) *The Lancet* 878.

Schick A., 'Can National Legislatures Regain an Effective Voice in Budget Policy?' (2002) 1 (3) *OECD Journal on Budgeting* 15.

Scott C. and Alston P., 'Adjudicating Constitutional Priorities in a Transnational Context: A Comment on Soobramoney's Legacy and Grootboom's Promise' (2000) 16 *South African Journal on Human Rights* 206.

Sepúlveda M., 'Colombia: The Constitutional Court's Role in Addressing Social Injustice' in M. Langford (ed) *Social Rights Jurisprudence: Emerging Trends in International Law* (Cambridge UP 2008).

Sepúlveda M., *The Nature of the Obligations under the International Covenant on Economic, Social and Cultural Rights* (Intersentia 2003).

Shah A., *Participatory Budgeting* (World Bank 2007).

Shanks P., 'Mortgage Rescue Packages' (2007) 13 *Housing Rights Review*, Winter.

Shue H., 'The Interdependence of Duties', in P. Alston and K. Tomasevski (eds), *The Right to Food* (Martinus Nijhoff Publishers 1984).

Shue H., *Basic Rights: Subsistence, Affluence, and US Foreign Policy* (Princeton UP 1980).

Smith A., 'The Unique Position of National Human Rights Institutions: A Mixed Blessing' (2006) 28 *Human Rights Quarterly* 904.

Snowdon C., *The Spirit Level Delusion: Fact-Checking the Left's New Theory of Everything* (Democracy Institute 2010).

Sohn L.B., 'The New International Law: Protection of Individuals Rather than States' (1982) 32 *American University Law Review* 1.

Spackman M., 'Public-Private Partnerships: Lessons from the British Approach' (2002) 26 *Economic Systems* 283.

Special Issue, 'Northern Ireland, the Belfast/Good Friday Agreement' (1999) 22 *Fordham International Law Journal*.

Ssenjoyonjo M., 'The Applicability of International Human Rights Law to Non-State Actors: What Relevance to Economic, Social and Cultural Rights?' (2008) 12 *International Journal of Human Rights* 725.

Stapenhurst R., Pelizzo R., Olson D. and von Tapp L., *Legislative Oversight and Budgeting: A World Perspective* (World Bank 2008).

Stapenhurst R., 'The Legislature and the Budget' in R. Pelizzo, R. Stapenhurst and D. Olson (eds), *The Role of Parliaments in the Budget Process* (World Bank Institute, Washington, DC 2008).

Steiner J.H., 'Political Participation as a Human Right' (1988) 1 *Human Rights Yearbook* 77.

Steiner H., Alston P. and Goodman R., *International Human Rights in Context* (Oxford UP 2008).

Sunstein C., 'Against Positive Rights: Why Social and Economic Rights Don't Belong in the Constitutions of Eastern Europe' (1993) (Winter) *East European Constitutional Review* 35.

Sunstein C., *The Second Bill of Rights: FDR's Unfinished Revolution and Why We Need It More Than Ever* (Basic Books 2004).

Thau A., *The Bond Book* (McGraw-Hill 2000).

Toebes B., 'Towards an Improved Understanding of the International Human Right to Health' (1999) 21 *Human Rights Quarterly* 661.

Tomlinson M.W., 'War, Peace and Suicide: The Case of Northern Ireland' (2012) 27 (4) *International Sociology* 464.

Van Bueren G., 'Alleviating Poverty through the Constitutional Court' (1999) 15 *South African Journal of Human Rights*, 52.

Van Bueren G., 'Combating Child Poverty – Human Rights Approaches' (1999) 21 *Human Rights Quarterly* 680.

Vasak K., 'A Thirty Year Struggle' (1977) 30 *UNESCO Courier* 29.

Vibert F., *The Rise of the Unelected: Democracy and the New Separation of Powers* (Cambridge UP 2007).

Weiss P., 'Economic and Social Rights Come of Age: United States Held to Account in IACHR' (2000) 7(2) *Human Rights Brief* (Center for Human Rights and Humanitarian Law).

Wehner J., 'Legislative Arrangements for Financial Scrutiny: Explaining Cross-National Variation' in R. Pelizzo, R. Stapenhurst and D. Olson (eds), *The Role of Parliaments in the Budget Process* (World Bank Institute, Washington, DC 2005).

Welling J.V., 'International Indicators and Economic, Social and Cultural' (2008) 30 *Human Rights Quarterly*, 933.

Wesson M., 'Grootboom and Beyond: Assessing the Socio-Economic Jurisprudence of the South African Constitutional Court' (2004) 20 *South African Journal of Human Rights* 284.

Whelan D., *Indivisible Human Rights: A History* (University of Pennsylvania Press 2010).

Whelan D. and Donnelly J., 'The West, Economic and Social Rights, and the Global Human Rights Regime: Setting the Record Straight' (2007) 29 *Human Rights Quarterly* 908.

Whelan D. and Donnelly H., 'Yes, a Myth: A Reply to Kirkup and Evans' (2009) 31 *Human Rights Quarterly* 239.

Whyte J., 'How Much Discrimination was There Under the Unionist Regime, 1921–68?' in T. Gallagher and J. O'Connell (eds), *Contemporary Irish Studies* (Manchester UP 1983).

Whyte J., *Interpreting Northern Ireland* (Clarendon 1991).

Wilkinson R. and Pickett K., *The Spirit Level: Why More Equal Societies Almost Always Do Better* (Penguin 2009).

Wilson R., 'Private Partners and the Public Good' (2002) 53 *Northern Ireland Legal Quarterly* 454.

Yamin A.E. and Parra-Vera O., 'How do Courts Set Health Policy? The Question of the Colombian Constitutional Court' (2009) (2) *PLoS Medicine* 61.

Yamin A.E. and Rosenthal E., 'Out of the Shadows: Using Human Rights Approaches to Secure Dignity and Well-being for People with Mental Disabilities' (2005) 2(4) *PLoS Medicine*, e71.

Young K., 'The Minimum Core of Economic and Social Rights: A Concept in Search of Content' (2008) 33 *Yale Journal on International Law* 113.

Reports

Advisory Committee on Equal Opportunities for Women and Men, *Opinion on the Gender Perspective on the Response to the Economic and Financial Crisis*, June 2009.

Amnesty International Ireland and Indecon, *Accountability in the Delivery of a Vision for Change* (2010).

Amnesty International Ireland and Indecon, *Review of Government Spending on Mental Health* (2009).

Amnesty International Ireland, *Pre-Budget Submission 2011* (16 July 2010).

Appleby J., *Independent Review of Health and Social Care Service in Northern Ireland* (2005).

APRODEV, *Budgeting Human Rights: Join the Efforts to Budget Human Rights* (2007).

Bamford Review of Mental Health and Learning Disability (Northern Ireland), *A Comprehensive Legislative Framework*, available at www.dhsspsni.gov.uk/legal-issue-comprehensive-framework.pdf (2007).

Blyberg A., *Notes From an International Budget Project Roundtable Discussion on the Obligation to Use 'Maximum of Available Resources'* (International Human Rights Internship Programme 2008).

Caliari A., Way S.A., Raaber N., Schoenstein A., Balakrishnan R. and Lusiani N., *Bringing Human Rights to Bear in Times of Crisis: A Human Rights Analysis of Government Response to the Economic Crisis,* Submission to the High–Level Segment 13th session of the UNHRC on the global economic and financial crises (2010).

Cameron Report, *Disturbances in Northern Ireland: Report of the Commission Appointed by the Governor of Northern Ireland* (HMSO, Belfast 1969) Cmnd. 532.

Centre for Economic and Social Rights, *Economic, Social and Cultural Rights: Guide to the Legal Framework* (2000).

COHRE, *Right to Water Manual* (2008).

Commission on a Bill of Rights, *Final Report: A UK Bill of Rights? The Choice Before Us* (Commission on a Bill of Rights, UK 2012).

Commission on the Future for Housing in Northern Ireland, *A Key Issues Paper from the Independent Commission* (2009).

Council of Mortgage Lenders, *Housing Finance* (2006).

Council of Mortgage Lenders, *Northern Ireland Factsheet: Housing and Mortgage Market Update* (2009).

Deloitte, *Research into the Financial Cost of the Northern Ireland Divide* (2008).

Department for Finance and Personnel, *Review of Domestic Rating: A Consultation Report* (2009).

Department for Social Development, *Building Solid Foundations – A Strategy for the Private Rented Sector* (2009).

Department for Social Development, *Northern Ireland Housing Statistics* 1999–2000 (2000).

Department for Social Development, *Northern Ireland Housing Statistics* 2000–01 (2001).

Department for Social Development, *Northern Ireland Housing Statistics* 2001–02 (2002).

Department for Social Development, *Northern Ireland Housing Statistics* 2003–04 (2004).

Department for Social Development, *Northern Ireland Housing Statistics* 2004–05 (2005).

Department for Social Development, *Northern Ireland Housing Statistics* 2008–09 (2009).

Department of Health and Children, *A Vision for Change: Report of the Expert Group on Mental Health Policy* (Stationery Office, Dublin 2006).

Department of the Environment, *Building for Success* (Northern Ireland Economic Development Office, Belfast 1996).

Diokno M.S.I., *A Rights-Based Approach Towards Budget Analysis* (1999).

Drudy P.J. and Punch M., *Out of Reach: Inequalities in the Irish Housing System,* (TASC at New Island Books Dublin 2005).

Economic Research Institute Northern Ireland/Oxford Economics, *Cutting Carefully – How Repairing UK Finances will Impact NI: A Report for NICVA*, July 2010 available at www.donegallpass.org/Oxford_Economics_Report_-_impact_on_NI_July_2010.pdf.

Elson D., *Budgeting for Women's Rights: Monitoring Government Budgets for Compliance with CEDAW* (UNIFEM 2006).

FAO, *Budget Work to Advance the Right to Food: Many a Slip* (2009).

Fundar, *Health Care: A Question of Rights, Not Charity* (2002).

Fundar, International Budget Project, International Human Rights Internship Program, *Dignity Counts: A Guide to Using Budget Analysis to Advance Human Rights* (2004).

Hall K. and Proudlock P. *Litigating for a Better Deal* Children's Institute Annual Report 2008 available at www.ci.org.za/depts/ci/pubs/pdf/general/annual/report08/litigating.pdf (accessed 7 April 2009).

Hewitt V. *Mitigating the Recession: Options for the Northern Ireland Executive* (Research Paper No. 37 Economic Research Institute of Northern Ireland 2009).

Hillyard P., Kelly G., McLaughlin E., Patsios D. and Tomlinson M., *Bare Necessities: Poverty and Social Exclusion in Northern Ireland* (2003) available at www.ofmdfmni.gov.uk/bare-necessities.pdf (accessed 30 August 2013).

Hofbauer H., *Sustained Work and Dedicated Capacity* (2006).

House of Commons Communities and Local Government Committee, *Housing and the Credit Crunch: Third Report of Session 2008–09* (HC 2008–2009 101).

House of Commons Northern Ireland Affairs Select Committee, *Social Housing Provision in Northern Ireland. Sixth Report of Session 2003–04* (HC 2003–2004 493).

Housing Rights Service, *Housing Rights Manual* (2008).

Housing Rights Service, *Response to Consultation Document: Building Solid Foundations – A Strategy for the Private Rented Sector in Northern Ireland* (2009).

IBP International Budget Partnership and IHRIP International Human Rights Internship Program, *Reading the Books: Governments' Budgets and the Right to Education* (2010).

IDASA and Judith Streak, *Budgeting for Child Socio-Economic Rights: Government Obligations and the Child's Right to Social Security and Education* (2002).

IDASA, *Child Specific Spending on the Right to Health in MTEF 2004/05– An Identification Problem* (2004).

IDASA, *Comparative Provincial Housing Brief* (2004).

IDASA and Judith Streak, *Monitoring Government Budgets to Advance Child Rights: A Guide for NGOs* (2003).

IHRIP International Human Rights Internship Program, *Government Human Rights Obligations and Budget Work* (2008).

Institute for Fiscal Studies, *The Distributional Effect of Tax and Benefit Reforms to be Introduced between June 2010 and April 2014: A Revised Assessment*, J. Browne and P. Levell (eds) IFS Briefing Note BN108 (2010) available at www.ifs.org.uk/bns/bn108.pdf (accessed 30 August 2013).

International Commission of Jurists, *Courts and the Legal Enforcement of Economic, Social and Cultural Rights: Comparative Experiences of Justiciability* (2008).

Iversen PB, *Program on Essential Drugs* WHO/DAP/98.12 (1998) available at http://apps.who.int/medicinedocs/pdf/s2237e/s2237e.pdf (accessed 30 August 2013).

Joint Committee on Human Rights, *Twenty-first Report The International Covenant on Economic, Social and Cultural Rights* (HL 183/HC 1188 2003–2004).

McKinsey Report: Reshaping the System: Implications for Northern Ireland's Health and Social Care Services of the 2010 Spending Review, available at www.dhsspsni.gov.uk/index/mckinseyreport.htm (accessed 30 August 2013).

National Housing and Planning Advise Unit, *Buy-to-let Mortgage Lending and the Impact on UK House Prices* (2008).

Nolan P., *Northern Ireland Peace Monitoring Report: Number One* (Community Relations Council, 2012).

Nolan P., *Northern Ireland Peace Monitoring Report: Number Two* (Community Relations Council, 2013).

Norton A. and Elson D., *What's Behind the Budget? Politics, Rights and Accountability in the Budget Project* (Overseas Development Institute 2002).

Northern Ireland Assembly Research and Library Services, *Funding for Social and Affordable Housing: The Potential Use of 'Prudential Borrowing' by the Northern Ireland Housing Executive* (2009).

Northern Ireland Federation of Housing Associations, *Evidence to the Commission on the Future for Housing in Northern Ireland* (2009).

Northern Ireland Housing Executive, *Housing Selection Scheme* available at www.nihe.gov.uk/housing_selection_scheme.pdf (accessed 30 August 2013).

Northern Ireland Housing Executive and Northern Ireland Federation Housing Association, *Response to the Recommendations of the Review into Affordable Housing Interim Report* (2007).

Northern Ireland Housing Executive, *Building on Success: Northern Ireland Housing Executive Response* (1996).

Northern Ireland Housing Executive, *Northern Ireland Housing Market: Review and Perspectives 2009–2012* (2009).

Northern Ireland Housing Executive, *The House Sales Scheme and the Housing Market* (2004).

Northern Ireland Housing Executive, *The NI Housing Market: Drivers and Policies* (2007).

Northern Ireland Housing Executive, *The Private Rented Sector in Northern Ireland* (2007).

Northern Ireland Human Rights Commission, *A Bill of Rights for Northern Ireland* (NIHRC 2008).

NYCWR New York City Welfare Reform and HRDP Human Rights Documentation Project, *Hunger is No Accident: New York and Federal Welfare Policies Violate the Human Right to Food* (2000).

Open Society Justice Initiative, *From Rights to Remedies: Structures and Strategies for Implementing International Human Rights Decisions* (Open Society 2013).

Open Society Justice Initiative, *From Judgment to Justice: Implementing International and Regional Human Rights Decisions* (Open Society 2010).

Potts H., *Participation and the Right to the Highest Attainable Standard of Health* (Human Rights Centre, University of Essex 2009).

PPR Participation and the Practice of Rights, *Participation and Mental Health: Monitoring your Engagement with Government*, available at www.pprproject.org/images/documents/mh%20participation%20pamphlet.pdf (accessed 30 August 2013).

Northern Ireland Assembly Public Accounts Committee, *Report on the Management of Social Housing rent Collection and Arrears* (2009).

QUB Budget Analysis Project, *Budget Analysis and Economic and Social Rights: A Review on Existing Guidance and Case Studies* (2010).

QUB Budget Analysis Project, *Budgeting for Human Rights: A Human Rights Framework* (2010).

QUB Budget Analysis Project, *Context Paper* (2010).

QUB Budget Analysis Project, *Human Rights Framework Paper* (2010).

QUB Budget Analysis Project, *The First Steps Towards a Human Rights Framework* Belfast (2010).

Ramkumar V., *Our Money, Our Responsibility: A Citizen's Guide to Monitoring Government Expenditures* (2009).

Rooney E., *Failing to Deliver* (Belfast, St Patrick's and St Joseph's Housing Committee 2007).

Samaritans, *Suicide Statistics Report 2013 Data for 2009–2011* available at www.samaritans.org/sites/default/files/kcfinder/files/research/Samaritans%20Suicide%20Statistics%20Report%202013.pdf (accessed 30 August 2013).

Shultz J., *Promises to Keep: Using Public Budgets as a Tool to Advance Economic, Social and Cultural Rights* (Fundar, Mexico 2002).

Select Committee on the Barnett Formula, *The Barnett Formula* (HL 2008–2009 139).

Semple J., *Review into Affordable Housing: Final Report* (2007).

Smyth M. and Bailey M., *Addressing the Economic Downturn: The Case for Increased Investment in Social Housing* (School of Economics, University of Ulster 2009).

Treaty Body Monitor, *Committee on Economic, Social and Cultural Rights , 42nd session, United Kingdom of Britain and Northern Ireland 4–5th report 12–13th of May 2009* Human Rights Monitor Series (2009).

UK Government, *Green Paper on Rights and Responsibilities: Developing Our Constitutional Framework*, Command Paper 7577 (2009).

UUJ, *Northern Ireland Quarterly House Prices Index* (2009).

Women's Budget Group, *The Impact on Women of the Budget 2012* (Women's Budget Group, 2012).

International: General Comments of the UN Treaty monitoring bodies

Committee on Economic, Social and Cultural Rights, *General Comment No. 3, The Nature of States Parties Obligations* UN Doc E/1991/23 Annex III at 86 (1990).

Committee on Economic, Social and Cultural Rights *General Comment No. 4, The Right to Adequate Housing* UN Doc E/1992 /23 annex III at 114 (1991).

Committee on Economic, Social and Cultural Rights, *General Comment No. 7 Forced Evictions and the Right to Adequate Housing* UN Doc E.1998/22, annex IV at 113 (1997).

Committee on Economic, Social and Cultural Rights, *General Comment No. 9, The Domestic Application of the Covenant* UN Doc E/C/.12/1998/24 (1998).

Committee on Economic, Social and Cultural Rights, *General Comment No. 12, The Right to Adequate Food* (Art.11) UN Doc E/C.12/1999/5 (1999).

Committee on Economic, Social and Cultural Rights, *General Comment No. 13, The Right to Education* UN Doc E/C.12/1999/10 (1999).

Committee on Economic, Social and Cultural Rights, *General Comment No. 14, The Right to the Highest Attainable Standard of Health* E/C.12/2000/4 (2000).

Committee on Economic, Social and Cultural Rights, *General Comment No. 15, The Right to Water (Article 11 and 12)* UNDoc E/C.12/2002/11 (2002).

Committee on Economic, Social and Cultural Rights, *General Comment No. 16: The Equal Right of Men and Women to the Enjoyment of all Economic, Social and Cultural Rights* UN Doc E/C.12/2005/3 (2005).

Committee on Economic, Social and Cultural Rights, *General Comment No. 19, The Right to Social Security* UN Doc E/C.12/GC/19 (2008).

Committee on Economic, Social and Cultural Rights, *General Comment No. 20, Non-Discrimination in Economic, Social and Cultural Rights* UN Doc E/C.12/GC/20 (2009).

Committee on the Elimination of All Forms of Discrimination Against Women, *General Recommendation No. 19, Violence against Women* UN Doc A/47/38 at 1 (1993).

Committee on the Rights of the Child, *General Comment No. 4, Adolescents' Health and Development in the Context of the Convention on the Rights of the Child* UN Doc CRC/GC/2003/4 (2003).

Committee on the Rights of the Child, *General Comment No. 5, General Measures of Implementation of the Convention on the Rights of the Child* UN Doc CRC/GC/2003/5 (2003).

Human Rights Committee, *General Comment No. 18, Non-discrimination* UN Doc HRI/GEN/1/Rev.6 at 146 (2003).

Human Rights Committee, *General Comment No. 20, Prohibition of Torture or Cruel, Inhuman or Degrading Treatment or Punishment* UN Doc HRI/GEN/1/Rev.1 at 30 (1994).

International: Reports and official documents from international organizations

Report of the High Commissioner for Human Rights on Implementation of Economic, Social and Cultural Rights UN Doc E/2009/90 (2009).

Report of the Special Rapporteur on Adequate Housing as a Component of the Right to an Adequate Standard of Living, Miloon Kothari A/HRC/4/18 (2007).

Committee on Economic, Social and Cultural Rights, *Conclusions and Recommendations of the Committee on Economic, Social and Cultural Rights, Canada* UN Doc E/C.12/1993/5 (1993).

Committee on Economic, Social and Cultural Rights, *Conclusions and Recommendations of the Committee on Economic, Social and Cultural Rights, Senegal* UN Doc E/C.12/1993/18 (1994).

Committee on Economic, Social and Cultural Rights, *Conclusions and Recommendations of the Committee on Economic, Social and Cultural Rights, United Kingdom of Great Britain and Northern Ireland* UN Doc E/C.12/1994/19 (1994).

Committee on Economic, Social and Cultural Rights, *Conclusions and Recommendations of the Committee on Economic, Social and Cultural Rights, Colombia* UN Doc E/C.12/1995/18 at 41 (1996).

Committee on Economic, Social and Cultural Rights, *Conclusions and Recommendations of the Committee on Economic, Social and Cultural Rights, United Kingdom of Great Britain and Northern Ireland* UN Doc E/C.12/1 Add.19 (1997).

Committee on Economic, Social and Cultural Rights, *Conclusions and Recommendations of the Committee on Economic, Social and Cultural Rights, Canada* in Volume UN Doc E/C/12/1/Add.31 (1998).

Committee on Economic, Social and Cultural Rights, *Conclusions and recommendations of the Committee on Economic, Social and Cultural Rights, Algeria* UN Doc E/C.12/1/Add.71 (2001).

Committee on Economic, Social and Cultural Rights, *Conclusions and Recommendations of the Committee on Economic, Social and Cultural Rights, Colombia* in Volume UN Doc E/C.12/1/Add.74 (2001).

Committee on Economic, Social and Cultural Rights, *Conclusions and recommendations of the Committee on Economic, Social and Cultural Rights, Republic of Korea* UN Doc E/C.12/1/Add.59 (2001).

Committee on Economic, Social and Cultural Rights, *Substantive Issues Arising in the Implementation of the International Covenant on Economic, Social and Cultural Rights; Poverty and the International Covenant on Economic, Social and Cultural Rights* E/C.12/2001/10 (2001).

Committee on Economic, Social and Cultural Rights, *Concluding Observations of the Committee on Economic, Social and Cultural Rights: United Kingdom of Great Britain and Northern Ireland* E/C.12/1/Add.79 (2002).

Committee on Economic, Social and Cultural Rights, *Concluding Observations of the Committee on Economic, Social and Cultural Rights: United Kingdom of Great Britain and Northern Ireland* UN Doc E/C.12/1/Add.79 (2002).

Committee on Economic, Social and Cultural Rights, *The Guidelines on Treaty-Specific Documents to be Submitted by State Parties under Articles 16 and 17 of the International Covenant on Economic, Social and Cultural Rights* UN Doc E/C.12/2008/2 (2008).

Committee on Economic, Social and Cultural Rights, *Concluding Observations of the Committee on Economic, Social and Cultural Rights United Kingdom* UNDoc E/C.12/GBR/CO/5 (2009).

Committee on Economic, Social and Cultural Rights, *The Guidelines on Treaty-Specific Documents to be Submitted by State Parties under Articles 16 and 17 of the International Covenant on Economic, Social and Cultural Rights* UN Doc E/C.12/2008/2 (2008).

Committee on Economic, Social and Cultural Rights, 'Letter from CESCR Chairperson to States Parties in the context of the economic and financial crisis', CESCR/48th/SP/MAB/SW, 16 May 2012.

Committee on the Rights of the Child, *General Guidelines Regarding the Form and Content of Periodic Reports to be Submitted by States Particle under Article 44, Paragraph 1(b) of the Convention* UN Doc CRC/C/58/Rev.1 (2005) at paragraph 5(f).

Human Rights Committee, *Concluding Observations Mongolia*, UN Doc CCPR/C/79/Add.120 (2000).

Human Rights Committee, *Concluding Observations Suriname*, UN Doc CCPR/CO/80/SUR (2004).

Hunt P., *Report of the Special Rapporteur on the Right of Everyone to the Highest Attainable Standard of Physical and Mental Health, Paul Hunt* E/CN.4/2005/51 (2005).

Hunt P., *Report of the Special Rapporteur on the Right of Everyone to the Enjoyment of the Highest Attainable Standard of Physical and Mental Health* UN Doc A/HRC/7/11 (2008).

Office of the High Commissioner for Human Rights, *Human Rights Indicators: A Guide to Measurement and Implementation* (2012) HR/PUB/12/5.

Raquel R., *Report of the Special Rapporteur on Adequate Housing as a Component of the Right to an Adequate Standard of Living, and the Right to Non-discrimination in this Context: Promotion and Protection of All Human Rights, Civil, Political, Economic, Social and Cultural Rights, including the Right to Development* UN Doc A/HRC/10/7 (2009).

Rolnik R., *Report of the Special Rapporteur on Adequate Housing as a Component of the Right to an Adequate Standard of Living A/67/286* (2012).

UN Habitat and OHCHR, *Monitoring Housing Rights*, Discussion Paper Prepared for Expert Group Meeting on Housing Rights Monitoring Geneva 26–28 November 2003.

United Nations, *Report on Indicators for Monitoring Compliance with International Human Rights Instruments* UN Doc HRI/MC/2006/7 (2006).

United Nations, *Report on Indicators for Promoting and Monitoring the Implementation of Human Rights* UN Doc HRI/MC/2008/3 (2008).

United Nations, *Report of the International Conference on Population and Development, Cairo, 5–13 September 1994* United Nations publication, Sales No. E.95.XIII.18, chapter I, resolution 1, annex, chaps. VII and VIII.

WHO, *Everybody's Business: Strengthening Health Systems to Improve Health Outcomes* (2007) available at www.who.int/healthsystems/strategy/everybodys_business.pdf (accessed 30 August 2013).

WHO, *Scaling Up Care for Mental, Neurological and Substance Use Disorders* (2008) available at www.who.int/mental_health/mhgap_final_english.pdf (accessed 30 August 2013).

WHO, *The World Health Report 2001: New Understanding, New Hope* (2001) available at www.who.int/whr/2001/en/ (accessed 30 August 2013).

WHO and Wonca (World Organization of Family Doctors), *Integrating Mental Health into primary care – A Global Perspective* (2008) taken from www.who.int/mental_health/policy/Mental%20health%20+%20primary%20care-%20final%20low-res%20140908.pdf (accessed 30 August 2013).

WHO Fact sheet no. 220, *Mental Health: Strengthening Mental Health Promotion* (2007) available at www.who.int/mediacentre/factsheets/fs220/en/print.html (accessed 30 August 2013).

International: Soft law documents

The Limburg Principles on the Implementation of the International Covenant on Economic, Social and Cultural Rights (1987) 9 Human Rights Quarterly, 122 and UN doc. E/CN.4/1987/17, Annex.

The Maastricht Guidelines on Violations of Economic, Social and Cultural Rights (1998) 20 Human Rights Quarterly, 691.

Legislation

Government of Ireland Act 1920.
Government of Wales Act 1998.
Government of Wales Act 2006.
Fair Employment (Northern Ireland) Act 1976.
Housing Executive Act (NI) 1971.
Housing (Northern Ireland) Order 1992.
Housing (Northern Ireland) Order 2003.
Ireland Act 1940.
Northern Ireland Act 1998.
Northern Ireland Act 2000.
Northern Ireland (St Andrew's Agreement) Act 2006.
Northern Ireland (Temporary Provisions) Act 1972.
Scotland Act 1998.
Scotland Act 2012.
Republic of Ireland Act 1948 (Ireland).

Case law

United Kingdom

Belfast Improved Housing Association Decision Notice FER 0152607.
R (on the application of Limbuela) v Secretary of State for the Home Department [2005] UKHL 66, [2006] 1 AC 396.
R (Weaver) v London and Quadrant Housing Trust [2009] EWCA Civ 587, [2010] 1 WLR 363.
R v Cambridge Health Authority, ex parte B [1995] 2 All ER 129 (CA).
R v East Sussex ex parte Tandy [1998] AC 714.
R v Gloucestshire County Council ex parte Mahfood, Barry, Grinham and Dartnell [1995] 1 CCLR 1997.
R v Shefton Metropolitcan BC, ex parte Help the Aged and Others [1997] 4 ALL ER 532.
Robinson [2002] UKHL 32, [2002] NI 390.
Wesley Housing Association Decision Notice FER 149772.

European Court of Human Rights

Guerra v Italy (1998) 26 EHRR 359.
Ireland v United Kingdom (1978) 2 EHRR 25.
Keenan v United Kingdom (2001) 33 EHRR 913.
Lopez Ostra v Spain (1995) 20 EHRR 277.
MSS v Belgium and Greece App no 30696/09, 21 January 2011.
Opuz v Turkey (2010) 50 EHRR 28.
Osman v United Kingdom (1998) 29 EHRR 245.
X v Ireland (1976) 7 DR 78.
Z v United Kingdom (2002) 34 EHRR 97.

European Committee of Social Rights

Marangopoulos Foundation for Human Rights (MFHR) v Greece Complaint Number 30/2005.

South Africa

Cele v The South African Social Security Agency and 22 related cases (2008) 7 BCLR 734 (D).
Certification of the Constitution of South Africa CCT 23/96, 6 September 1996.
City of Cape Town v Various Occupiers of the Road Reserve of Applicant Parallel to Sheffield Road Philipi unreported judgment Cape Town High Court delivered 30 September 2003,case number A5/2003.
City of Johannesburg v L Mazibuko 489/08 [2009] ZASCA 20.
City of Johannesburg v Rand Properties (PTY) Ltd. and Others 2006 (6) BCLR 728 (W).
Government of the Republic of South Africa and Others v Grootboom and Others 2000 (11) BCLR 1169 (CC).
Jaftha v Schoeman and Others Van Rooyen v Stoltz and Others 2005 (1) BCLR 78 (CC).
Khosa and Others v Minister of Social Development and Others 2004(6) BCLR 569 (CC).
Lingwood Michael an Another v The Unlawful Occupiers of R/E of Erf 9 Highlands unreported case No. 2006/ 16243 (WLD).

Minister of Health v Treatment Action Campaign (No.2) 2002 (5) SA 721 (CC).
Ncamile and the Children's Institute v the Minister of Social Development and Minister of Finance (unreported).
Occupiers of 51 Olivia Road, Berea Township and 197 Main Street, Johannesburg v City of Johannesburg and Others case No. CCT 24/ 07.
Port Elizabeth Municipality v Various Occupiers 2004 (12) BCLR 1268 (CC).
President of the Republic of South Africa and Another v Modderklip.
Boerdery (PTY) Ltd and Others 2005 (8) BCLR 786 (CC) (4) SA 385 (W).
Soobramoney v Minister of Health (Kwazulu-Natal) 1998 (1) SA 765 (CC).

African Commission on Human and Peoples' Rights

Free Legal Assistance v Zaire Free Legal Assistance Group and Others v. Zaire, Comm. No. 25/89, 47/90, 56/91, 100/93 (2005).
OMCT et al v Zaïre, Communications 25/89, 47/90, 56/91 and 100/93.
Purohit and Moore v The Gambia Communication No. 241/2001.
Social and Economic Rights Action Center and the Center for Economic and Social Rights v Nigeria Communication No. 155/96.

Canada

Eldridge v The Attorney General of British Colombia [1997] 3 SCR 624.

Germany

Asylum case, 1 BvL 10/10, 18 July 2012 available at www.bundesverfassungsgericht.de/en/decisions/ls20120718_1bvl001010en.html (accessed 30 August 2013).
Hartz IV case BverfG,1BvL 1/09 vom 9.2.2010 Absatz-Nr (1–220) available at www.bundesverfassungsgericht.de/en/decisions/ls20100209_1bvl000109en.html (accessed 30 August 2013).

Human Rights Committee

KL v Peru 22 November 2005 communication No. 1153/2003.

Hungary

Decision 4/2006.

Argentina

Menores Comunidad Paynemil s/accion de amparo, Expte. 311-CA-1997. Sala II. Cámara de Apelaciones en lo Civil, Neuquen, 19 May, 1997.

India

Paschim Banga Khet Samity v State of West Bengal Case no. 169 Judgment 6 May 1996 Petition No. 796.

Philippines

Reofisto T. Guingona, Jr., et al. v Guillermo Carague, et al.G.R. No. 94571 1991 Supreme Court.

Portugal

Decision 187/2013.

United States

Marbury v Madison 5 US 137 Cranch 137 (1803).

Media reports and press releases

BBC News, *Public sector borrowing soaring* (19/09/09) Available at http://news.bbc.co.uk/1/hi/business/8262434.stm (accessed 30 August 2013).

Clarke L., 'This is going to hurt you more than it hurts him; George Osborne's slash and burn Budget risks a return to oldstyle class war politics. As usual the poorest will bear the brunt of the pain' Belfast Telegraph, June 24, 2010.

Curtis P. and Wintour P., 'Coalition cuts will hit poor 10 times harder than rich, says TUC' guardian.co.uk, 10 September 2010.

Department for Social Development 'A New Agenda for Housing' 26 February 2008 available at www.dsdni.gov.uk/index/publications/ministers_speeches/offps-new-agenda-housing.htm (accessed 30 August 2013).

Department for Social Development '£21 million of Private Funding for Social Housing' 31 March 2010 available at www.northernireland.gov.uk/news/news-dsd/news-dsd-310310-private-funding-for.htm (accessed 30 August 2013).

McAdam N., *Cutbacks of £128m . . . but it could have been worse*, Belfast Telegraph 25 May 2010.

Murphy J., 'Robert Chote named chief of Office for Budget Responsibility' 9 September 2010, *London Evening Standard*, available at www.standard.co.uk/news/robert-chote-named-chief-of-office-for-budget-responsibility-6512030.html (accessed 30 August 2013).

Northern Ireland Executive, *Dodds Announces Decision Not to Introduce Derelict Land Tax*, 23 October 2008, available at www.northernireland.gov.uk/news-dfp-231008-derelict-land-tax (accessed 30 August 2013).

Northern Ireland Executive, *Record £30 million European Housing Investment*, 3 December 2009, available at www.northernireland.gov.uk/news/news-dsd/news-dsd-0312009-record-european-housing.htm (accessed 30 August 2013).

Northern Ireland Executive, *Landlords to be regulated for the first time announces Ritchie*, 24 March 2010 available at www.northernireland.gov.uk/news/news-dsd/news-dsd-240310-landlords-to-be.htm (accessed 30 August 2013).

Parker G., *UK coalition reveals £6.2bn budget cuts* Financial Times (24/05/10) Available at www.ft.com/cms/s/0/e7704314–6721–11df-bf08–00144feab49a.html (accessed 30 August 2013).

Sparrow A., 'Nick Clegg says report attacking emergency budget is "partial" Deputy prime minister hits out at Institute of Fiscal Studies, which said budget was "clearly regressive"' guardian.co.uk, Wednesday 25 August 2010 taken from www.guardian.co.uk/politics/2010/aug/25/nick-clegg-budget-report-partial/print (accessed 30 August 2013).

Index

Page references to figures or tables are in *italics*

Taylor & Francis

eBooks

FOR LIBRARIES

ORDER YOUR FREE 30 DAY INSTITUTIONAL TRIAL TODAY!

Over 23,000 eBook titles in the Humanities, Social Sciences, STM and Law from some of the world's leading imprints.

Choose from a range of subject packages or create your own!

Benefits for you

- Free MARC records
- COUNTER-compliant usage statistics
- Flexible purchase and pricing options

Benefits for your user

- Off-site, anytime access via Athens or referring URL
- Print or copy pages or chapters
- Full content search
- Bookmark, highlight and annotate text
- Access to thousands of pages of quality research at the click of a button

For more information, pricing enquiries or to order a free trial, contact your local online sales team.

UK and Rest of World: **online.sales@tandf.co.uk**

US, Canada and Latin America:
e-reference@taylorandfrancis.com

www.ebooksubscriptions.com

ALPSP Award for BEST eBOOK PUBLISHER 2009 Finalist

Taylor & Francis eBooks
Taylor & Francis Group

A flexible and dynamic resource for teaching, learning and research.

For Product Safety Concerns and Information please contact our EU representative GPSR@taylorandfrancis.com
Taylor & Francis Verlag GmbH, Kaufingerstraße 24, 80331 München, Germany

www.ingramcontent.com/pod-product-compliance
Ingram Content Group UK Ltd.
Pitfield, Milton Keynes, MK11 3LW, UK
UKHW011001180926
475701UK00004B/497